Pro Android Python with SL4A

Paul Ferrill

Apress®

Pro Android Python with SL4A

ISBN 978-1-4302-3569-9

ISBN 978-1-4302-3570-5 (eBook)

President and Publisher: Paul Manning
Lead Editor: Tom Welsh
Technical Reviewer: Justin Grammens
Editorial Board: Steve Anglin, Mark Beckner, Ewan Buckingham, Gary Cornell, Jonathan Gennick, Jonathan Hassell, Michelle Lowman, James Markham, Matthew Moodie, Jeff Olson, Jeffrey Pepper, Frank Pohlmann, Douglas Pundick, Ben Renow-Clarke, Dominic Shakeshaft, Matt Wade, Tom Welsh
Coordinating Editors: Mary Tobin, Corbin Collins
Copy Editor: Nancy Sixsmith
Production Support: Patrick Cunningham
Indexer: SPI Global
Artist: April Milne
Cover Designer: Anna Ishchenko

Distributed to the book trade worldwide by Springer Science+Business Media, LLC., 233 Spring Street, 6th Floor, New York, NY 10013. Phone 1-800-SPRINGER, fax (201) 348-4505, e-mail orders-ny@springer-sbm.com, or visit www.springeronline.com.

For information on translations, please e-mail rights@apress.com, or visit www.apress.com.

Apress and friends of ED books may be purchased in bulk for academic, corporate, or promotional use. eBook versions and licenses are also available for most titles. For more information, reference our Special Bulk Sales–eBook Licensing web page at www.apress.com/bulk-sales.

The source code for this book is available to readers at www.apress.com. You will need to answer questions

pertaining to this book in order to successfully download the code.

To my wife, Sandy, for your tireless support of me and our family. I could not have done this without you. And to my wonderful children who put up with a preoccupied daddy for way too long.

—Paul Ferrill

Contents at a Glance

Contents

About the Author

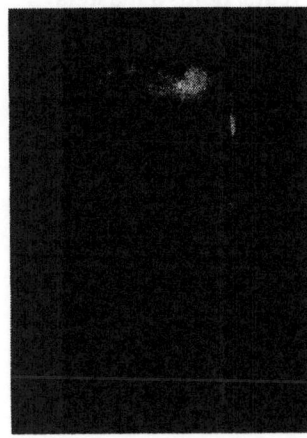

Paul Ferrill has a BS and MS in electrical engineering and has been writing about computers for more than 25 years. He currently serves as CTO for Avionics Test and Analysis Corporation, working on multiple DoD projects. Software development has been his primary focus, along with architecting large-scale data management and storage systems. He also serves on several DoD standards committees, providing input to the next generation of data recording and transmission standards.

He has a long history with both Microsoft and open source technologies. His two favorite languages are Visual Basic and Python. He's had articles published in *PC Magazine, PC Computing, InfoWorld, Computer World, Network World, Network Computing, Federal Computer Week, Information Week*, and multiple web sites.

About the Technical Reviewer

Justin Grammens has been writing software for 12 years, holds a masters degree in Software Systems, and has a patent pending on the process of a system to collect and rate digital media. He has written applications for a variety of mobile platforms in a number of different market sectors and is the cofounder of Recursive Awesome, LLC; owner of Localtone, LLC; and founder of Mobile Twin Cities.

Justin has built online e-commerce systems, real-time mapping solutions, large-scale tax accounting software, and technology for Internet radio stations. Having worked with Android since version 1.0, Justin has spoken on mobile technology at conferences and software development groups since 2008.

Justin has developed Android applications for Best Buy, McDonald's, BuzzFeed, and Consolidated Knowledge; and is co-creator of a cross-platform streaming video service called Mobile Vidhub. Justin is employed by Code 42 as a Director of Mobile Technology and lives in St. Paul, MN, with his wife.

Acknowledgments

I would like to acknowledge the excellent staff at Apress who managed to get this book completed on time through multiple delays and reworking of the original title. You've made the process much less frightening for a first-time author than I expected.

A special thanks goes to coordinating editors Mary Tobin and Corbin Collins, and to Tom Welsh, the lead editor.

I'd also like to thank Frank Pohlmann for convincing me to do this project in the first place.

Thank you to the technical reviewer, Justin Grammens, for a keen set of eyes and helpful comments. A big thank you to Robbie Matthews, who has become one of the primary contributors to the SL4A project and provided help when things didn't make sense.

Thanks also to the folks at TechSmith, and Betsy Weber in particular, for their fantastic Snagit product, without which the screenshots would have been so much harder.

Final thanks go to my son Micah Ferrill for his help with the Python code.

Preface

It's no secret that traditional computing patterns are undergoing a radical change. The proliferation of smartphones with ever-increasing processing power will only accelerate the process. Tablet devices have seen a much broader adoption as extensions of the smartphone platform where previous attempts to downsize general-purpose computers failed. While the operating system of the most popular mobile devices may be different from the user's perspective, it has more in common with a desktop system than you might think.

Google's Android platform has seen a huge increase over the last year and is challenging Apple's iOS for market share. Apple's wide lead in applications has been steadily dwindling although the jury is still out when it comes to quality. Building those applications has, for the most part, been restricted to Objective C for iOS and Java for Android. There are a few other options if you take into consideration the MonoTouch and MonoDroid projects, but that's about it.

Mobile devices will probably never completely replace traditional computers, although the division of activity will continue to swing toward the one you have access to the most. This book is about bringing some of the flexibility you get with a desktop computer in the form of writing simple programs or scripts to accomplish a specific task. I know I've learned a lot along the way, and it is my sincere hope that through reading this book you will glean a thing or two as well.

CHAPTER 1

Introduction

This book is about writing real-world applications for the Android platform primarily using the Python language and a little bit of JavaScript. While there is nothing wrong with Java, it really is overkill when all you need to do is turn on or off a handful of settings on your Android device. The Scripting Layer for Android (SL4A) project was started to meet that specific need. This book will introduce you to SL4A and give you the power to automate your Android device in ways you never thought possible.

Why SL4A?

One of the first questions you probably have about this book is, "Why would I want to use SL4A instead of Java?" There are several answers to that question. One is that not everyone is a fan of Java. The Java language is too heavyweight for some and is not entirely open source. It also requires the use of an edit / compile / run design loop that can be tedious for simple applications. An equally legitimate answer is simply "I want to use X", where X could be any number of popular languages.

Google provides a comprehensive software development kit (SDK) aimed specifically at Java developers, and most applications available from the Android market are probably written in Java. I'll address the Android SDK in Chapter 3 and use a number of the tools that come with it throughout the book.

Note SL4A currently supports Beanshell, JRuby, Lua, Perl, PHP, Python, and Rhino.

SL4A is really targeted at anyone looking for a way to write simple scripts to automate tasks on an Android device using any of the supported languages, including Java through Beanshell. It provides an interactive console in which you can type in a line of code and immediately see the result. It even makes it possible, in many cases, to reuse code you've written for a desktop environment. The bottom line is that SL4A makes it possible both to write code for Android-based devices in languages other than Java and to do it in a more interactive way.

The World of Android

Google jumped into the world of mobile operating systems in a big way when it bought Android, Inc. in 2005. It's really pretty amazing how far it has come in such a short time. The Android community is huge and has spawned a wide range of conferences, books, and support materials that are easily available over the Internet.

This is a good point to define a few terms that you'll see throughout the rest of this book. Android applications are typically packaged into `.apk` files. These are really just `.zip` files containing everything needed by the application. In fact, if you rename an `.apk` file to `.zip,` you can open it with any archive tool and examine the contents.

Most Android devices come from the manufacturer with the systems files protected to prevent any inadvertent or malicious manipulation. The Android operating system (OS) is essentially Linux at the core and provides much of the same functionality you would find on any Linux desktop. There are ways to unlock the system areas and provide *root*, or unrestricted, access to the entire filesystem on an Android device. This process is appropriately called *rooting* your device, and once complete, the device is described as *rooted*. SL4A does not require a rooted device, but will work on one if you have chosen this path.

Android Application Anatomy

Android is based on the Linux operating system (at the time of writing, version 2.6 of the Linux kernel). Linux provides all the core plumbing such as device drivers, memory and process management, network stack, and security. The kernel also adds a layer of abstraction between the hardware and applications. To use an anatomical analogy, you might think of Linux as the skeleton, muscles, and organs of the Android body.

The next layer up the Android stack is the Dalvik Virtual Machine (DVM). This piece provides the core Java language support and most of the functionality of the Java programming language. The DVM is the brains in which the majority of all processing takes place. Every Android application runs in its own process space in a private instance of the DVM. The application framework provides all the necessary components needed by an Android application. From the Google Android documentation:

"Developers have full access to the same framework APIs used by the core applications. The application architecture is designed to simplify the reuse of components. Any application can publish its capabilities, and any other application may then make use of those capabilities (subject to security constraints enforced by the framework). This same mechanism allows components to be replaced by the user.

Underlying all applications is a set of services and systems, including:

- *A rich and extensible set of Views that can be used to build an application, including lists, grids, text boxes, buttons, and even an embeddable web browser*

- *Content Providers that enable applications to access data from other applications (such as Contacts) or to share their own data*

- *A Resource Manager, providing access to non-code resources such as localized strings, graphics, and layout files*

- *A Notification Manager that enables all applications to display custom alerts in the status bar*

- *An Activity Manager that manages the lifecycle of applications and provides a common navigation backstack"*

All Android applications are based on three core components: activities, services, and receivers. These core components are activated through messages called *intents*. SL4A gives you access to much of the core Android functionality through its API facade, so it's a good idea to understand some of the basics. Chapters 3 and 5 look at the Android SDK and Android application programming interface (API) in detail, so I'll save the specifics for later. For now, I'll introduce you to activities and intents, as they will be used extensively.

Activities

The Android documentation defines an *activity* as "an application component that provides a screen with which users can interact in order to do something, such as dial the phone, take a photo, send an e-mail, or view a map. Each activity is given a window in which to draw its user interface. The window typically fills the screen but may be smaller than the screen and float on top of other windows."

Android applications consist of one or more activities loosely coupled together. Each application will typically have a "main" activity that can, in turn, launch other activities to accomplish different functions.

Intents

From the Google documentation: "An intent is a simple message object that represents an *intention* to do something. For example, if your application wants to display a web page, it expresses its *intent* to view the URI by creating an intent instance and handing it off to the system. The system locates some other piece of code (in this case, the browser) that knows how to handle that intent and runs it. Intents can also be used to broadcast interesting events (such as a notification) system-wide."

An intent can be used with `startActivity` to launch an *activity*, `broadcastIntent` to send it to any interested `BroadcastReceiver` components, and `startService(Intent)` or `bindService(Intent, ServiceConnection, int)` to communicate with a background service. Intents use primary and secondary attributes that you must provide in the form of arguments.

There are two primary attributes:

- **action:** The general action to be performed, such as `VIEW_ACTION`, `EDIT_ACTION`, `MAIN_ACTION`, and so on

- **data:** The data to operate on, such as a person record in the contacts database, expressed as a Uniform Resource Identifier (URI)

---

[1] `http://developer.android.com/guide/basics/what-is-android.html`

There are four types of secondary attributes:

- **category:** Gives additional information about the action to execute. For example, `LAUNCHER_CATEGORY` means it should appear in the Launcher as a top-level application, while `ALTERNATIVE_CATEGORY` means it should be included in a list of alternative actions the user can perform on a piece of data.

- **type:** Specifies an explicit type (a MIME type) of the intent data. Normally, the type is inferred from the data itself. By setting this attribute, you disable that evaluation and force an explicit type.

- **component:** Specifies an explicit name of a component class to use for the intent. Normally this is determined by looking at the other information in the intent (the action, data/type, and categories) and matching that with a component that can handle it. If this attribute is set, none of the evaluation is performed, and this component is used exactly as is. By specifying this attribute, all the other intent attributes become optional.

- **extras:** A bundle of any additional information. This can be used to provide extended information to the component. For example, if we have an action to send an e-mail message, we could also include extra pieces of data here to supply a subject, body, and so on.

SL4A History

SL4A was first announced on the Google Open Source blog in June of 2009 and was originally named Android Scripting Environment (ASE). It was primarily through the efforts of Damon Kohler that this project came to see the light of day. Others have contributed along the way as the project has continued to mature. The most recent release as of this writing is r4, although you'll also find experimental versions available on the SL4A web site (`http://code.google.com/p/android-scripting`).

SL4A Architecture

At its lowest level, SL4A is essentially a scripting host, which means that as an application it hosts different interpreters each of which processes a specific language. If you were to browse the SL4A source code repository, you would see a copy of the source tree of each language. This gets cross-compiled for the ARM architecture using the Android Native Development Kit (NDK) and loads as a library when SL4A launches a specific interpreter. At that point, the script will be interpreted line by line.

The basic architecture of SL4A is similar to what you would see in a distributed computing environment. Figure 1-1 shows in pictorial form the flow of execution when you launch SL4A and then run a script (in this case, `hello.py`). Every SL4A script must import or source an external file, such as `android.py` for Python, which will define a number of proxy functions needed to communicate with the Android API.

The actual communication between SL4A and the underlying Android operating system uses a remote procedure call (RPC) mechanism and JavaScript Object Notation (JSON). You normally find RPC used in a distributed architecture in which information is passed between a client and a server. In the case of SL4A, the server is the Android OS, and the client is an SL4A script. This adds a layer of separation between SL4A and the Android OS to prevent any malicious script from doing anything harmful.

Security is a concern and is one of the reasons that SL4A uses the RPC mechanism. Here's how the SL4A wiki describes it:

> *"**RPC Authentication:** SL4A enforces per-script security sandboxing by requiring all scripts to be authenticated by the corresponding RPC server. In order for the authentication to succeed, a script has to send the correct handshake secret to the corresponding server. This is accomplished by:*
>
> 1. *reading the AP_HANDSHAKE environment variable.*
>
> 2. *calling the RPC method _authenticate with the value of AP_HANDSHAKE as an argument.*
>
> *The _authenticate method must be the first RPC call and should take place during the initialization of the Android library. For example, see Rhino's or Python's Android module".[2]*

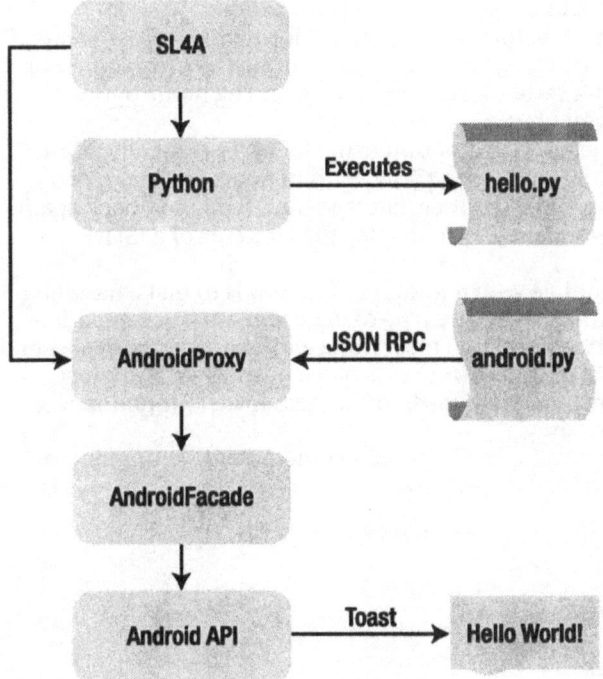

Figure 1-1. *SL4A execution flow diagram*

---

[2] http://code.google.com/p/android-scripting/wiki/InterpreterDeveloperGuide

SL4A Concepts

There are a number of concepts used by SL4A that need to be introduced before we actually use them. At a very high level, SL4A provides a number of functional pieces working in concert together. Each supported language has an interpreter that has been compiled to run on the Android platform. Along with the interpreters is an abstraction layer for the Android API. This abstraction layer provides a calling interface in a form expected for each language. The actual communication between the interpreters and the native Android API uses inter-process communication (IPC) as an extra layer of protection. Finally, there is support for an on-device environment to test scripts interactively.

Although Figure 1-1 shows Python as the interpreter, the concept works pretty much the same for all supported languages. Each interpreter executes the language in its own process until an API call is made. This is then passed along to the Android OS using the RPC mechanism. All communication between the interpreter and the Android API typically uses JSON to pass information.

JavaScript Object Notation (JSON)

SL4A makes heavy use of JSON to pass information around. You might want to visit the http://www.json.org web site if you've never seen JSON before. In its simplest form JSON is just a way of defining a data structure or an object in much the same way you would in the context of a program. For the most part, you will see JSON structures appear as a series of name/value pairs. The name part will always be a string while the value can be any JavaScript object.

In SL4A, you will find that many of the API calls return information using JSON. Fortunately, there are multiple options when it comes to creating, parsing, and using JSON. Python treats JSON as a first-class citizen with a full library of tools to convert from JSON to other native Python types and back again. The Python Standard Library `pprint` module is a convenient way to display the contents of a JSON response in a more readable format.

The Python Standard Library includes a JSON module with a number of methods to make handling JSON much easier. Because JSON objects can contain virtually any type of data, you must use encoders and decoders to get native Python data types into a JSON object. This is done with the `json.JSONEncoder` and `json.JSONDecoder` methods. When you move a JSON object from one place to another, you must serialize and then deserialize that object. This requires the `json.load()` and `json.loads()` functions for decoding, and `json.dump()` plus `json.dumps()` for encoding.

There are a large number of web services that have adopted JSON as a standard way to implement an API. Here's one from Yahoo for images:

```
{
  "Image": {
    "Width":800,
    "Height":600,
    "Title":"View from 15th Floor",
    "Thumbnail":
    {
      "Url":"http:\/\/scd.mm-b1.yimg.com\/image\/481989943",
      "Height": 125,
      "Width": "100"
    },
  "IDs":[ 116, 943, 234, 38793 ]
  }
}
```

Events

The Android OS uses an event queue as a means of handling specific hardware-generated actions such as when the user presses one of the hardware keys. Other possibilities include any of the device sensors such as the accelerometer, GPS receiver, light sensor, magnetometer, and touch screen. Each sensor must be explicitly turned on before information can be retrieved.

The SL4A API facade provides a number of API calls that will initiate some type of action resulting in an event. These include the following:

- `startLocating()`
- `startSensing()`
- `startTrackingPhoneState()`
- `startTrackingSignalStrengths()`

Each of these calls will begin gathering some type of data and generate an event such as a "location" event or a "phone" event. Any of the supported languages can register an event handler to process each event. The `startLocating()` call takes two parameters, allowing you to specify the minimum distance and the minimum time between updates.

Languages

One of the things that SL4A brings to the table is lots of language choices. As of the writing of this book, those choices include Beanshell, Lua, JRuby Perl, PHP, Python, and Rhino (versions given in the following sections). You can also write or reuse shell scripts if you like. Without question, the most popular of all these languages is Python. Support for the others has not been near the level of Python, up to this point, but it is possible to use them if you're so inclined.

Beanshell 2.0b4

Beanshell is an interesting language in that it's basically interpreted Java. It kind of begs the question of why you would want an interpreted Java when you could just write native Java using the Android SDK. The Beanshell interpreter does provide an interactive tool to write and test code. It's definitely not going to be the fastest code, but you might find it useful for testing code snippets without the need to go through the whole compile/deploy/test cycle.

Examining the `android.bsh` file shows the code used to set up the JSON data structures for passing information to and receiving information from the Android OS. Here's what the basic call function looks like:

```
call(String method, JSONArray params) {
  JSONObject request = new JSONObject();
  request.put("id", id);
  request.put("method", method);
  request.put("params", params);
  out.write(request.toString() + "\n");
  out.flush();
  String data = in.readLine();
```

```
    if (data == null) {
      return null;
    }
    return new JSONObject(data);
  }
```

Here's a simple `hello_world.bsh` script:

```
source("/sdcard/com.googlecode.bshforandroid/extras/bsh/android.bsh");
droid = Android();
droid.call("makeToast", "Hello, Android!");
```

Lua 5.1.4

Lua.org describes Lua as "an extension programming language designed to support general procedural programming with data description facilities".[3] The term *extension programming language* means that Lua is intended to be used to extend an existing program through scripting. This fits in well with the concept of SL4A.

From a syntax perspective, Lua resembles Python somewhat in that it doesn't use curly braces to wrap code blocks or require a semicolon for statement termination, although you can do this if you want to. In the case of a function definition, Lua uses the reserved word `function` to begin the code block and then the reserved word `end` to mark the end.

Lua has most of the standard data types you would expect in a modern language and also includes the concept of a table. In Lua, a table is a dynamically created object that can be manipulated much like pointers in conventional languages. Tables must be explicitly created before use. Tables can also refer to other tables, making them well suited to recursive data types. The list of generic functions for manipulating tables includes `table.concat`, `.insert`, `.maxn`, `.remove`, and `.sort`.

From the Lua web site, here's a short Lua code snippet that creates a circular linked list:

```
list = {}                    -- creates an empty table
current = list
i = 0
while i < 10 do
  current.value = i
  current.next = {}
  current = current.next
  i = i+1
end
current.value = i
acurrent.next = list
```

---

[3] http://www.lua.org/manual/5.1/manual.html

Here's the Lua code that implements the RPC call function:

```lua
function rpc(client, method, ...)
  assert(method, 'method param is nil')
  local rpc = {
    ['id'] = id,
    ['method'] = method,
    params = arg
  }
  local request = json.encode(rpc)
  client:send(request .. '\n')
  id = id + 1
  local response = client:receive('*l')
  local result = json.decode(response)
  if result.error ~= nil then
    print(result.error)
  end
  return result
end
```

The obligatory Lua hello world script:

```lua
require "android"

name = android.getInput("Hello!", "What is your name?")
android.printDict(name)  -- A convenience method for inspecting dicts (tables).
android.makeToast("Hello, " .. name.result)
```

The Lua wiki has links to sample code with a large number of useful snippets.

Perl 5.10.1

Perl probably qualifies as the oldest of the languages available in SL4A if you don't count the shell. It dates back to 1987 and has been used in just about every type of computing application you can think of. The biggest advantage of using Perl is the large number of code examples to draw from. Coding the hello_world.pl script looks a lot like that of other languages:

```perl
use Android;
my $a = Android->new();
$a->makeToast("Hello, Android!");
```

Here's the Perl code needed to launch an SL4A script:

```perl
# Given a method and parameters, call the server with JSON,
# and return the parsed the response JSON.  If the server side
# looks to be dead, close the connection and return undef.
sub do_rpc {
    my $self = shift;
    if ($self->trace) {
        show_trace(qq[do_rpc: $self: @_]);
    }
```

```perl
    my $method = pop;
    my $request = to_json({ id => $self->{id},
                            method => $method,
                            params => [ @_ ] });
    if (defined $self->{conn}) {
        print { $self->{conn} } $request, "\n";
        if ($self->trace) {
            show_trace(qq[client: sent: "$request"]);
        }
        $self->{id}++;
        my $response = readline($self->{conn});
        chomp $response;
        if ($self->trace) {
            show_trace(qq[client: rcvd: "$response"]);
        }
        if (defined $response && length $response) {
            my $result = from_json($response);
            my $success = 0;
            my $error;
            if (defined $result) {
                if (ref $result eq 'HASH') {
                    if (defined $result->{error}) {
                        $error = to_json( { error => $result->{error} } );
                    } else {
                        $success = 1;
                    }
                } else {
                    $error = "illegal JSON reply: $result";
                }
            }
            unless ($success || defined $error) {
                $error = "unknown JSON error";
            }
            if (defined $error) {
                printf STDERR "$0: client: error: %s\n", $error;
            }
            if ($Opt{trace}) {
                print STDERR Data::Dumper->Dump([$result], [qw(result)]);
            }
            return $result;
        }
    }
    $self->close;
    return;
}
```

PHP 5.3.3

PHP is, without a doubt, one of the most successful general-purpose scripting languages for creating dynamic web pages. From humble beginnings as the Personal Home Page, the acronym PHP now stands for PHP: Hypertext Preprocessor. PHP is a free and open source language with implementations for virtually every major operating system available free of charge.

Here's the PHP code needed to launch an SL4A script via an RPC:

```php
public function rpc($method, $args)
{
    $data = array(
        'id'=>$this->_id,
        'method'=>$method,
        'params'=>$args
    );
    $request = json_encode($data);
    $request .= "\n";
    $sent = socket_write($this->_socket, $request, strlen($request));
    $response = socket_read($this->_socket, 1024, PHP_NORMAL_READ) or die("Could not
 read input\n");
    $this->_id++;
    $result = json_decode($response);

    $ret =  array ('id' => $result->id,
        'result' => $result->result,
        'error' => $result->error
    );
    return $ret;
}
```

The PHP version of hello_world.php looks like this:

```php
<?php
require_once("Android.php");
$droid = new Android();
$name = $droid->getInput("Hi!", "What is your name?");
$droid->makeToast('Hello, ' . $name['result']);
```

You get a number of other example scripts when you install PHP along with the basic hello_world.php.

Rhino 1.7R2

The Rhino interpreter gives you a way to write stand-alone JavaScript code. JavaScript is actually standardized as ECMAScript under ECMA-262. You can download the standard from http://www.ecma-international.org/publications/standards/Ecma-262.htm. The advantages of having a JavaScript interpreter are many. If you plan on building any type of custom user interface using HTML and JavaScript, you could prototype the JavaScript part and test it with the Rhino interpreter.

The **android.js** file for Rhino resembles that of the other languages in many aspects. Here's what the RPC call definition looks like:

```
this.rpc = function(method, args) {
  this.id += 1;
  var request = JSON.stringify({'id': this.id, 'method': method,
                                'params': args});
  this.output.write(request + '\n');
  this.output.flush();
  var response = this.input.readLine();
  return eval("(" + response + ")");
},
```

Here's a simple Rhino **hello_world.js** script:

```
load("/sdcard/sl4a/extras/rhino/android.js");
var droid = new Android();
droid.makeToast("Hello, Android!");
```

JRuby 1.4

One of the potential hazards of any open source project is neglect. At the time of this writing, based on SL4A r4, the JRuby interpreter has suffered from neglect and doesn't even run the **hello_world.rb** script. In any case, here's what that script looks like:

```
require "android"
droid = Android.new
droid.makeToast "Hello, Android!"
```

The JRuby interpreter does launch, and you can try out some basic JRuby code with it. Here's what the Android class looks like in Ruby:

```
class Android

  def initialize()
    @client = TCPSocket.new('localhost', AP_PORT)
    @id = 0
  end

  def rpc(method, *args)
    @id += 1
    request = {'id' => @id, 'method' => method, 'params' => args}.to_json()
    @client.puts request
    response = @client.gets()
    return JSON.parse(response)
  end

  def method_missing(method, *args)
    rpc(method, *args)
  end

end
```

Shell

If you're a shell script wizard, then you'll feel right at home with SL4A's shell interpreter. It's essentially the same bash script environment you would see at a typical Linux terminal prompt. You'll find all the familiar commands for manipulating files like cp, ls, mkdir, and mv.

Python

Python has a wide usage and heavy following, especially within Google. In fact, its following is so significant they hired the inventor of the language, Guido van Rossum. Python has been around for quite a while and has many open source projects written in the language. It also has seen the most interest as far as SL4A is concerned, so you'll find more examples and discussions in the forums than for any of the other languages. For that reason, I will spend a little more time introducing the language, trying to hit the highlights of things that will be important from an SL4A perspective.

Language Basics

Knowing the Python language is not an absolute requirement for this book, but it will help. The first thing you need to know about Python is that everything is an object. The second thing is that whitespace is meaningful in Python. By that, I mean Python uses either tabs or actual spaces (ASCII 32) instead of curly braces to control code execution (see Figure 1-2). Third, it's important to remember that Python is a case-sensitive language.

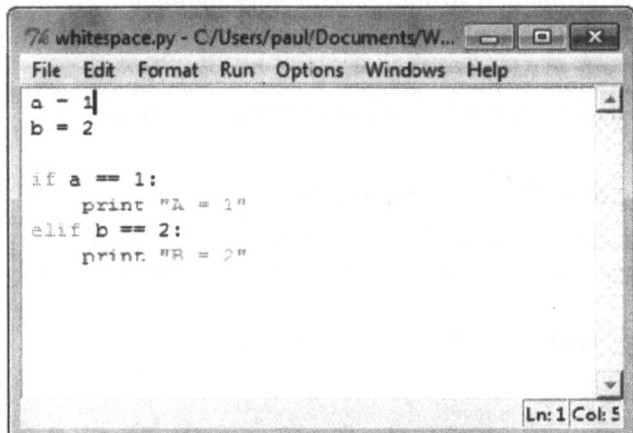

Figure 1-2. *Example of whitespace usage in Python*

Python is a great language to use when teaching an "introduction to computer programming" course. Every installation of standard Python comes with a command-line interpreter where you can type in a line of code and immediately see the result. To launch the interpreter, simply enter python at a command prompt (Windows) or terminal window (Linux and Mac OS X). At this point, you should see a few lines with version information followed by the triple arrow prompt (>>>), letting you know that you're inside the Python interpreter as shown here:

```
C:\Users\paul>python
Python 2.6.6 (r266:84297, Aug 24 2010, 18:13:38) [MSC v.1500 64 bit (AMD64)] on
win32
Type "help", "copyright", "credits" or "license" for more information.
>>>
```

Python uses a number of naming conventions that you will see if you examine much Python code. The first is the double underscore, which is used in Python to "mangle" or change names as a way to define private variables and methods used inside a class. You will see this notation used for "special" methods such as __init_(self). If a class has the special __init__ method, it will be invoked whenever a new instantiation of that class occurs.

For example:

```
>>> class Point:
        def __init__(self, x, y):
                self.x = x
                self.y = y


>>> xy = Point(1,2)
>>> xy.x, xy.y
(1, 2)
```

As you can see from the example, self is used as a reserved word in Python and refers to the first argument of a method. It's actually a Python convention and, in reality, has no special meaning to Python. However, because it's a widely accepted convention, you'll want to stick with it to avoid any potential issues. Technically, self is a reference to the class or function itself. Methods within a class may call other methods in the same class by using the method attributes of the self argument.

Python has a short list of built-in constants. The main ones you'll run into are False, True, and None. False and True are of type bool and show up primarily in logical tests or to create an infinite loop.

One of the things that frequently confuses new users of the language is the variety of data types. The following sections give quick overview of the key data types you'll need to use Python and SL4A.

Dictionary: An Unordered Set of Key/Value Pairs Requiring Unique Keys

A Python dictionary maps directly to a JSON data structure. The syntax for defining a dictionary uses curly braces to enclose entries and a colon between the key and value. Here's what a simple dictionary definition looks like:

```
students = {'barney' : 1001, 'betty' : 1002, 'fred' : 1003, 'wilma' : 1004}
```

To reference entries, use the key, as shown here:

```
students['barney'] = 999
students['betty'] = 1000
```

You can also use the dict() constructor to build dictionaries. When the key is a simple string, you can create a new dictionary using arguments passed to dict() such as the following:

```
students = dict(barney=1001, betty=1002, fred=1003, wilma=1004)
```

Because everything in Python is an object, you can expect to see methods associated with a dictionary object. As you might expect, there are methods to return the keys and the values from a dictionary. Here's what that would look like for the `students` dictionary:

```
>>> students
{'barney': 1001, 'betty': 1002, 'fred': 1003, 'wilma': 1004}
>>> students.keys()
['barney', 'betty', 'fred', 'wilma']
>>> students.values()
[1001, 1002, 1003, 1004]
```

The square bracket convention denotes a list. Evaluating the `students.keys()` statement returns a list of keys from the `students` dictionary.

List: A Built-In Python Sequence Similar to an Array in Other Languages

In Python, a *sequence* is defined as "an iterable which supports efficient element access using integer indices via the __getitem__() special method and defines a `len()` method that returns the length of the sequence." An *iterable* is defined as "a container object capable of returning its members one at a time." Python provides direct language support for iteration because it's one of the more common operations in programming. List objects provide a number of methods to make working with them easier. From the Python documentation:

- `list.append(x)`: Add an item to the end of the list; equivalent to `a[len(a):] = [x]`.

- `list.extend(L)`: Extend the list by appending all the items in the given list; equivalent to `a[len(a):] = L`.

- `list.insert(I,x)`: Insert an item at a given position. The first argument is the index of the element before which to insert, so `a.insert(0, x)` inserts at the front of the list, and `a.insert(len(a), x)` is equivalent to `a.append(x)`.

- `list.remove(x)`: Remove the first item from the list whose value is *x*. It is an error if there is no such item.

- `list.pop([i])`: Remove the item at the given position in the list and return it. If no index is specified, `a.pop()` removes and returns the last item in the list. (The square brackets around the *i* in the method signature denote that the parameter is optional, not that you should type square brackets at that position.) You will see this notation frequently in the Python Library Reference.

- `list.index(x)`: Return the index in the list of the first item whose value is *x*. It is an error if there is no such item.

- `list.count(x)`: Return the number of times *x* appears in the list.

- `list.sort`: Sort the items of the list, in place.

- `list.reverse(x)`: Reverse the elements of the list, in place.

String: An Immutable Sequence Made Up of Either ASCII or Unicode Characters

The key word in the string definition is *immutable,* meaning not changeable after creation. This makes for speedy implementation of many operations and is why Python can process strings in a very efficient manner. The backslash (\) character is used to escape characters that would otherwise have a special meaning, including the backslash character itself. If you prefix a string literal with either lower or uppercase "r," you don't need the backslash character because every character will be treated as a "raw" string. You can define a string literal using either single or double quotes, as shown here:

```
name = "Paul Ferrill"
initials = 'PF'
directory = r'C:\users\paul\documents'
```

There are a large number of methods available for the string class. Here's the list from the Python documentation:[4]

```
capitalize()
center(width[, fillchar])
count(sub[, start[, end]])
decode( [encoding[, errors]])
encode( [encoding[,errors]])
endswith( suffix[, start[, end]])
expandtabs( [tabsize])
find( sub[, start[, end]])
index( sub[, start[, end]])
isalnum( )
isalpha( )
isdigit( )
islower( )
isspace( )
istitle( )
isupper( )
join( seq)
ljust( width[, fillchar])
lower( )
lstrip( [chars])
partition( sep)
replace( old, new[, count])
rfind( sub [,start [,end]])
rindex( sub[, start[, end]])
rjust( width[, fillchar])
rpartition( sep)
rsplit( [sep [,maxsplit]])
rstrip( [chars])
split( [sep [,maxsplit]])
splitlines( [keepends])
startswith( prefix[, start[, end]])
```

---

[4] http://docs.python.org/release/2.6/library/stdtypes.html#string-methods

```
strip( [chars])
swapcase( )
title( )
translate( table[, deletechars])
upper( )
zfill( width)
```

With Python 2.6, the built-in `str` and `unicode` classes provide a very full-featured formatting and substitution capability through the `str.format()` method. There's also a `Formatter` class with an even more extensive set of methods suitable for implementing a templating capability. Python uses the percent sign with strings for formatting as well. Here's an example of using the percent sign in a print statement:

```
>>> Pi = 3.141593
>>> print "Pi = %10.2f" % Pi
Pi =       3.14
>>> print "Long Pi = %10.6f" % Pi
Long Pi =    3.141593
```

This is a good place to talk about the use of *slices* in Python. Any object with multiple items, such as a string, can be addressed using a notation called a slice. To reference the items from j to k of string s, use `s[j:k]`. Adding a third item to the slice notation includes a step so that `s[j:k:l]` references the items from j to k, incremented by l. To reference items from the beginning of the list to the *n*th item, use `s[:n]`, and from the *n*th item to the end would use `s[n:]`. For example:

```
>>> mylist = [1,2,3,4,5,6,7,8,9]
>>> mylist[:3]
[1, 2, 3]
>>> mylist[3:]
[4, 5, 6, 7, 8, 9]
```

Note that Python uses zero-based referencing. So, the first or zeroth element of mylist would be equal to 1. The syntax `mylist[:3]` says "return all elements of mylist from the beginning up to, but not including, the fourth element." Negative indices count from the end of the list.

Tuple: An Immutable List

As with the string type, a *tuple* is immutable, meaning it can't be changed once created. Tuples are defined using the same syntax as a list, except they are enclosed by parentheses instead of square brackets. Here's an example of a tuple:

```
>>> Sentence = ("Today", "is", "the", "first", "day", "of", "the", "rest", "of", "your", ↵
 "life.")
>>> Sentence
('Today', 'is', 'the', 'first', 'day', 'of', 'the', 'rest', 'of', 'your', 'life.')
>>> Sentence[0]
'Today'
>>> Sentence[1:3]
('is', 'the')
>>> Sentence[-1]
'life.'
```

Python Standard Library

One of the biggest strengths of the Python language has to be the Python Standard Library, which includes a wide variety of routines to make your coding life much simpler. Although there's not enough space available in this introduction to walk through the entire library, I'll try to point out some of the key functions that will show up in later chapters.

All documentation for the Python language can be found at http://docs.python.org, including older releases. SL4A uses Python 2.6, so you'll want to look under the older releases to get the right information. For the Python Standard Library, you'll want to start with http://docs.python.org/release/2.6.5/library/index.html.

The Python interpreter has a large number of built-in functions that are always available. One of those functions is dir(), which displays all the names that a module defines. If you type dir() at a Python prompt you'll receive a list of names in the current local scope, as seen here:

```
>>> dir()
['__builtins__', '__doc__', '__name__', '__package__']
>>> import sys
>>> dir()
['__builtins__', '__doc__', '__name__', '__package__', 'sys']
>>> import os
>>> dir()
['__builtins__', '__doc__', '__name__', '__package__', 'os', 'sys']
```

If you pass an argument to dir(), you'll get a list of all attributes for that object. Many of the modules from the Python Standard Library implement a method named __dir__(), which is what actually produces the list of attributes when called. If there is no __dir__() method, the function will attempt to use the object's __dir__() attribute to get the information it needs.

You can use dir() on any object to inspect the module's attributes. Here's what you get when you use dir() on the android object:

```
>>> import android
>>> dir(android)
['Android', 'HANDSHAKE', 'HOST', 'PORT', 'Result', '__author__', '__builtins__', '__doc__',↵
 '__file__', '__name__', '__package__', 'collections', 'json', 'os', 'socket', 'sys']
```

Another example is to define a string to see what methods are available:

```
>>> a = "Hello"
>>> dir(a)
['__add__', '__class__', '__contains__', '__delattr__', '__doc__', '__eq__', '__format__',↵
 '__ge__', '__getattribute__', '__getitem__', '__getnewargs__', '__getslice__', '__gt__',↵
 '__hash__', '__init__', '__le__', '__len__', '__lt__', '__mod__', '__mul__', '__ne__',↵
 '__new__', '__reduce__', '__reduce_ex__', '__repr__', '__rmod__', '__rmul__',↵
 '__setattr__', '__sizeof__', '__str__', '__subclasshook__', '_formatter_field_name_split',↵
 '_formatter_parser', 'capitalize', 'center', 'count', 'decode', 'encode', 'endswith',↵
 'expandtabs', 'find', 'format', 'index', 'isalnum', 'isalpha', 'isdigit', 'islower',↵
 'isspace', 'istitle', 'isupper', 'join', 'ljust', 'lower', 'lstrip', 'partition',↵
 'replace', 'rfind', 'rindex', 'rjust', 'rpartition', 'rsplit', 'rstrip', 'split',↵
 'splitlines', 'startswith', 'strip', 'swapcase', 'title', 'translate', 'upper', 'zfill']
```

There are times when you may be working with the Python Standard Library, or even some other library, and you don't know the type of a returned variable. For this, you can use the **type( )** built-in function like this:

```
>>> type(a)
<type 'str'>
```

Number conversion is one of those frequently needed functions, and Python has that down in spades. Here are a few examples:

```
>>> bin(12345678)
'0b101111000110000101001110'
>>> hex(12345678)
'0xbc614e'
>>> oct(12345678)
'057060516'
```

The result of these functions is a string. To convert from a string to an integer, use the int( ) function as follows:

```
>>> print int('0xbc614e',16)
12345678
```

File input and output in Python use a very simplified approach. To open a file, use **open**, as shown in Figure 1-3.

```
>>> infile = open('
                  open(name[, mode[, buffering]]) -> file object
```

Figure 1-3. Example of the Python file open

Supported file modes include append ('a'), read ('r'), and write ('w'). **open** returns an object of type **file** with a full selection of methods and attributes. Here's what that looks like:

```
>>> infile = open(r'c:\users\paul\documents\dependents.txt')
>>> type(infile)
<type 'file'>
>>> dir(infile)
['__class__', '__delattr__', '__doc__', '__enter__', '__exit__', '__format__',↵
 '__getattribute__', '__hash__', '__init__', '__iter__', '__new__', '__reduce__',↵
 '__reduce_ex__', '__repr__', '__setattr__', '__sizeof__', '__str__', '__subclasshook__',↵
 'close', 'closed', 'encoding', 'errors', 'fileno', 'flush', 'isatty', 'mode', 'name',↵
 'newlines', 'next', 'read', 'readinto', 'readline', 'readlines', 'seek', 'softspace',v
 'tell', 'truncate', 'write', 'writelines', 'xreadlines']
```

The os module provides platform-independent interfaces to the underlying operating system. If you plan to do anything with filenames, you'll want to get to know the os module. Here's what you get if you import os and then do a dir(os):

```
>>> dir(os)
['F_OK', 'O_APPEND', 'O_BINARY', 'O_CREAT', 'O_EXCL', 'O_NOINHERIT', 'O_RANDOM', 'O_RDONLY',
 'O_RDWR', 'O_SEQUENTIAL', 'O_SHORT_LIVED', 'O_TEMPORARY', 'O_TEXT', 'O_TRUNC', 'O_WRONLY',
 'P_DETACH', 'P_NOWAIT', 'P_NOWAITO', 'P_OVERLAY', 'P_WAIT', 'R_OK', 'SEEK_CUR', 'SEEK_END',
 'SEEK_SET', 'TMP_MAX', 'UserDict', 'W_OK', 'X_OK', '_Environ', '__all__', '__builtins__',
 '__doc__', '__file__', '__name__', '__package__', '_copy_reg', '_execvpe', '_exists',
 '_exit', '_get_exports_list', '_make_stat_result', '_make_statvfs_result',
 '_pickle_stat_result', '_pickle_statvfs_result', 'abort', 'access', 'altsep', 'chdir',
 'chmod', 'close', 'closerange', 'curdir', 'defpath', 'devnull', 'dup', 'dup2', 'environ',
 'errno', 'error', 'execl', 'execle', 'execlp', 'execlpe', 'execv', 'execve', 'execvp',
 'execvpe', 'extsep', 'fdopen', 'fstat', 'fsync', 'getcwd', 'getcwdu', 'getenv', 'getpid',
 'isatty', 'linesep', 'listdir', 'lseek', 'lstat', 'makedirs', 'mkdir', 'name', 'open',
 'pardir', 'path', 'pathsep', 'pipe', 'popen', 'popen2', 'popen3', 'popen4', 'putenv',
 'read', 'remove', 'removedirs', 'rename', 'renames', 'rmdir', 'sep', 'spawnl', 'spawnle',
 'spawnv', 'spawnve', 'startfile', 'stat', 'stat_float_times', 'stat_result',
 'statvfs_result', 'strerror', 'sys', 'system', 'tempnam', 'times', 'tmpfile', 'tmpnam',
 'umask', 'unlink', 'unsetenv', 'urandom', 'utime', 'waitpid', 'walk', 'write']
```

As you can see, there are quite a few methods available. Another handy module for dealing with files and directories is glob, which you can use to get a list of files in a specific directory based on wild cards like this:

```
>>> import glob
for file in glob.glob("*.jpg"):
    print file
```

This would print a list of all the .jpg files in the current working directory. The next module on the hit list is datetime. If you need to do anything with dates or times, you'll need datetime. Here are a few examples of using this module:

```
>>> print datetime.date.today()
2011-04-26
>>> print datetime.datetime.now()
2011-04-26 14:35:25.045000
>>> print datetime.date.weekday(datetime.datetime.now())
1
```

Last on the list of file utilities is shutil. This module provides a number of file utilities such as shutil.copy, shutil.copytree, shutil.move, and shutil.rmtree. Here's what you get if you import shutil and use dir() to see the methods:

```
>>> import shutil
>>> dir(shutil)
['Error', '__all__', '__builtins__', '__doc__', '__file__', '__name__', '__package__',
 '_basename', '_samefile', 'abspath', 'copy', 'copy2', 'copyfile', 'copyfileobj',
 'copymode', 'copystat', 'copytree', 'destinsrc', 'fnmatch', 'ignore_patterns', 'move',
 'os', 'rmtree', 'stat', 'sys']
```

Processing data stored in comma-separated value (CSV) files is another common task. Python 2.6 includes the csv module for just such a task. Here's a simple script that uses the csv module to simply print out all rows in a file:

```
import csv
reader = csv.reader(open("some.csv", "rb"))
for row in reader:
    print row
```

You can also write to a CSV file in a similar manner:

```
import csv
writer = csv.writer(open("some.csv", "wb"))
writer.writerows(someiterable)
```

This example shows how you could parse the data into separate items in a list:

```
>>> import csv
>>> for row in csv.reader(['one,two,three']):
        print row

['one', 'two', 'three']
```

You could use the string.count method if you didn't know how many columns were in the file like this:

```
>>> import string
>>> string.count('one,two,three,four,five',',')
4
```

The last method from the csv module we'll look at is DictReader. In most cases, you should know what fields are contained in your CSV file. If that is indeed the case, you can use the DictReader function to read the file into a dictionary. Here's a sample text file with name, address, and phone number:

```
John Doe|Anycity|ST|12345|(800) 555-1212
Jane Doe|Anycity|ST|12345|(800) 555-1234
Fred Flinstone|Bedrock|ZZ|98765|(800) 555-4321
Wilma Flinstone|Bedrock|ZZ|98765|(800) 555-4321
Bambam Flinston|City|ST|12345|(800) 555-4321
Barney Rubble|Bedrock|ZZ|98765|(800) 555-1111
```

We need one more module for our sample code: itertools. This module provides functions for creating efficient iterators used by Python with the for keyword. The code to read the file and print out the results looks like this:

```
import itertools
import csv

HeaderFields = ["Name", "City", "State", "Zip", "PhoneNum"]

infile = open("testdata.txt")

contacts = csv.DictReader(infile, HeaderFields, delimiter="|")

for header in itertools.izip(contacts):
    print "Header (%d fields): %s" % (len(header), header)
```

Finally, here's what the output looks like:

```
Header (1 fields): ({'City': 'Anycity', 'State': 'ST', 'PhoneNum': '(800) 555-1212', 'Name':↩
 'John Doe', 'Zip': '12345'},)
Header (1 fields): ({'City': 'Anycity', 'State': 'ST', 'PhoneNum': '(800) 555-1234', 'Name':↩
 'Jane Doe', 'Zip': '12345'},)
Header (1 fields): ({'City': 'Bedrock', 'State': 'ZZ', 'PhoneNum': '(800) 555-4321', 'Name':↩
 'Fred Flinstone', 'Zip': '98765'},)
Header (1 fields): ({'City': 'Bedrock', 'State': 'ZZ', 'PhoneNum': '(800) 555-4321', 'Name':↩
 'Wilma Flinstone', 'Zip': '98765'},)
Header (1 fields): ({'City': 'City', 'State': 'ST', 'PhoneNum': '(800) 555-4321', 'Name':↩
 'Bambam Flinston', 'Zip': '12345'},)
Header (1 fields): ({'City': 'Bedrock', 'State': 'ZZ', 'PhoneNum': '(800) 555-1111', 'Name':↩
 'Barney Rubble', 'Zip': '98765'},)
Header (1 fields): ({'City': 'Bedrock', 'State': 'ZZ', 'PhoneNum': '(800) 555-1111', 'Name':↩
 'Betty Rubble', 'Zip': '98765'},)
```

The weekday method returns 0 for Monday, 1 for Tuesday, and so on. One of the things you might need later is the ability to convert from a system timestamp value to a human-readable string. Here's a snippet of code used in a later chapter that converts the timestamp for an SMS message into a string:

```
b = ''
for m in SMSmsgs:
  millis = int(message['date'])/1000
  strtime = datetime.datetime.fromtimestamp(millis)
  b += strtime.strftime("%m/%d/%y %H:%M:%S") + ',' + m['address'] + ',' + m['body'] + '\n'
```

Writing code for mobile devices will inevitably involve communicating with a web site in some fashion. The Python Standard Library has two modules to help with this task: urllib and urllib2. Although the two modules provide similar functionality, they do it in different ways. Here's what you get when you import both and examine their methods:

```
>>> import urllib
>>> dir(urllib)
['ContentTooShortError', 'FancyURLopener', 'MAXFTPCACHE', 'URLopener', '__all__',↩
 '__builtins__', '__doc__', '__file__', '__name__', '__package__', '__version__',↩
 '_ftperrors', '_have_ssl', '_hextochr', '_hostprog', '_is_unicode', '_localhost',↩
 '_noheaders', '_nportprog', '_passwdprog', '_portprog', '_queryprog', '_safemaps',↩
 '_tagprog', '_thishost', '_typeprog', '_urlopener', '_userprog', '_valueprog', 'addbase',↩
 'addclosehook', 'addinfo', 'addinfourl', 'always_safe', 'basejoin', 'ftpcache',↩
 'ftperrors', 'ftpwrapper', 'getproxies', 'getproxies_environment', 'getproxies_registry',↩
 'localhost', 'main', 'noheaders', 'os', 'pathname2url', 'proxy_bypass',↩
 'proxy_bypass_environment', 'proxy_bypass_registry', 'quote', 'quote_plus', 'reporthook',↩
 'socket', 'splitattr', 'splithost', 'splitnport', 'splitpasswd', 'splitport', 'splitquery',↩
 'splittag', 'splittype', 'splituser', 'splitvalue', 'ssl', 'string', 'sys', 'test',↩
 'test1', 'thishost', 'time', 'toBytes', 'unquote', 'unquote_plus', 'unwrap',↩
 'url2pathname', 'urlcleanup', 'urlencode', 'urlopen', 'urlretrieve', 'warnings']
>>> import urllib2
>>> dir(urllib2)
```

```
['AbstractBasicAuthHandler', 'AbstractDigestAuthHandler', 'AbstractHTTPHandler',↵
 'BaseHandler', 'CacheFTPHandler', 'FTPHandler', 'FileHandler', 'HTTPBasicAuthHandler',↵
 'HTTPCookieProcessor', 'HTTPDefaultErrorHandler', 'HTTPDigestAuthHandler', 'HTTPError',↵
 'HTTPErrorProcessor', 'HTTPHandler', 'HTTPPasswordMgr', 'HTTPPasswordMgrWithDefaultRealm',↵
 'HTTPRedirectHandler', 'HTTPSHandler', 'OpenerDirector', 'ProxyBasicAuthHandler',↵
 'ProxyDigestAuthHandler', 'ProxyHandler', 'Request', 'StringIO', 'URLError',↵
 'UnknownHandler', '__builtins__', '__doc__', '__file__', '__name__', '__package__',↵
 '__version__', '_cut_port_re', '_opener', '_parse_proxy', 'addinfourl', 'base64', 'bisect',↵
 'build_opener', 'ftpwrapper', 'getproxies', 'hashlib', 'httplib', 'install_opener',↵
 'localhost', 'mimetools', 'os', 'parse_http_list', 'parse_keqv_list', 'posixpath',↵
 'proxy_bypass', 'quote', 'random', 'randombytes', 're', 'request_host', 'socket',↵
 'splitattr', 'splithost', 'splitpasswd', 'splitport', 'splittype', 'splituser',↵
 'splitvalue', 'sys', 'time', 'unquote', 'unwrap', 'url2pathname', 'urlopen', 'urlparse']
```

If you simply want to download the contents of a URL as you might do with a right-click and Save As on a desktop machine, you can use urllib.urlretrieve. There are a number of helper methods in urllib to build or decode a URL, including pathname2url, url2pathname, urlencode, quote, and unquote. Here's a snippet of code for urllib:

```
import urllib

class OpenMyURL(urllib.FancyURLopener):
    # read a URL with HTTP authentication

    def setpasswd(self, user, passwd):
        self.__user = user
        self.__passwd = passwd

    def prompt_user_passwd(self, host, realm):
        return self.__user, self.__passwd

urlopener = OpenMyURL()
urlopener.setpasswd("user", "password")

f = urlopener.open("http://www.aprivatesite.com")
print f.read()
```

If you need to download files over FTP, you'll want to use urllib2. Here's a sample I found on stackoverflow.com:

```
>>> files = urllib2.urlopen('ftp://ftp2.census.gov/geo/tiger/TIGER2008/01_ALABAMA/')↵
.read().splitlines()
>>> for l in files[:4]: print l
...
drwxrwsr-x    2 0         4009          4096 Nov 26  2008 01001_Autauga_County
drwxrwsr-x    2 0         4009          4096 Nov 26  2008 01003_Baldwin_County
drwxrwsr-x    2 0         4009          4096 Nov 26  2008 01005_Barbour_County
drwxrwsr-x    2 0         4009          4096 Nov 26  2008 01007_Bibb_County
```

For implementing a basic HTTP server there's SimpleHTTPServer. Here's what you get:

```
>>> import SimpleHTTPServer
>>> dir(SimpleHTTPServer)
['BaseHTTPServer', 'SimpleHTTPRequestHandler', 'StringIO', '__all__', '__builtins__',
 '__doc__', '__file__', '__name__', '__package__', '__version__', 'cgi', 'mimetypes',
 'os', 'posixpath', 'shutil', 'test', 'urllib']
```

I'll use this module in Chapter 7 to build a quick script to give you access to any directory on your Android device from a web browser. You might have occasion to need the value of your local IP address. The socket library comes to the rescue here. One trick to get your own address is to connect to a well-known site and retrieve your address from the connection details. Here's how to do that:

```
>>> s = socket.socket(socket.AF_INET, socket.SOCK_DGRAM)
>>> s.connect(("gmail.com",80))
>>> print s.getsockname()
('192.168.1.8', 64300)
```

There are some functions that return a decimal or hexadecimal number representing the IP address. The socket library provides two functions to help you go from a decimal number to the four numbers in standard IP address notation or vice versa. You'll also need the Python **struct** module. Here's the code:

```
>>> import socket, struct
>>> struct.unpack('L', socket.inet_aton('192.168.1.8'))[0]
134326464
>>> socket.inet_ntoa(struct.pack('L',134326464))
'192.168.1.8'
```

To access any of the Android API functions from Python, you must **import android** and then instantiate an object like this:

```
>>> import android
>>> droid = android.Android()
```

Once that's done, you have full access to all API functions. Here's what the Android class looks like from **android.py**:

```
class Android(object):

  def __init__(self, addr=None):
    if addr is None:
      addr = HOST, PORT
    self.conn = socket.create_connection(addr)
    self.client = self.conn.makefile()
    self.id = 0
    if HANDSHAKE is not None:
      self._authenticate(HANDSHAKE)

  def _rpc(self, method, *args):
    data = {'id': self.id,
            'method': method,
            'params': args}
    request = json.dumps(data)
    self.client.write(request+'\n')
    self.client.flush()
```

```
      response = self.client.readline()
      self.id += 1
      result = json.loads(response)
      if result['error'] is not None:
        print result['error']
      # namedtuple doesn't work with unicode keys.
      return Result(id=result['id'], result=result['result'],
                    error=result['error'], )

  def __getattr__(self, name):
    def rpc_call(*args):
      return self._rpc(name, *args)
    return rpc_call
```

Here's a simple Python hello_world.py script from the SL4A installation:

```
>>> import android
>>> droid = android.Android()
>>> name = droid.getInput("Hello!", "What is your name?")
>>> print name
Result(id=0, result=u'Paul', error=None)
>>> droid.makeToast("Hello, %s" % name.result)
Result(id=1, result=None, error=None)
>>>
```

When you combine the simplicity of the Python language with the breadth of the Python Standard Library, you get a great tool for implementing useful scripts on the desktop, server, or Android device with SL4A.

Figure 1-4 shows the first thing you'll see onscreen when you run the simple hello_world.py script. When you type in your name as I have done and press the Ok button, you should see the little popup message shown in Figure 1-5 as a result of the makeToast API call.

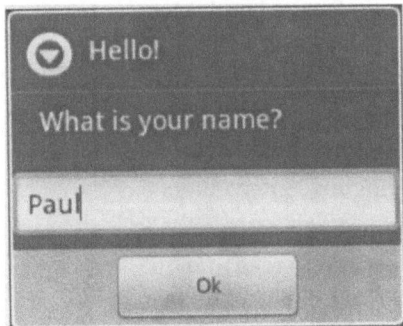

Figure 1-4. Hello World input dialog box

Figure 1-5. *Result of makeToast API call*

Summary

This chapter introduces the Android platform in a general sense and SL4A more specifically. There are a few things here that are worth noting and remembering as you continue along through the rest of the book.

Here's what you should hold on to from this chapter:

- **Linux underpinnings**: The Android OS is essentially Linux under the hood. Many of the same directories and programs are there.

- **Java is the language of Android**: Applications built on top of the Android SDK run inside a Java DVM. Although it's not an absolute necessity, it doesn't hurt to know a little Java to help you understand some of the plumbing behind SL4A.

- **SL4A is a container application**: It hosts all the different language interpreters and provides the interface using RPC to the underlying OS.

- **JSON is the way to pass data**: Nicely formatted JSON is not hard to read and, in fact, has a very logical structure. Once you get used to the syntax, you should be able to handle any of the API functions.

- **Language options**: Although Python is the most popular, you also have other options including Beanshell, JRuby, Lua, Perl, PHP, and Rhino.

CHAPTER 2

Getting Started

This chapter will give you all the information you need to get going with Google's Scripting Layer for Android (SL4A).

■ **Note** A number of topics will be introduced in this chapter and covered in more detail later.

Okay. Let's get started. Here's what I'll cover in this chapter:

- Installing the core files on your device
- Installing the Android SDK
- Remotely connecting to your device
- Executing simple programs

By using the instructions given here, you will be able to get up and running with SL4A in a very short time. Pay close attention to the sections on configuring your device and desktop as the instructions will need to be accomplished to get the two communicating. You will find it helpful to follow along with the examples as I walk you through them.

Installing SL4A on the Device

The quickest way to get started with SL4A is to simply install it on an Android device. There are several ways of doing this. If you navigate to the SL4A home page (http://code.google.com/p/android-scripting), you'll find download links for the .apk files and a QR code for use with a barcode scanner to install on your device. Here's a list of the steps you need to accomplish to get SL4A installed:

1. Download the SL4A .apk file (see Figure 2-1).

Figure 2-1. Downloading the .apk file

2. Launch the .apk file from the notifications screen (see Figure 2-2).

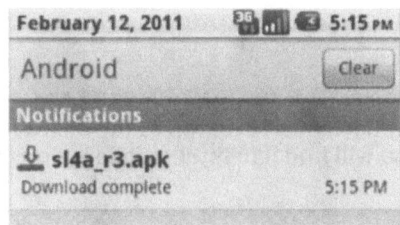

Figure 2-2. Launching the .apk file

3. Select Install on the next screen to actually install SL4A (see Figure 2-3).

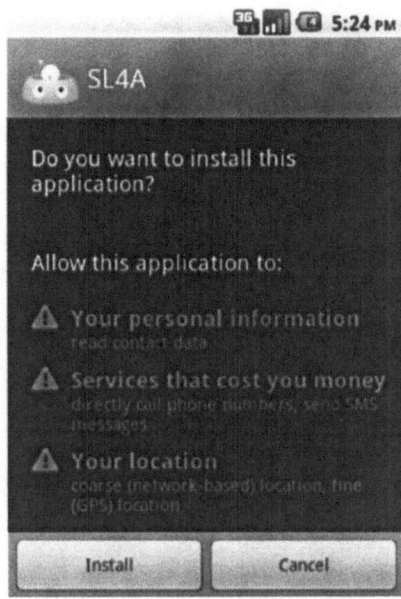

Figure 2-3. *Installing SL4A*

Don't worry about the warnings as they simply indicate that SL4A has the capability to perform any of those tasks, but won't unless you actually write a script to do so. If you choose to install in the emulator, simply navigate to the SL4A web site from the browser inside the emulator and click either the QR code or the s14a_rx.apk link under Downloads.

The first time you start the SL4A application you'll be asked if you want to allow the collection of anonymous usage information. Either way, you can always change your mind later through the Preferences menu.

Now that you have the main SL4A application installed you'll still need to install your favorite interpreter. This is done by starting the SL4A application and then pressing the menu button (see Figure 2-4).

Figure 2-4. *SL4A menu button popup*

This will present a number of buttons across the bottom of the screen including one labeled View. Touching this button causes a popup selection dialog box with options including Interpreters (see Figure 2-5).

■ **Note** Because this book is primarily about working with Android devices using touch as the primary user interaction, you will see the words *touch* or *select* frequently used. There will also be references to other finger-based motions such as drag down or swipe from left to right.

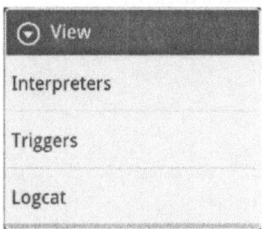

Figure 2-5. *SL4A view button popup*

Choosing the Interpreters option will bring you to a default screen listing only Shell as an available option. To install additional interpreters, press the menu button again and then touch the Add button (see Figure 2-6).

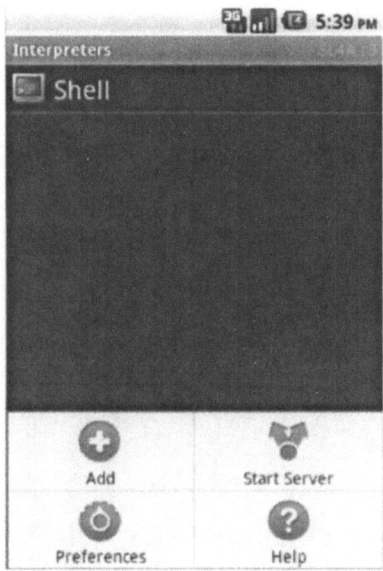

Figure 2-6. *Interpreters screen options menu*

This will display a list of available interpreters for you to download and install (see Figure 2-8). Selecting one such as Python 2.6.2 will initiate a download of the primary Python interpreter package from the main SL4A website. You must again access the Notification bar by swiping down from the top of the display to launch the Python installer by touching the filename (see Figure 2-7).

▦ **Note** It would be worth your time at this point to review the Terminal Help available from the Interpreters screen menu option. With the Interpreters screen visible, press the hardware menu button and then choose Help. From there, select Terminal Help and read about entering and editing text.

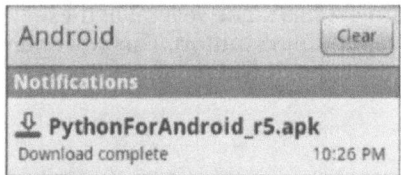

Figure 2-7. *Python interpreter download notification*

Figure 2-8. *SL4A add an Interpreter*

I should mention at this point that there is an alternative way to install a Python interpreter. This method consists of downloading the .apk file and then using the Android Debug Bridge (ADB) to install it. You'll need to use this method if you wish to try any of the newer Python for Android releases as the base SL4A installation typically points at the last official-release version. In this case you would use a web browser to navigate to the Google code site (http://code.google.com/p/python-for-android) and then use the right-click and save-as method to download the PythonForAndroid_rx.apk file where the x represents the version you wish to test. Next you would use the following ADB command to install the .apk file onto either an emulator or a physical device:

```
adb install PythonForAndroid_r6.apk
```

Touching the Install button starts the actual installation and presents you with the same "Open" and "Done" buttons as you saw when the SL4A installation completed. With early versions of the Python interpreter you would see a single Install button after touching "Open" (see Figure 2-9). More recent versions of Python for Android will present a screen like the one in Figure 2-10. Three new buttons have been added to facilitate module management. By modules I mean additional library modules not included with a normal Python distribution. The Python for Android project has made several of these modules available and you can see them when you click on the "Browse Modules" button. This will open a web page on the Python for Android wiki site and give you the opportunity to download them (see Figure 2-11).

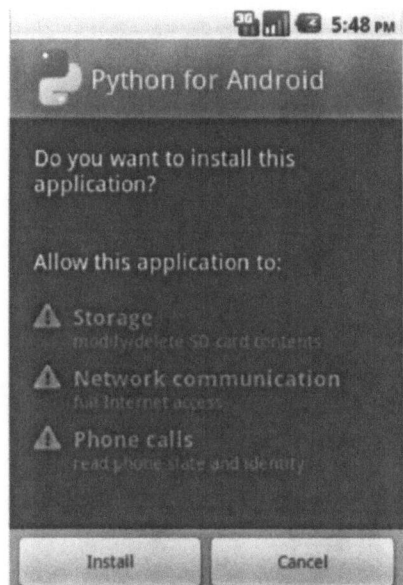

Figure 2-9. *Installing Python for Android*

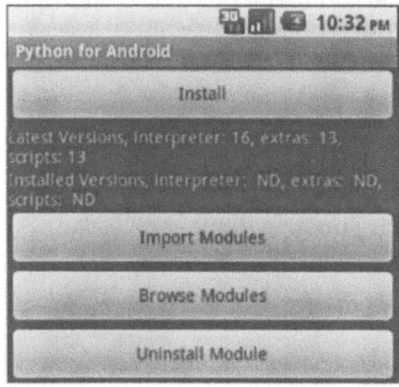

Figure 2-10. *Python for Android Installer*

You should see a quick popup dialog box with the words *Installation Successful* if everything runs without error. At this point there will be a screen with the Shell and Python 2.6.2 interpreters listed. Additional interpreters can be added in a similar fashion. Choosing the Python 2.6.2 option will launch the Python interpreter.

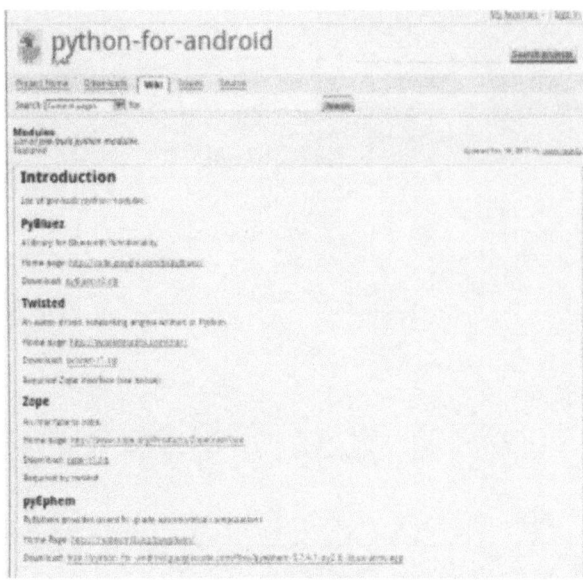

Figure 2-11. *Python-for-android modules page*

Now you're finally ready to start entering code at a standard Python command prompt, as shown in Figure 2-13. You can type any valid Python code and immediately see the results. If you want to access any Android functions, you must import the android module. It takes a total of three lines of code to implement the typical "Hello World" program as follows:

```
>>> import android
>>> droid = android.Android()
>>> droid.makeToast('Hello, Android World')
```

When you hit return after the third line, you should see a dialog box popup with the text "Hello, Android World" (see Figure 2-12). The dialog box will automatically close after a few seconds.

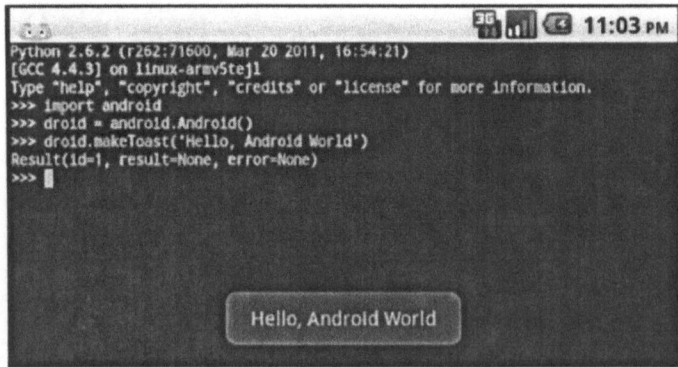

Figure 2-12. *Results of makeToast function call*

Figure 2-13. SL4A Python interpreter prompt

If you press the menu button while in the interpreter, you will see four buttons at the bottom of the screen labeled Force Size, Email, Preferences, and Exit & Edit. These buttons are generic to every interpreter so you'll be able to access them from Python, BeanShell, or any of the other interpreters you choose to install. Figure 2-14 shows what these buttons look like.

■ **Note** All scripts are stored on the SD card of your device in the directory /sdcard/sl4a/scripts. If you have your device connected to a host computer using the USB cable, the SD card will not be available, and your scripts won't be visible.

Figure 2-14. SL4A Python interpreter menu

The Force Size button allows you to change the screen dimensions of the interpreter. The default is 80 × 25, which fits the screen in landscape mode fairly well. Once you choose your dimensions and select the Resize button your screen will adjust to the new size. Figure 2-15 shows the resize dialog box.

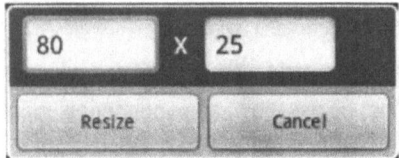

Figure 2-15. SL4A interpreter screen resize dialog box

The Email menu option will capture all text in the interpreter screen and load it into an e-mail message, allowing you to send everything you've typed to yourself (or anyone else, for that matter). Here's what the text of the e-mail looks like for the previous "Hello World" code with a little editing to the actual message to add carriage returns for clarity:

```
Python 2.6.2 (r262:71600, Sep 19 2009, 11:03:28)
[GCC 4.2.1] on linux2
Type "help", "copyright", "credits" or "license" for more information.
>>> import android
>>> droid = android.Android()
>>> droid.makeToast('Hello, Android World')
Result(id=1, result=None, error=None)
>>>
```

This is a good point to stop and talk about moving files between your host computer and the device. The absolute easiest way is to connect your device using a USB cable and set the connection type to Disk drive. With this set, you should be able to browse the files on the device using your normal file manager application on any operating system (OS). At this point, moving files between host and device becomes a simple drag-and-drop operation. We'll take a look at a few other methods in a later chapter when we discuss the Android SDK in more detail.

Now back to the Interpreter Options menu. The Exit & Edit button is grayed-out for SL4A R3, meaning it is not currently implemented. Selecting the Preferences button presents a new scrollable page with multiple entries, grouped by functional area, allowing you to configure any number of different options. Some of these options, such as Font size, are repeated under different headings, making it possible to change the font size in both the Editor Tool and the Interpreter window.

There are a few of the options that you should take note of. If you selected Allow Usage Tracking when you first installed SL4A, you can change that with the first entry on the Preferences screen. Figure 2-16 shows the first four options of the Preferences screen including General Usage Tracking, Script Manager Show all files, Script Editor Font size, and Terminal Scrollback size. Most of these are pretty self-explanatory, but I'll highlight a few things of interest.

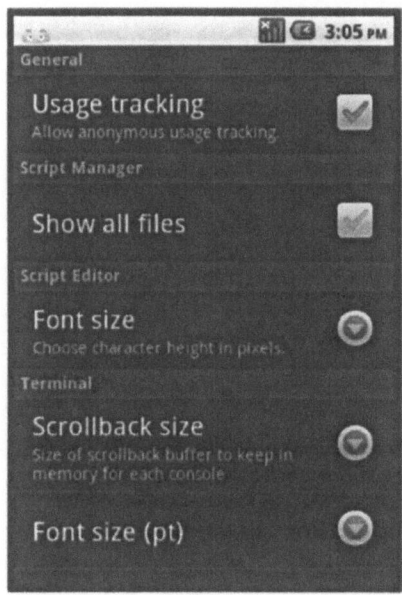

Figure 2-16. First part of SL4A Preferences Menu

Enabling the Show all files option under the Script Manager heading will display all files in the /sdcard/sl4a/scripts directory on the device. This can come in handy if you're using other files as a part of your application and you want to verify that they are actually in the right directory. The Font size option under the Script Editor heading will set the font size for the text editor only. There's another Font size option under the Terminal heading that will set the size of characters in the terminal window when you open an interpreter command prompt.

The Terminal heading has a few other settings of interest. Rotation mode lets you choose how the screen behaves when the terminal window is visible. Options include Default, Force landscape, Force portrait, and Automatic. You might want your terminal window to always open in landscape mode, which is a little easier to see but gives you limited screen real estate to work with. The Automatic option will rotate the screen for you when you rotate the device.

Default screen colors in the terminal window are white text on a black background. You can change them to be virtually anything you'd like using a color-wheel picker or a slider control. For screenshot purposes I set the colors exactly opposite of the default, meaning black text on a white background. The color picker dialog box displays the HSV, RGB, and YUB values of the current color, along with a hex code you could use with CSS. Figure 2-17 shows what the color picker looks like. You can accept your change by selecting the Accept button or revert to what you previously had with the Revert button.

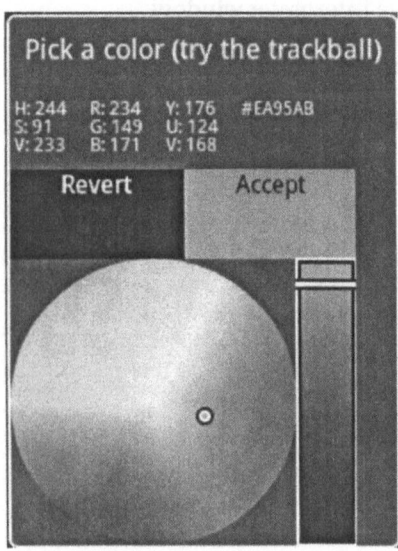

Figure 2-17. *Terminal window color picker*

There is one more Terminal heading option you probably want to enable, and that's the Keep screen awake option. It should be on by default, but if your screen starts disappearing on you while you're thinking about the next line of code, you'll know which option to look for. Next I'll take you through installing the Android SDK on a development machine to take advantage of some of the tools there.

Installing the Android SDK

There are a number of tools provided with the Android SDK that make life much easier for the developer. I'll address installing the SDK here and do a deep dive on what's inside in a later chapter. Step one is to download the appropriate install file for your operating system. Google provides installers for Linux, Mac OS X, and Windows. You'll also need the Java Development Kit (JDK) installed first if you don't already have that loaded on your machine. I'll address installation on all three platforms to make sure the bases are covered.

Linux

To walk through installing the SDK on Linux I'll start with a fresh install of a 64-bit version of Ubuntu 10.10 desktop. You also want to make sure the system is up-to-date with the latest security patches before you proceed. The first thing you must install are the base Java packages. This can be accomplished with the following commands from a terminal window:

```
$ sudo add-apt-repository ppa:sun-java-community-team/sun-java6
$ sudo apt-get update
$ sudo apt-get install sun-java6-jre sun-java6-bin sun-java6-jdk
```

To get this to work properly, you'll need to execute another command line install to get the SDK to fully function. This has to do with the use of 32-bit packages by the SDK. Creating a new Android virtual device (AVD) uses the mksdcard utility, which depends on the ia32-libs package. To install this dependency you'll need to enter another command in a terminal window:

```
$ sudo apt-get install ia32-libs
```

For Linux there's a .tgz file containing all the base SDK files on the Android SDK download page (http://developer.android.com/sdk). If you're using Firefox for your web browser, you should be presented with the option to open the file using the File Roller utility. Extract the entire directory to somewhere convenient. Once you have the files extracted you need to run the SDK Manager app to actually install one or more versions of the Android platform.

The SDK Manager application looks virtually identical on all three platforms so I'll describe the process of downloading specific versions only once. On Linux, the manager app is named android and exists in the tools subdirectory below the main SDK root directory. You can launch it from a Nautilus file manager window by double-clicking the android file. If you're really curious, you can open the file in a text editor because it is, in fact, a shell script that will launch sdkmanager.jar. This will bring up the main SDK Manager screen, as shown in Figure 2-18.

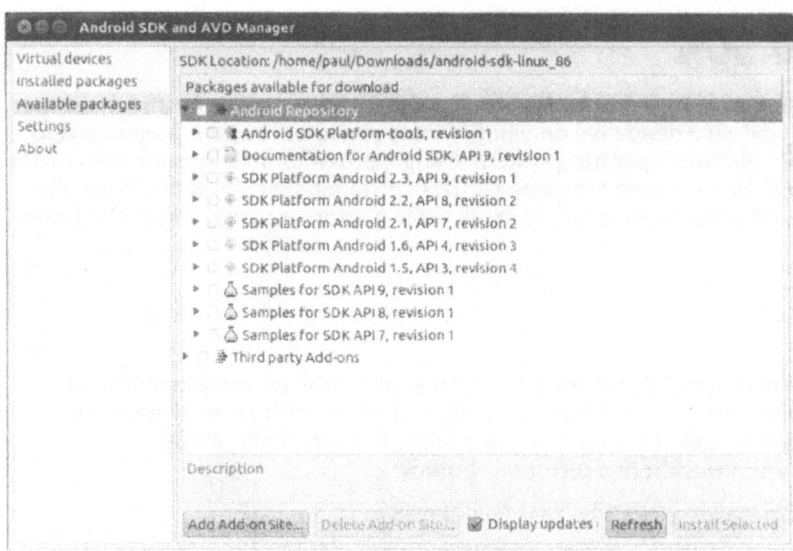

Figure 2-18. *Android SDK Manager screen*

Note   If you access the Internet through a proxy, you will need to add that information in the Settings menu, as shown in Figure 2-19.

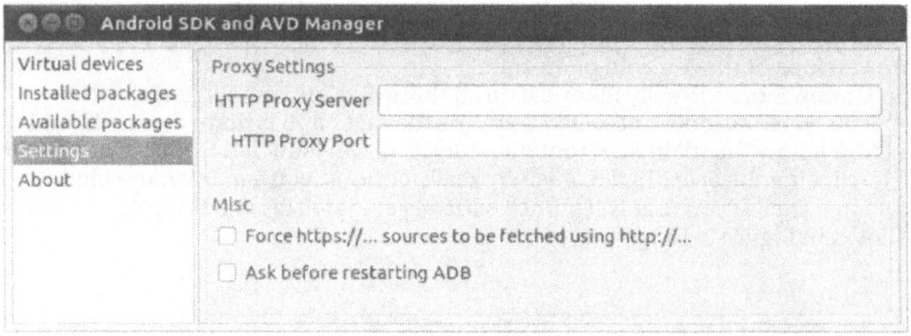

Figure 2-19. *Proxy server Settings page*

Choosing which versions to install depends primarily upon the versions of Android running on the devices you will be supporting. For the examples in this book, I'll install all the 2.x versions and samples. To do this you simply click the checkbox next to those items, along with the Android SDK Platform tools and Documentation entries, and then click the Install Selected button. The whole process should take less than ten minutes with a reasonably fast Internet connection.

It makes sense to create a few shortcuts on your desktop to frequently used programs installed by the SDK for later use. You can do this with GNOME by right-clicking the desktop and selecting Create Launcher. The dialog box prompts for a name to display underneath the icon along with a command to execute. If you click the Browse button next to the Command text box, you'll be able to navigate to the SDK tools directory. Clicking the android file will set it as the target for execution for the new launcher. Now you have quick access to the SDK Manager application from an icon on the desktop.

The SDK installation instructions recommend that you also add the tools and platform-tools directories to your path. If you unpacked the SDK files in your home directory, you could set this from the command line with the following:

```
export PATH=${PATH}:~/android-sdk-linux-x86/tools:~/android-sdk-linux-x86/platform-tools
```

■ **Note** Watch out for subtle changes between SDK releases that could throw you for a loop. Google changed conventions from SDK version 8 to 9 (Android 2.2 to 2.3), including the directories for several of the most commonly used utility programs.

Mac OS X

Installing on a Mac consists of downloading a zip file and then unpacking the contents. You must run the Android SDK and AVD Manager application and then choose which versions you want to install. To start the process, you can either launch the Android application from the Finder or from a terminal window in the directory where you unpacked the SDK download with this command:

```
$ tools/android
```

The first time you run the SDK Manager application you will be presented with a list of SDK versions to choose from. OS X will look almost identical to Linux from a command-line perspective, including setting the path statement. You can use the same syntax as before, taking care to specify the correct path to the SDK directory. In my case, I unpacked the SDK at the top level of my home directory and used this export statement:

```
export PATH=${PATH}:~/android-sdk-mac-x86/tools:~/android-sdk-linux-x86/platform-tools
```

You'll need to add this same line to your .bash_profile file to make the path modification the next time you log in. You will probably want to create a shortcut on your dock to quickly launch the SDK Manager. All you have to do is drag the android file from the tools directory to the right side of the dock. Now you'll have one-click access to the SDK Manager and from there you can launch a device emulator. We'll take an in-depth look at using a device emulator in Chapter 3.

Windows

Google provides both a zip file and an executable to install the SDK on Windows. The download file size is almost the same, so that shouldn't make any difference in choosing one over the other. If you download the .exe file, you'll have one fewer step to perform to unpack the files. It's also the recommended choice, so that's what I will address. I'll be using the 64-bit version of Windows 7 Ultimate for all Windows development and examples. To start the process, I simply clicked the installer_r08-windows.exe link on the Android SDK download page. Once that file has downloaded, you need to double-click it to launch the installer. If you don't have the Java Development Kit (JDK), you'll see a screen like the one shown in Figure 2-20.

▓ **Note** The Android SDK .exe installer looks for the 32-bit version of the JDK and won't continue if you don't have it installed.

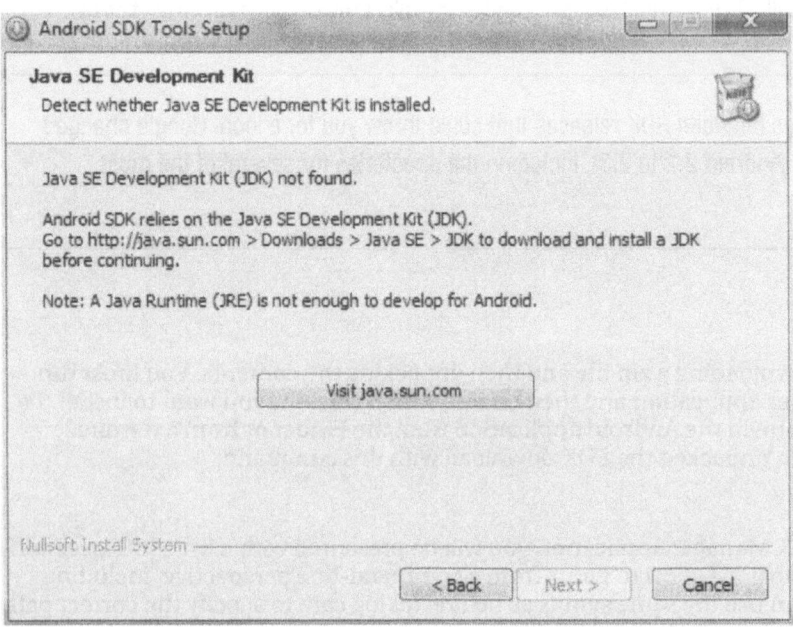

Figure 2-20. *Missing JDK screen*

Even though I'm testing on 64-bit Windows, I discovered that you must install the 32-bit JDK for the Android SDK to install. Once you have the JDK downloaded, you simply double-click the filename to start the installation. With that step complete you can now proceed to install the Android SDK. At the completion of the installation you'll be given the option to launch the SDK Manager. Launching the SDK Manager for the first time on Windows looks slightly different from Linux and Mac OS X. Figure 2-21 shows the dialog box you will see, allowing you to choose specific packages to install.

You'll notice the dialog box for choosing SDK versions is slightly different and requires you to select a specific line in the dialog box and then click the Reject radio button to unselect a version. Since I'll only be using 2.x versions of the SDK, I deselected the 1.5 and 1.6 version options. With that complete, I clicked on the Install button, and everything then ran without intervention. When you choose the .exe installer, you'll get a new option added to your Windows programs menu labeled Android SDK Tools. You can also right-click the SDK Manager icon and drag it to the desktop for quick access. Be aware that if you simply drag the icon from the Windows Programs menu you'll actually move it to the desktop.

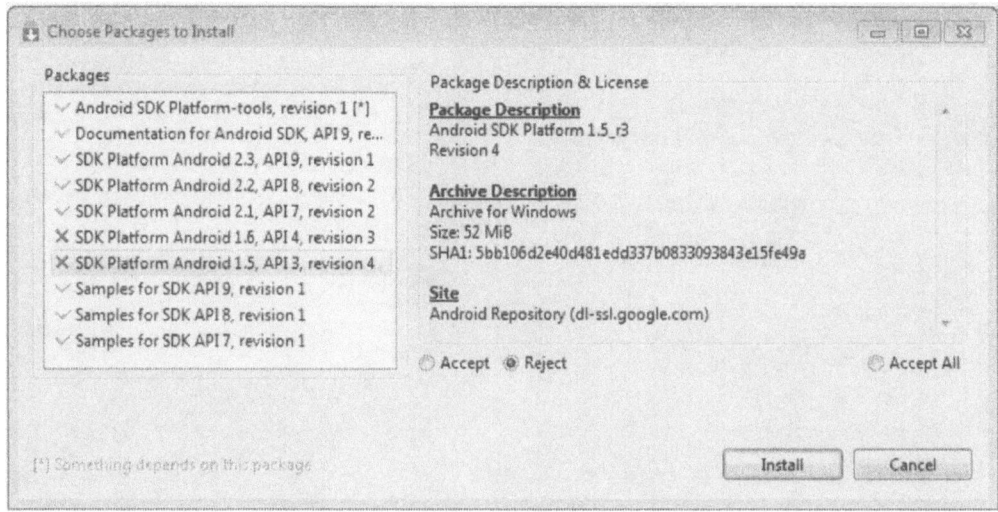

Figure 2-21. *Initial Android SDK Manager Screen*

Installing Python

Although you can type in code directly on your device, you'll quickly find the process quite tedious unless you happen to have a full-size keyboard attached. Connecting remotely from a host computer provides a much more productive environment for developing and testing applications. I'll look at using Eclipse for this purpose in Chapter 4, but for now I'll show you how to use the Android SDK tools to do essentially the same thing.

There is one more thing, however, that needs to be done first. If you happen to be using either Linux or Mac OS X, you will more than likely have a version of Python already installed. On both platforms you can tell for sure by opening a terminal window and launching Python. Figure 2-22 shows what this looks like on my Mac Mini running OS X Snow Leopard version 10.6.5.

▓ **Note** Any 2.6 version of Python should work on the host computer, but be aware that SL4A is based on 2.6.2 just in case you see some peculiar behavior when running scripts from the host remotely to the device.

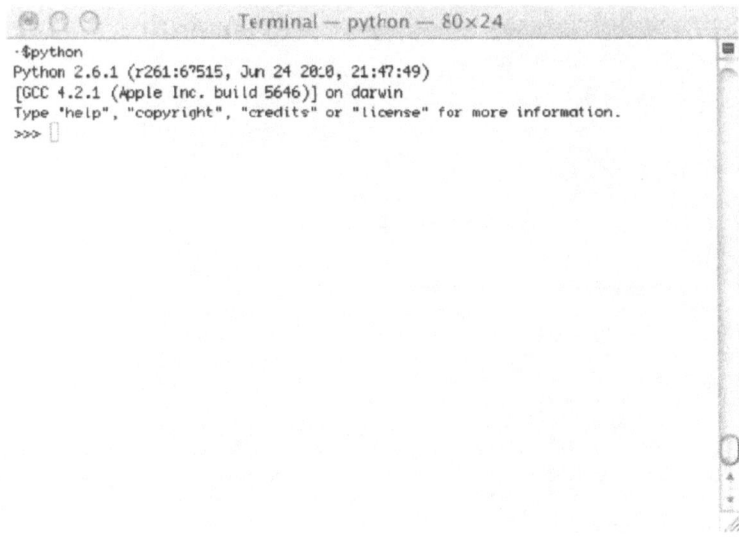

```
          Terminal — python — 80×24
·$python
Python 2.6.1 (r261:67515, Jun 24 2010, 21:47:49)
[GCC 4.2.1 (Apple Inc. build 5646)] on darwin
Type "help", "copyright", "credits" or "license" for more information.
>>> []
```

Figure 2-22. *Python running on Mac OS X*

Python is not installed by default on Windows. To install Python, go to http://python.org and find the releases page (http://python.org/download/releases). There you will find all the major version releases, including version 2.6.6. Options include versions for 32- and 64-bit Windows. I chose the 64-bit version for my testing purposes. Double-clicking the .msi file launches the installer, which prompts you for permission to install.

Once that completes, you can modify your Windows path to add the Python26 directory. The quickest way to accomplish that task is to press the Windows key and type in the word **system**. You should see the option Edit the System Environment Variables under the Control Panel heading. Click that line to launch the System Properties dialog box and then click the Environment Variables button. Locate the Path variable in the System variables section and click the Edit button. This will display a single text box with the current system path statement. Navigate to the end of the string and add the following text:

;C:\Python26

This will add the Python directory to the search path and make Python available from any command window. To verify that you have Python installed correctly and the path set properly, launch a command window and type the word **Python**. You should see something like Figure 2-23.

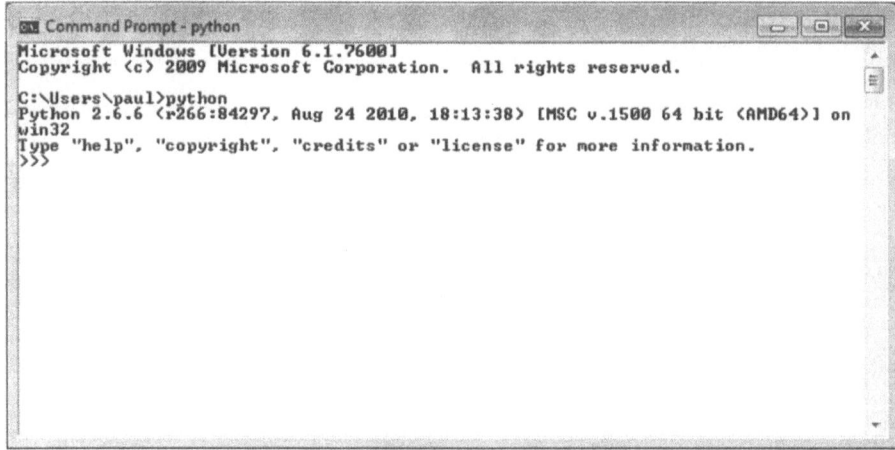

Figure 2-23. *Python running on Windows 7*

Remotely Connecting to the Device

Connecting from a host computer to your device requires the Android SDK and ADB tool. I'll take an in-depth look at that tool in a later chapter, but for now I'll talk about how to use the command for remotely connecting to the device. In essence, you are setting up a proxy that passes communication over a specific port to the device.

There are a few hurdles to overcome in order to connect to your device from Windows. The first and probably biggest hurdle is getting Windows to recognize your device. One of the optional components when you download the SDK package is a USB driver for Windows. This is required if you want your computer to recognize your device. Figure 2-24 shows this item under the Available Packages window.

Select this option and then click the Install Selected button. This will download the driver files into a subdirectory below the root SDK directory. The next steps you take will depend on the type of device you're trying to connect to your Windows computer.

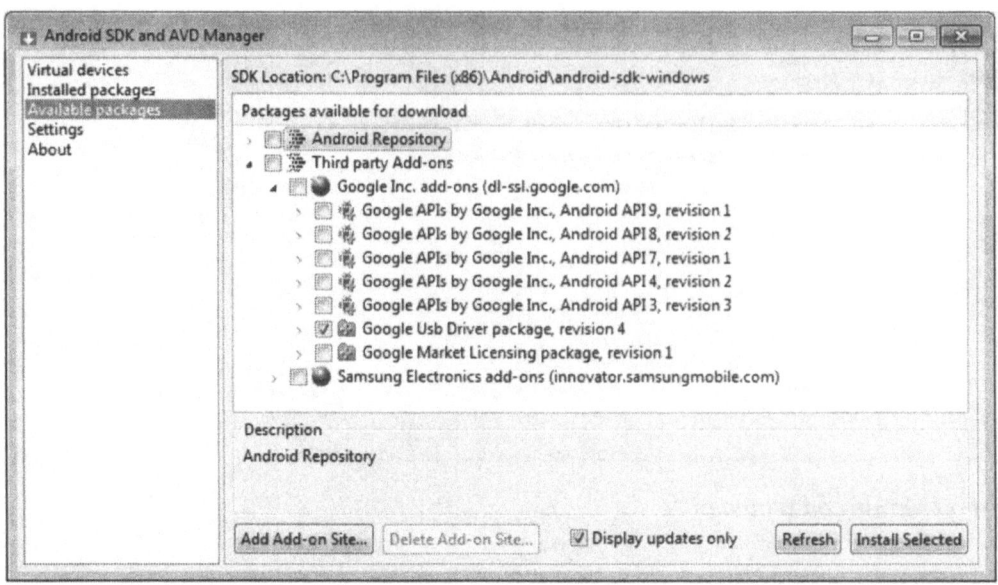

Figure 2-24. *USB driver for Windows*

If your device happens to be a G1, myTouch 3G, Verizon Droid, or Nexus One, you should be all set. If not, you'll have a little more work to do. Connecting to another device, such as the HTC EVO 4G smartphone, requires additional information to be added to the driver .inf file in order for the driver to recognize the device. This file can be found in the same directory tree with the SDK in the google-usb_driver subdirectory. The only thing you really need to know is the vendor ID (VID) and the product ID (PID) for your device. You can probably find the right numbers for your device with a few Google searches. Another good place to look for answers about ADB connectivity issues is the Android Developers group on Google groups (http://groups.google.com/group/android-developers).

As a last resort, you'll have to go into sleuthing mode. When you connect your device to Windows, it will try to install the appropriate driver for you. If it can't find one, you'll get a popup message indicating that the device failed to install properly. At this point you'll have to use Device Manager to discover the information needed. The easiest way to launch Device Manager is to press the Windows key and start typing **device** in the search box. This should give you a list of options, including Device Manager. Choosing Device Manager will bring up a dialog box similar to Figure 2-25.

Since Windows did not recognize the device when you connected it, you'll see ADB listed under Other Devices. Now you have to right-click the ADB device and choose Properties to find the VID and PID listings for your device. I'll show you what it looks like for the HTC EVO 4G, and hopefully, you can use the same approach to get your device connected.

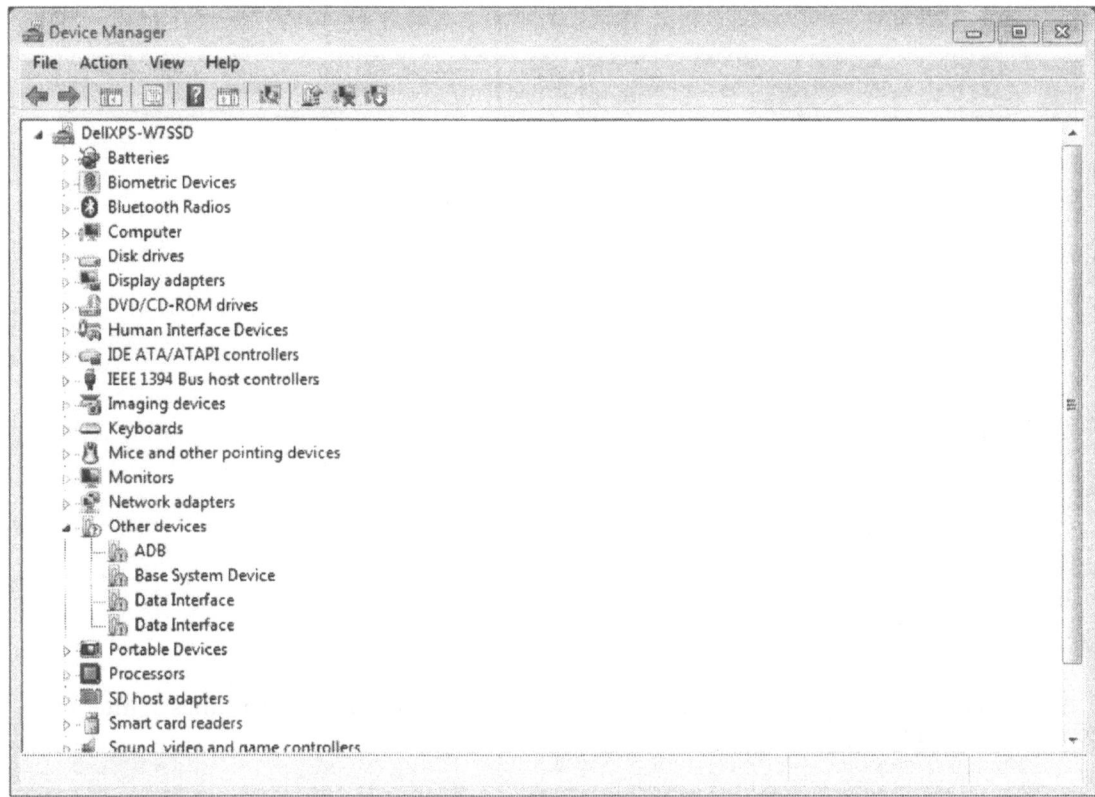

Figure 2-25. *Windows Device Manager showing unknown devices*

With the ADB Properties screen displayed you need to select the Details tab and then choose Hardware Ids from the dropdown box. Figure 2-26 shows the information you should see for an HTC EVO 4G. You'll need the VID and PID information to modify the driver .inf file next.

■ **Note** If you took the defaults for the Android SDK .exe installer, you will find the USB driver files in the following directory: C:\Program Files (x86)\Android\android-sdk-windows\google-usb_driver.

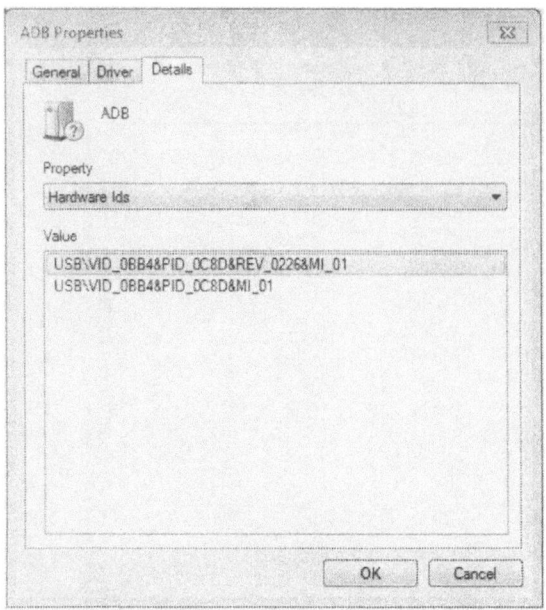

Figure 2-26. *Device properties for an ADB device*

Armed with the VID and PID, you'll need to edit the android_winusb.inf file. The lines of interest you need to add are as follows:

```
;
;HTC EVO 4G
%SingleAdbInterface%        = USB_Install, USB\VID_0BB4&PID_0C8D⏎
%CompositeAdbInterface%     = USB_Install, USB\VID_0BB4&PID_0C8D&MI_01
```

The simplest way to make the changes is to edit the file using Notepad. You will have to launch Notepad as administrator if you want to be able to save it back to the same directory. To do this, you can press the Windows key and start typing **notepad**. Right-click Notepad in the popup window and select Run As Administrator. Once Notepad is open, navigate to the google-usb_driver directory and then double-click the android_winusb.inf file. When you have the file open, you need to find the section with the label [Google.NTx86] and copy the first three lines right below. In my case, this was an entry for the HTC Dream device. Paste those lines at the end of both [Google.NTx86] and [Google.NTamd64] sections, changing the VID and PID values you discovered previously. I didn't have to change the VID since the EVO 4G is an HTC device.

Now you should be ready to connect your device to the host computer using a USB cable. I also had to change USB Connection Type on the device to HTC Sync. This will bring up a dialog box on the phone as it tries to connect to an HTC Sync application on the host computer. At this point you can either press the back key on the device or wait for the connection attempt to time out. Update the driver for the ADB device by launching Device Manager again and right-clicking the ADB device under Other Devices. Choose Update Driver from the popup dialog box and then select Browse My Computer For Driver Software from the next screen. This dialog box will allow you to browse for the directory where you placed the edited .inf file. Make sure you choose the google-usb_driver directory and then click Next. If all goes well, you should see a screen indicating that Windows Has Successfully Updated Your Driver Software.

Finally, enable USB debugging on your device. This happens from the Device Settings screen. From Settings, touch Applications and then Development. On the Development screen, you must select the checkbox next to USB debugging to enable that feature.

If you managed to get everything configured correctly, you will be able to open a command window or terminal session and issue adb commands. On Windows, you should be able to see your device with the command shown in Figure 2-27.

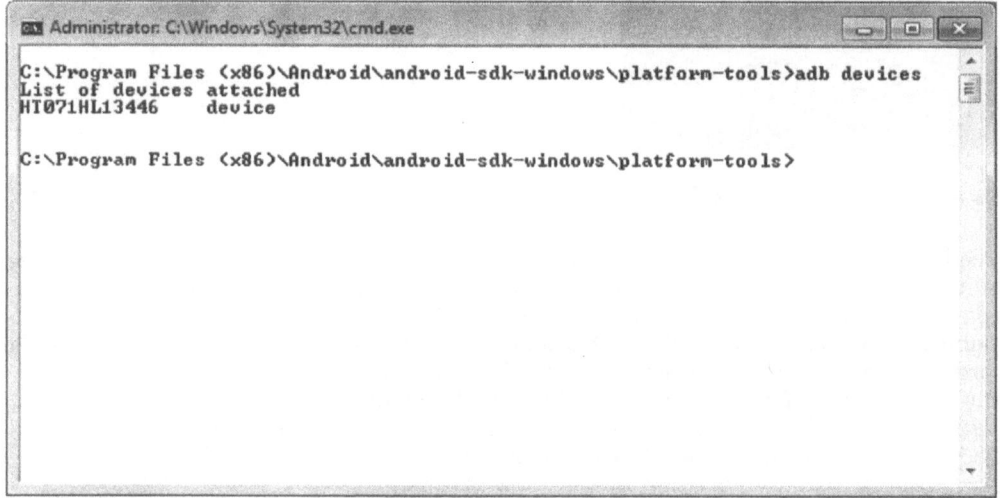

Figure 2-27. Output of adb devices command

If you're using Linux or Mac OS X, you shouldn't have any issues connecting your device. I was able to see the HTC EVO 4G with the adb devices command on both platforms after connecting the USB cable without any additional steps.

Device Settings

Connecting to your device remotely requires a few steps on both the device and the desktop. On the device, you have to launch a server from the Interpreters screen. The steps you must accomplish to do this are as follows:

1. Start SL4A from the All apps screen on the device.

2. Press the Menu button and then select the View option.

3. Choose the Interpreters from the list.

4. Press the Menu button again and then choose Start Server.

5. Select either Public, if you want to connect over WiFi, or Private, if you are connected over USB.

At this point, your server should be started and ready for access over a specific port. To find out what port number was assigned you must open the Script Monitor by dragging down the status window from the top of the device screen. This will show the SL4A service and the number of running scripts that should be 1 at this point. To determine the port number, you must click (touch) the SL4A service line to bring up the Script Monitor. You should see something like Figure 2-28 with the port number displayed after the localhost: string.

Figure 2-28. *SL4A server mode with port address*

You're now ready to connect to your device remotely. To get this to work, you must enter a few more commands to define an environment variable and enable port forwarding. These commands and Python itself need to run from a command window started with the Run As Administrator option. The environment variable must be named AP_PORT with a default value of 9999 for the examples to work. To enable port forwarding, an adb command is used to forward all internal tcp traffic for port 9999 to the port number of the remote server. Figure 2-29 shows what this should look like on Windows.

There are slight differences for the commands between Linux, Mac OS X, and Windows. On both Linux and Mac OS X you create an environment variable with the export command:

```
$ export AP_PORT=9999
```

You'll probably want to add that to your startup script as well. On Linux, this will be either ~/.bash_profile or ~/.bashrc. On Mac OS X, it will be .bash_profile in your home directory.

```
C:\Windows\system32>set AP_PORT=9999

C:\Windows\system32>adb forward tcp:9999 tcp:53973

C:\Windows\system32>python
Python 2.6.6 (r266:84297, Aug 24 2010, 18:13:38) [MSC v.1500 64 bit (AMD64)] on
win32
Type "help", "copyright", "credits" or "license" for more information.
>>> import android
>>> droid = android.Android()
>>> droid.makeToast("Hello Android from PC")
Result(id=0, result=None, error=None)
>>>
```

Figure 2-29. *Windows environment variable and adb commands for remoting*

On Windows-based computers, you can make this a permanent environment variable by adding it through the Environment Variables screen used earlier. This time you create a new User variable with the new button and then enter the name **AP_PORT** and value **9999**, as shown in Figure 2-30.

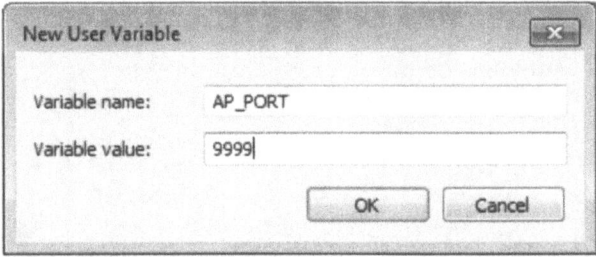

Figure 2-30. *Creating a permanent Windows environment variable for AP_PORT*

Executing Simple Programs

Once you get everything connected, you might want to start exploring using Python and IDLE. IDLE is a simple cross-platform integrated development environment (IDE) written in Python and the Tkinter GUI toolkit. First of all, it provides a Python interpreter command line where you can type in lines of code and get immediate feedback on the results of the code. You can also open an editor window for creating and modifying Python scripts. These scripts can be saved and then run with output occurring in the main interpreter window. You also get feedback on any syntax errors in the editor window before you execute the script.

The neat thing about this approach is that you can code on your desktop machine and test the code on your device. Keep in mind that any library you source will need to be available on your desktop machine. The other thing you need to note is Python version numbers. As of the writing of this book, SL4A uses version 2.6.2 of Python. You can probably get away with any 2.6 version after 2.6.2, but be aware that you run the risk of some obscure compatibility issue if you use something different than 2.6.2 on the desktop. Figure 2-31 shows IDLE running the "Hello World" program.

You will need to copy the android.py file into the same directory as your code or into the default Python installation directory on your development machine. The interpreter must be able to locate android.py when you execute the import android code in your script.

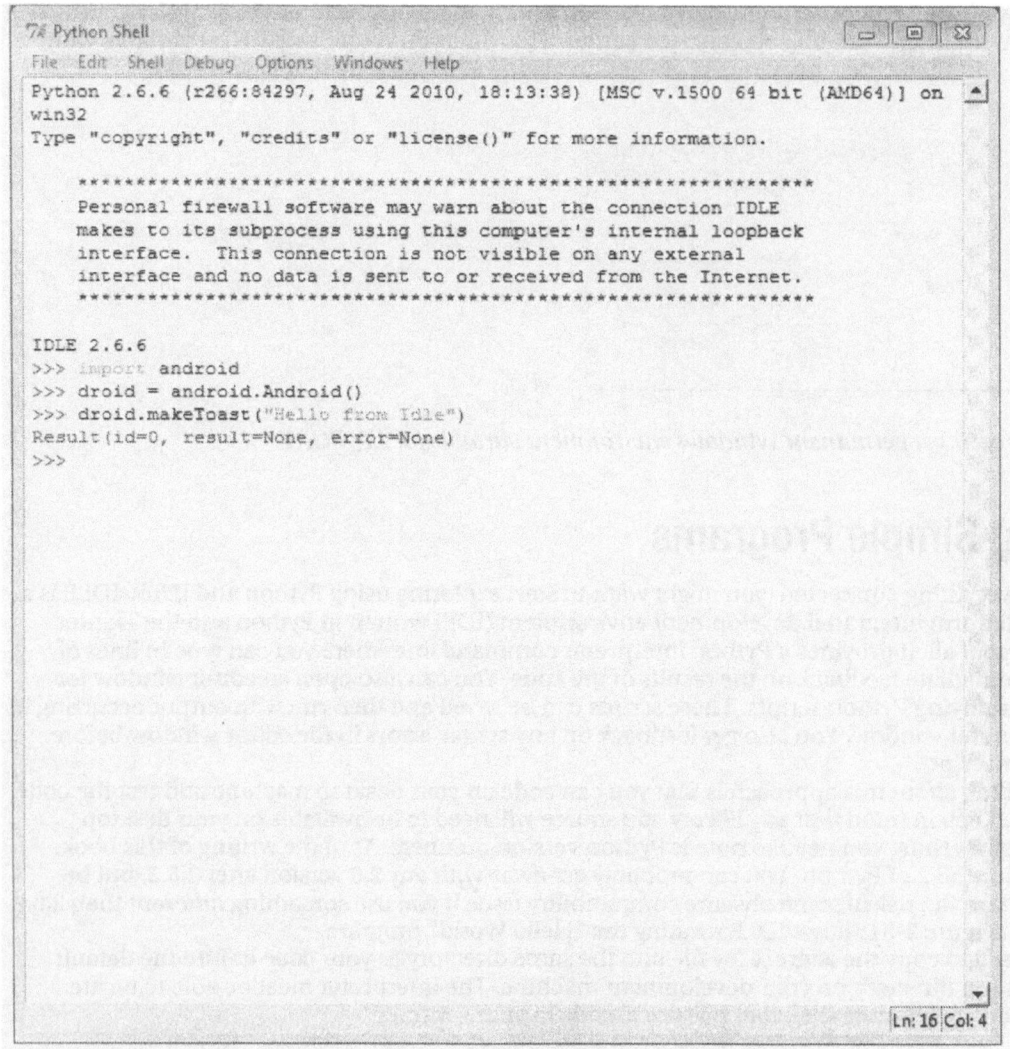

Figure 2-31. Python IDLE program connected to device

You can also use IDLE to edit and run scripts in a separate editor window. If you click the File menu and select New Window, you'll be presented with a blank editor screen for entering Python code. You can also cut and paste between the immediate window and the editor window. Giving this a try with the "Hello Android World" code will require a minor amount of editing to remove the extra prompt characters. Figure 2-32 shows the results.

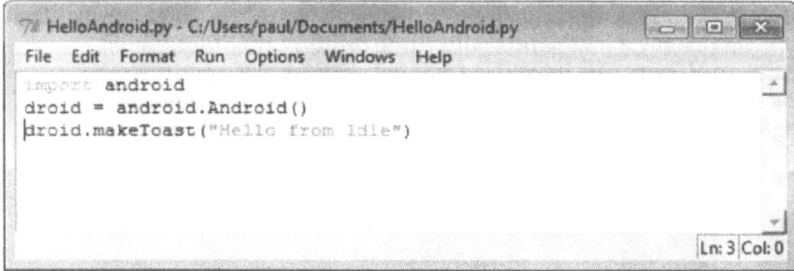

Figure 2-32. Python IDLE editor window

Another great way to start exploring with SL4A is to take a look at some of the sample programs installed along with the Python interpreter. One of those is Test.py, a sample program that exercises many of the dialog types supported by SL4A along with a few other test cases. This is one of those programs that imports several modules that are installed by default on the device but probably won't be on your host computer unless you explicitly install them.

You can give Test.py a run on your device by launching SL4A and selecting Test.py from the list of files. When you select one of the files from the main SL4A window, you'll see a little dialog box pop up with a number of icons. Figure 2-33 shows what you should see.

Figure 2-33. SL4A script launch options

The terminal icon launches the script in a terminal window on the device so you can see any error or debug messages while the cog-wheel icon launches the script in the background. Selecting the pencil icon will open the script in a text editor, and the disk icon will let you rename a script. If you choose the trash can icon, you will have one more chance to change your mind about deleting because a yes/no dialog box will open with a prompt to make sure that's what you want to do.

The script editor provides a simple way to enter or edit scripts on your device. It's not very efficient on small devices, but works relatively well on devices with larger screens such as tablets. You can use it in the emulator as well to test your scripts before loading them on an actual device. Once you're done editing, you must press the Menu button to bring up the options menu to Save & Exit or Save & Run. Figure 2-34 shows what this will look like on your device.

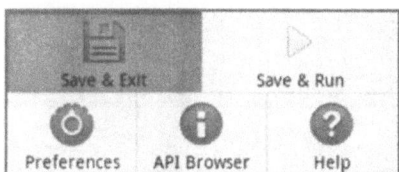

Figure 2-34. SL4A script editor options menu

The Preferences button will bring up the same menu as before with options for the SL4A application as a whole. Selecting the Help button will display a dialog box with three options, including Wiki Documentation, YouTube Screencasts, and Terminal Help. The first two options will open a web browser and redirect to the same pages you'll find if you go to the home page of the SL4A project.

The API Browser button will present a screen with all the available API functions listed (see Figure 2-35).

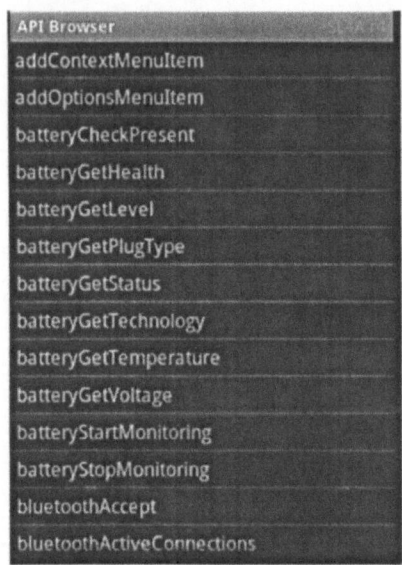

Figure 2-35. *API browser tool*

If you long-press (meaning touch one line and hold) you'll see a screen like the one in Figure 2-36. Selecting Prompt will bring up an additional dialog with individual text boxes for you to fill in the necessary parameters needed by that API function call (see Figure 2-37). This makes for a great way to explore some of the more complex API functions and have the SL4A interpreter walk you through the process of filling in the correct entries.

Figure 2-36. API browser options

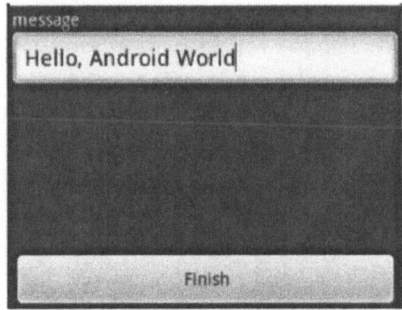

Figure 2-37. API browser prompt option

Summary

This chapter has a lot of information in it, but hopefully, by the time you get to this point you will have your SL4A test environment fully configured both on the device and on a host computer. The OS for the host computer shouldn't matter, so you're free to go with whatever platform you're most comfortable with. Google search is your friend if you happen to get stuck somewhere along the way.

As a recap, let's identify the key points from this chapter:

- **Installing SL4A**: This happens on a physical device or in the emulator. You first install the SL4A .apk file and then add interpreters from an SL4A menu.

- **Installing the Android SDK**: This happens on your development machine, which can run Linux, Mac OS X, or Windows. You might also have to install Java first if your OS doesn't have it installed already.

- **Configuring the USB driver on Windows**: This is probably the trickiest step, and unfortunately there's no way around it if you're developing on a Windows machine. You must have this working to establish communication between your development machine and a physical device.

- **Installing Python on Windows**: Again, you won't find Python on any stock Windows machine, so you'll have to install it yourself. Fortunately this is pretty simple.

Don't be afraid to kick the tires here. If you're not comfortable trying some of this stuff out on your shiny new phone, use the emulator. That's what it's there for. Understand that there will come a time that you will have to use the device because not every function of a real device can be simulated in the emulator. The good news is that the list of those capabilities is pretty short.

CHAPTER 3

Navigating the Android SDK

This chapter will take an in-depth look at the Android Software Development Kit (SDK) and how to use it for developing code targeted at the Scripting Layer for Android.

Note All examples in this chapter are based on release 8 of the Android SDK.

Here's how I'll break it down in this chapter:

- Wading through the SDK documentation
- Examining the different SDK components
- Testing with the Android emulator
- Exploring with the Android Debug Bridge (ADB)
- Debugging and more with the Dalvik Debug Monitor Service (DDMS)

Get ready to dive right into the world of the Android SDK. Each release of Android brings with it an SDK specific to that release. When building native Android apps you have the option to target a specific release in order to take advantage of the latest features. That means you can use the latest SDK release and still build and test apps running on older versions. I'll be using release 8 (r8) for the target as that is the version of Android on all the devices I will be testing with.

Wading Through the SDK Documentation

If you look in the root directory of the SDK installation, you'll see an entry named docs. This is essentially a copy of the documentation on the main Android developer site for local access. Open the docs directory and you'll see several .html files. Index.html is what you would see if you opened your web browser and navigated to developer.android.com. Offline.html has links to help you get the SDK installed if you haven't already done that along with a note pointing you to the main site "for the most current documentation and a fully-functional experience."

It's not hard to get overwhelmed the first time you browse the Android developer site. The amount of information there is pretty staggering. The best thing to do is to step back and pick a few areas you want to read up on and then focus your exploring on those topics. There's a search box at the top of every page that will return your request in sorted order, along with a list of tabs to let you quickly narrow the results to specific areas of the documentation tree including Dev Guide, Reference, Developer Groups, Android Source, and Blog.

If you haven't looked at the Android platform from an architectural perspective, then you probably want to start with the Application Fundamentals (`developer.android.com/guide/topics/fundamentals.html`) section to get a good overview of what makes Android tick. There are a number of top-level concepts discussed in great detail that will help you understand how applications communicate with lower-level functionality provided by specific Android application programming interfaces (APIs). Of particular interest in the context of this book is how different processes communicate using remote procedure calls (RPCs). Scripting Layer for Android (SL4A) uses this mechanism to pass information from a script interpreter process to an Android API.

Understanding content providers in Android will make it easier to work with the information available to your scripts. Figure 3-1 shows a snapshot from the Dev Guide section of the Android developer documentation of what a content Uniform Resource Identifier (URI) looks like and how to interpret it. The key piece of a content URI is the authority part, which looks a lot like a web address. Once you see the pattern, you will be able to read one of these URIs and know exactly what it means.

Figure 3-1. *Android content provider description*

Another good place to spend some time reading is the User Interface Guidelines section. Any program that will interact in some way with the user should try to adhere to Google's conventions for buttons, icons, and text entry. SL4A provides access to a wide range of user interface elements, and you will do well to invest some time in understanding how and when to use them. A good example here would be when to use a context menu versus an option menu. An *option menu* typically appears when the user presses the menu button, while a *context menu* is similar to what you would get on a desktop operating system when you right-click the mouse. On Android, the long-press or touch-and-hold actions are equivalent to a right-click with a mouse.

In Chapter 2, I introduced an Android utility function called `makeToast`. This little function creates a short popup message that appears on the screen, but doesn't take focus or pause the current activity. It's part of a class of messages falling under the heading of notifications. A *toast notification* is an easy way to give users feedback about something they just did, like setting an alarm to go off at a specific time. Android also supports status bar notifications to add an icon and optional short message to the system's status bar along with an expanded message in the Notifications window. You can also generate things like a sound or vibration to give additional feedback.

Dialog boxes are other user interface elements worth reading up on. DatePickerDialog and TimePickerDialog are two special dialog boxes that make entering dates and times much easier on a small screen. ProgressDialog is a user feedback element for providing progress information for a long-running activity. AlertDialog is without question the most flexible and probably the most used dialog box of them all. Alert dialog boxes can also contain lists of items, check boxes, and radio buttons. Figure 3-2 shows an alert dialog box with text and buttons.

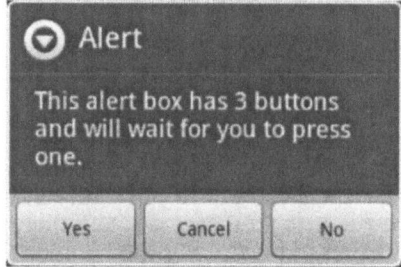

Figure 3-2. *Alert dialog box with text and buttons*

One more area of interest in the documentation is the WebView. If you want to build any user interface with something more than buttons and dialog boxes, you'll have to use a WebView. I'll spend a lot of time in Chapter 9 on building interfaces using a WebView, so understanding the basics will help.

Examining the Different SDK Components

If you take a look at the directory tree where you installed the Android SDK, you should see a list of folders containing documentation, sample code, and a number of tools. There's also a directory named `market_licensing` with information on how to market your finished application. With release 8 of the SDK, Google made some changes to the directory structure, affecting where some of the more common tools are located. If you set up shortcuts or modified your path for a previously installed version of the SDK, you'll need to change the target directories.

Figure 3-3 shows a screen capture of the top-level directory on a Windows 7 machine. This shows the 32-bit SDK installed on a 64-bit version of Windows 7, hence the **Program Files (x86)** parent directory.

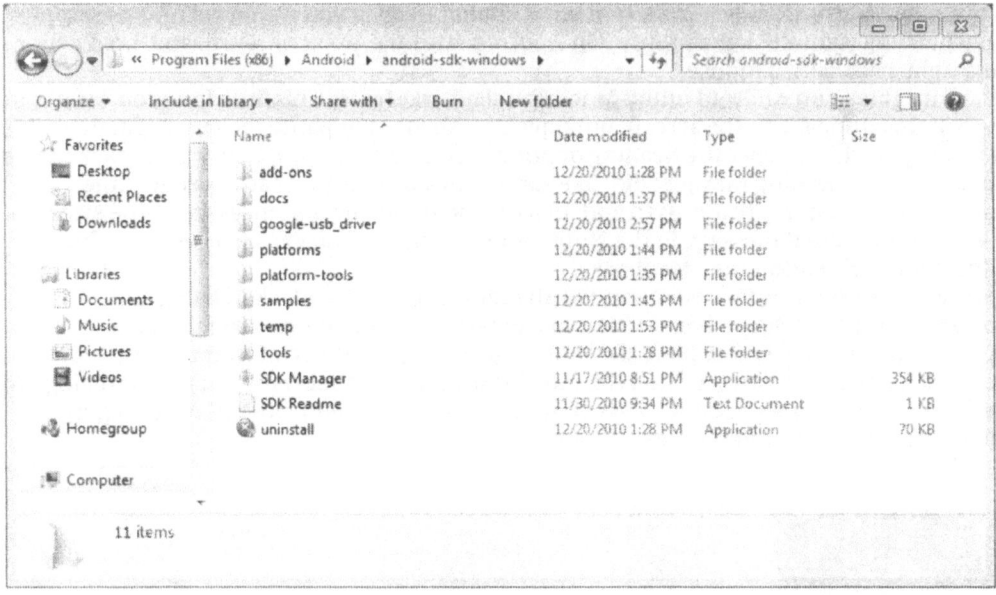

Figure 3-3. *Android SDK file structure on Windows*

If you want to create a shortcut to the SDK Manager application on Windows, be sure you right-click the SDK Manager Application in the **android-sdk-windows** directory, drag it onto your desktop, and then select Create shortcuts here. If you don't do that, you'll move the application or make a copy of it which won't run from the desktop.

Navigating to the tools subdirectory will reveal a number of executable files. The first and arguably most important is the Android Debug Bridge (ADB) tool. You can use ADB for moving files from your local machine to the device in much the same way you would copy files from a command line. I'll dive into the ADB in depth a little later in the chapter. The SDK Manager application is your starting place for SDK updates, creating and launching virtual devices, and finding third-party add-ons.

Testing With the Android Emulator

The first thing you must do before you can use the Android emulator is to configure a target device. An Android virtual device (AVD) consists of a number of different files, including configuration and virtual storage, which the emulator needs to do its job. You can create as many AVDs as you need for simulating different devices. The easiest way to create an AVD is to use the SDK and AVD Manager application, as shown in Figure 3-4.

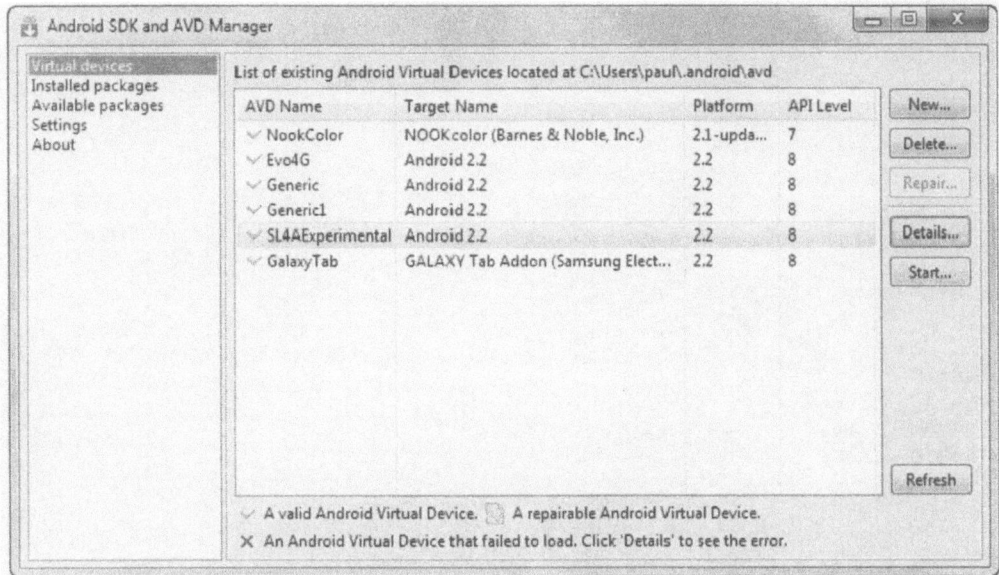

Figure 3-4. Android SDK and AVD Manager tool

To start the process of creating a new AVD, you simply click the New button. That will bring up a dialog box as shown in Figure 3-5. The first thing you have to do is give your new AVD a name. You should make it descriptive, but the name cannot have any spaces. After picking a name you must select a target environment. Finally, you'll want to choose a size for your SD card. You shouldn't need a lot of space if you're using it exclusively for testing SL4A. A value of 100 MB was used for this example.

___

■ **Tip**   Additional target devices such as the Samsung Galaxy Tab are available through the SDK Manager, whereas others may be available directly from the vendor as in the case of the Barnes & Noble Nook Color. You can also modify one of the generic devices to accommodate features of a real device such as the presence of a hardware keyboard or a specific screen size.

___

Screen resolution will default to one of the built-in devices unless you check the Resolution radio button and specify specific dimensions. To add or remove hardware features, click the New button next to the Hardware section and choose a feature from the drop-down list. To remove a feature such as a keyboard, first add Keyboard support by clicking the New button and then changing its value by clicking in the Value column and choosing No.

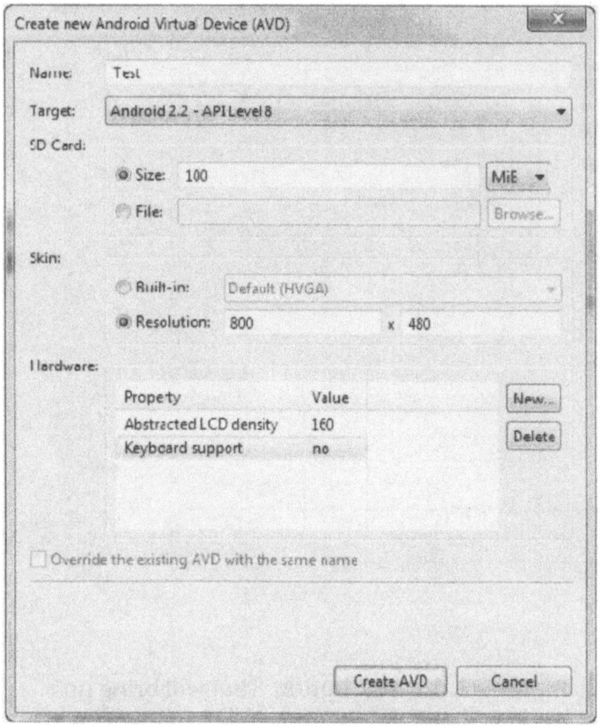

Figure 3-5. *New AVD dialog box*

You can start any of the defined AVDs from the SDK Manager screen by selecting your device and then clicking the Start button. That will bring up another dialog box, giving you the chance to set a few options before it starts. One of the options you will want to change is the Scale Display To Real Size check box. This enables the Screen Size and Monitor DPI text boxes, in which you can choose how big you want the emulator to appear on your screen. This will depend on your actual monitor size, although I found 10 inches a good choice for a typical 20-inch display.

The last check box, Wipe User Data, gives you a quick way to start your virtual device with no data from any previous sessions. This feature allows you to test applications with first-time-run behavior that differs from normal behavior without re-creating a new AVD each time. Figure 3-6 shows what this dialog box looks like with the Screen Size option set to ten inches.

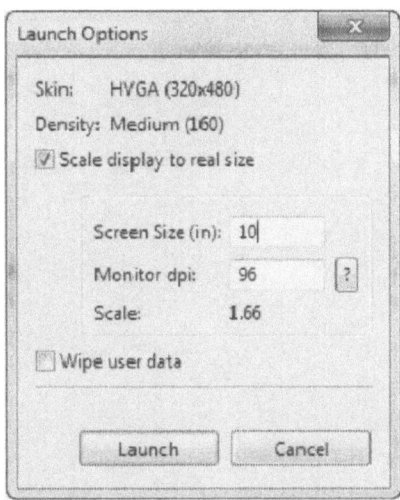

Figure 3-6. *AVD Launch Options dialog box*

For devices with keyboards, there is a standard set of mappings from the host keyboard to actions on the device. Table 3-1 shows the default set of definitions stored in the **.android** subdirectory below your home directory in the file **default.keyset**. You can change these settings by editing the **default.keyset** file or by creating your own **keyset** file and then adding the **-keyset** option on the emulator command line.

Table 3-1. *Emulator Key Mappings*

BUTTON_CALL	F3
BUTTON_HANGUP	F4
BUTTON_HOME	Home
BUTTON_BACK	Escape
BUTTON_MENU	F2, PageUp
BUTTON_STAR	Shift+F2, PageDown
BUTTON_POWER	F7
BUTTON_SEARCH	F5
BUTTON_CAMERA	Ctrl+Keypad_5, Ctrl+F3
BUTTON_VOLUME_UP	Keypad_Plus, Ctrl+F5

Continued

BUTTON_VOLUME_DOWN	Keypad_Minus, Ctrl+F6
TOGGLE_NETWORK	F8
TOGGLE_TRACING	F9
TOGGLE_FULLSCREEN	Alt-Enter
BUTTON_DPAD_CENTER	Keypad_5
BUTTON_DPAD_UP	Keypad_8
BUTTON_DPAD_LEFT	Keypad_4
BUTTON_DPAD_RIGHT	Keypad_6
BUTTON_DPAD_DOWN	Keypad_2
TOGGLE_TRACKBALL	F6
SHOW_TRACKBALL	Delete
CHANGE_LAYOUT_PREV	Keypad_7, Ctrl+F11
CHANGE_LAYOUT_NEXT	Keypad_9, Ctrl+F12
ONION_ALPHA_UP	Keypad_Multiply
ONION_ALPHA_DOWN	Keypad_Divide

Launching a generic AVD with the keyboard will bring up a screen that should look like Figure 3-7.

Figure 3-7. *Generic emulator window*

The emulator should function just like a real device, with a few minor exceptions. You should remember which keys on your PC keyboard mimic the hardware button keys because you will use them frequently. By default, the mappings for PC to Device are Home to Home, F2 to Menu, Esc to Back, and F5 to Search. The mouse on the PC takes the place of your finger on a real device. Left-clicking the mouse is the same as touching or pressing on the screen. If you click the icon at the bottom-center of the screen resembling a checkerboard, you will launch the Applications screen as shown in Figure 3-8.

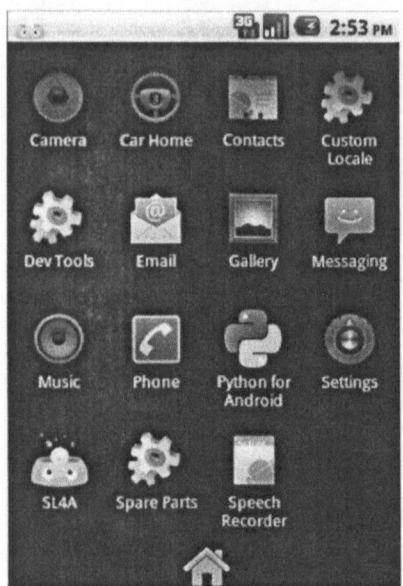

Figure 3-8. Emulator application launcher screen

To view messages in the notification area, you first have to click and hold your mouse near the top of the device screen, in the same white bar area as the signal strength, battery level, and time icons. Next, you perform a drag-downward movement with the mouse as you would with your finger. It is similar to pulling a window shade down. This motion will reveal the notification window at any time and display a "No notifications" message if none is present. The same technique can be used to simulate swiping from left to right or vice versa, using the mouse to click, hold, and drag across the emulator device screen.

Bluetooth is not functional in the emulator, so if you have any need to test using Bluetooth you'll have to do that on a real device. WiFi is also not available. The emulator does support 3G data connections, meaning that you will have connectivity to the Internet. You can simulate calls by selecting a contact or by directly entering a phone number. All calls show up in the call log, providing another data source for you to test against. While you can simulate making and receiving calls, there is no real voice capability, so don't expect to actually make a real call. That also means you won't be able to test any of the voice recognition capabilities on an emulator.

You'll probably want to configure the e-mail account on your emulator for testing purposes, which works just like on a real device. Figure 3-9 shows the opening screen when you first launch the app.

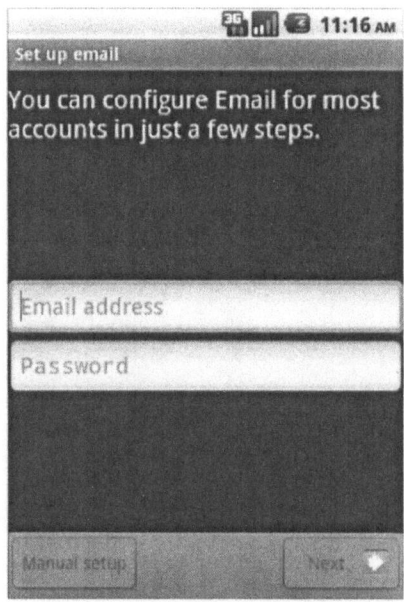

Figure 3-9. *Emulator e-mail configuration screen*

To configure a Gmail account, enter your full address including the @gmail.com part. After entering your password, click the Next button. If you entered your information correctly, you should then see a screen asking you for an (optional) account name and a name (signature) to be added on outgoing messages.

For convenience, you can add a shortcut on your emulator home screen to the SL4A application and the scripts folder. To do this, click and hold the mouse anywhere on the home screen. That will launch the Add to Home screen dialog box. At this point you have the option to add a Shortcut, Widget, Folder, or Wallpaper. Select the Shortcuts entry to add one for the SL4A application. This will display another dialog box with all available applications and actions that support a shortcut. Select Applications and from the Select activity dialog box, choose SL4A.

Another handy way to quickly access your scripts is to add a folder to your home screen. You do this the same way as adding a shortcut except you select Folder from the Add to Home dialog box. After choosing Folder, you should see a new dialog box labeled Select Folder with a list of available folders. Choose the entry labeled Scripts, and you should be all set. Now you should see a screen like Figure 3-10 when you click the Scripts icon on your home screen. This will display a list of all scripts in that folder and give you one-click access to running any of them. I will use this feature in Chapter 8 to build a handy phone settings script to change multiple settings with just two clicks.

Figure 3-10. *Home screen scripts folder*

Another thing that does not work on the emulator is live SMS messages. You can open the messaging application and type in a message, but nothing will actually go out. It will populate a database with outgoing messages if you need that for testing. To simulate an incoming SMS message you'll have to use the ADB tool, which is the next topic of discussion.

Android Debug Bridge

Chapter 2 has a brief introduction to the Android Debug Bridge (ADB), but really only brushes the surface of the things you can do with this tool. ADB actually requires three separate components to do its job. On your development machine, ADB consists of a client and a server. The ADB server handles all communication between the client running on the development machine and a daemon running on either an emulator or a target device.

Command-line options are used to instruct ADB to perform a specific task. Table 3-2 shows each of these commands with a brief description. For the Install, Sync, and Uninstall commands there are options available to modify how the command behaves. If you happen to have an emulator running and a real device connected, you must specify where you want the ADB commands to execute. To direct ADB commands to a real device, use the option –d and for the emulator, use –e.

Table 3-2. *List of ADB Commands*

`adb push <local> <remote>`	Copy file/dir to device
`adb pull <remote> [<local>]`	Copy file/dir from device
`adb sync [ <directory> ]`	Copy host->device only if changed (-l means list but don't copy)
`adb shell`	Run remote shell interactively

`adb push <local> <remote>`	Copy file/dir to device
`adb shell <command>`	Run remote shell command
`adb emu <command>`	Run emulator console command
`adb logcat [ <filter-spec> ]`	View device log

`adb forward <local> <remote>`	Forward socket connections
	
	Forward specs are one of the following:
	
	`tcp:<port>`
	`localabstract:<unix domain socket name>`
	`localreserved:<unix domain socket name>`
	`localfilesystem:<unix domain socket name>`
	`dev:<character device name>`
	`jdwp:<process pid>` (remote only)

`adb jdwp`	List PIDs of processes hosting a JDWP transport
`adb install [-l] [-r] [-s] <file>`	Push this package file to the device and install it (`-l` means forward-lock the app) (`-r` means reinstall the app, keeping its data) (`-s` means install on SD card instead of internal storage)
`adb uninstall [-k] <package>`	Remove this app package from the device (`-k` means keep the data and cache directories)
`adb bugreport`	Return all information from the device that should be included in a bug report
`adb help`	Show this help message
`adb version`	Show version number

Files and Applications

There are three commands that deal with copying files between a host computer and either the emulator or a physical device. `push` will copy a file from the host to a target, while `pull` will copy from the target to the host. `sync` attempts to synchronize files between directories on the host and target. You can also pass the -l option to `sync` and it will simply list the contents of the directory.

Installing or uninstalling .apk files to either the emulator or a physical device uses the adb `install` or `uninstall` command, respectively. Options for the `install` command include -l to forward-lock the app, -r to reinstall keeping all old data, and -s to install the app on the SD card instead of internal device storage.

■ **Tip**   You can use the adb push tool to quickly load contacts on an emulated device for testing purposes. If you have contacts stored in a Gmail account, you can easily export those to a vCard file and then use adb push to move it to the SD card on the device. All that's left is to start contacts and import the vCard file from the SD card.

The Shell

The adb shell command provides a way to send shell commands to the device and display the results or to launch an interactive shell locally. One of the things you can use the shell command for is to automate testing on a device. This uses the shell input keyevent and sendevent commands. Input is an application that lives in the /system/bin directory on a device, making it possible to simulate keyboard input of any kind. You can push a text string with this command:

```
adb shell input text "ANDROID"
```

To simulate pressing a key on either a physical or virtual keyboard, use the keyevent qualifier to the input command along with an integer representing the specific keycode you wish to invoke. A list of keycodes is shown in Table 3-3. You would simulate pressing the menu key with the following:

```
adb shell input keyevent 1
```

Table 3-3. *Listing of Keycodes*

Keycode	Key sent	Keycode	Key sent
0	UNKNOWN	55	COMMA
1	MENU	56	PERIOD
2	SOFT_RIGHT	57	ALT_LEFT
3	HOME	58	ALT_RIGHT
4	BACK	59	SHIFT_LEFT
5	CALL	60	SHIFT_RIGHT
6	ENDCALL	61	TAB
7	0	62	SPACE
8	1	63	SYM
...	...	64	EXPLORER
15	8	65	ENVELOPE

Keycode	Key sent	Keycode	Key sent
16	9	66	ENTER
17	STAR	67	DEL
18	POUND	68	GRAVE
19	DPAD_UP	69	MINUS
20	DPAD_DOWN	70	EQUALS
21	DPAD_LEFT	71	LEFT_BRACKET
22	DPAD_RIGHT	72	RIGHT_BRACKET
23	DPAD_CENTER	73	BACKSLASH
24	VOLUME_UP	74	SEMICOLON
25	VOLUME_DOWN	75	APOSTROPHE
26	POWER	76	SLASH
27	CAMERA	77	AT
28	CLEAR	78	NUM
29	A	79	HEADSETHOOK
30	B	80	FOCUS
31	C	81	PLUS
...	...	82	MENU
52	X	83	NOTIFICATION
53	Y	84	SEARCH
54	Z	85	TAG_LAST_KEYCODE

If you plan to develop any applications to interact with functionality of the phone (initiating a phone call; sending or receiving SMS messages), you must use the `telnet` command to connect to the emulator console. On Windows 7 there is no Telnet program installed by default. Fortunately, it is a part of the operating system and just needs to be enabled. To enable Telnet, you must open the Control Panel and select the Programs category. This will bring up a window like the one in Figure 3-11. You can also directly launch the Windows Features dialog box by pressing the Windows key and typing the word **features**. This will show a list of options including several under the heading Control Panel. Selecting the "Turn Windows features on or off" item will bring up the dialog box shown in Figure 3-12.

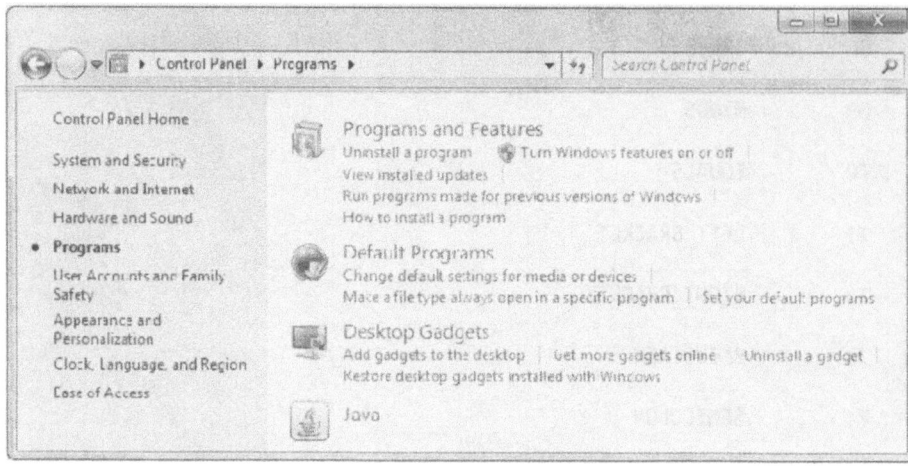

Figure 3-11. *Windows 7 Control Panel programs page*

To enable the Telnet client program, you simply click the check box next to Telnet Client in the Windows Features dialog box. as shown in Figure 3-12. If you would like your machine to also function as a Telnet server, you can check the Telnet Server box, although most Windows firewalls will block incoming Telnet traffic for security reasons.

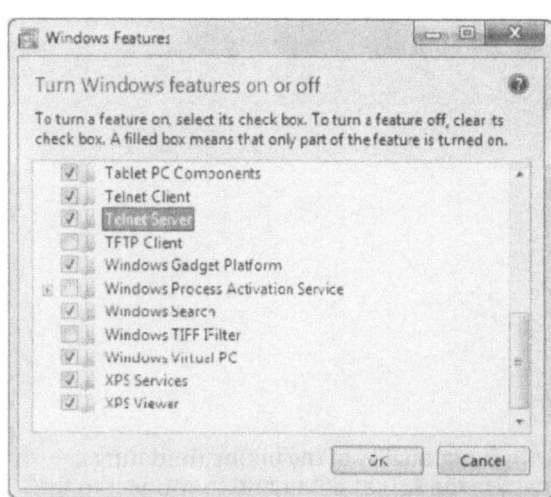

Figure 3-12. *Windows 7 Features dialog box*

Assuming you have started an ADB device with the normal defaults, you would initiate a telnet session on Linux or Mac OS X from a terminal window or from a command prompt in Windows with this command:

```
telnet localhost 5554
```

Now you're ready to issue commands directly to the device. Figure 3-13 shows the output of the help command with a telnet session started.

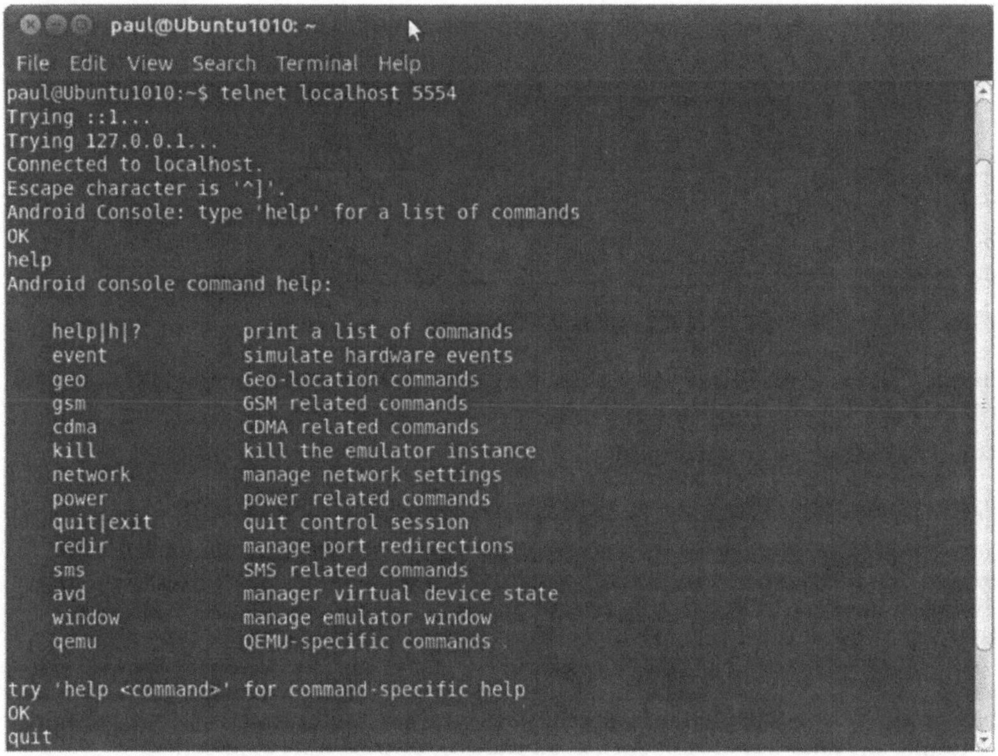

```
paul@Ubuntu1010: ~
File Edit View Search Terminal Help
paul@Ubuntu1010:~$ telnet localhost 5554
Trying ::1...
Trying 127.0.0.1...
Connected to localhost.
Escape character is '^]'.
Android Console: type 'help' for a list of commands
OK
help
Android console command help:

    help|h|?          print a list of commands
    event             simulate hardware events
    geo               Geo-location commands
    gsm               GSM related commands
    cdma              CDMA related commands
    kill              kill the emulator instance
    network           manage network settings
    power             power related commands
    quit|exit         quit control session
    redir             manage port redirections
    sms               SMS related commands
    avd               manager virtual device state
    window            manage emulator window
    qemu              QEMU-specific commands

try 'help <command>' for command-specific help
OK
quit
```

Figure 3-13. Telnet session on Linux to emulator

Emulating an incoming SMS message would require a command such as this:

```
sms send 3015551212 "This is a test SMS message from Telnet"
```

On the emulator you should see a message arrive. Open the Messaging application, and you should see something like Figure 3-14.

Figure 3-14. *Messaging app with simulated SMS message displayed*

For testing location-based applications you can use the geo command, which will send either a GPS NMEA sentence or a simple GPS fix. These two commands would look like this:

```
geo fix -82.411629 28.054553
```

```
geo nmea $GPGGA,001431.092,0118.2653,N,10351.1359,E,0,00,,-19.6,M,4.1,M,,0000*5B
```

You'll have to use the NMEA command if you want to do anything more than simulate the current latitude and longitude. The $GPGGA code stands for *Global Positioning System Fix Data.* Fields in order, left to right, are Sentence Identifier ($GPGGA), Time (00:14:31.092), Latitude, North, Longitude (103 degrees, 51 minutes and 13.59 seconds, number of satellites, horizontal dilution of precision (HDOP), Altitude, Height of geoid above WGS84 ellipsoid, Time since last DGPS update, DGPS reference station ID, and a checksum.

There is a shell command to allow you to change the date and time on the emulator. This can come in handy if you're testing any time-based logic such as an alarm or elapsed time application:

```
adb shell date secs
```

The only downside to using this command is you must enter the time in seconds since January 1, 1970; otherwise known as the *UNIX epoch.* There is a way from a Linux or Mac OS X terminal prompt to determine the value for secs of the current time with this command:

```
date +%s
```

The Python language has many handy features and functions as a part of the Python standard library. Time and date manipulation is one task Python can handle with just a few lines of code. Here's a short script to convert any date and time into the proper seconds value:

Listing 3-1. *Python Epoch Time Converter*

```
#!/usr/bin/python
#-----------------------------
# This script will convert arg1 (Date) and arg2 (Time) to Epoch Seconds
#
import sys, time, datetime

if len(sys.argv) < 3:
    print "Usage pyEpoch YYYY-MM-DD HH:MM"
else:
    intime = sys.argv[1] + " " + sys.argv[2]

t = time.strptime(intime, "%Y-%m-%d %H:%M")
t = datetime.datetime(*t[:6])
print "Epoch Seconds:", time.mktime(t.timetuple())
```

A quick Google search for **UNIX epoch converter** turns up several web sites that will convert to/from a date and seconds. Be advised that executing this command will generate an error message that **settimeofday** failed, but it does actually work. Figure 3-15 shows a Windows command prompt with several times set and the time of day read using the same date command with no argument to show the current time.

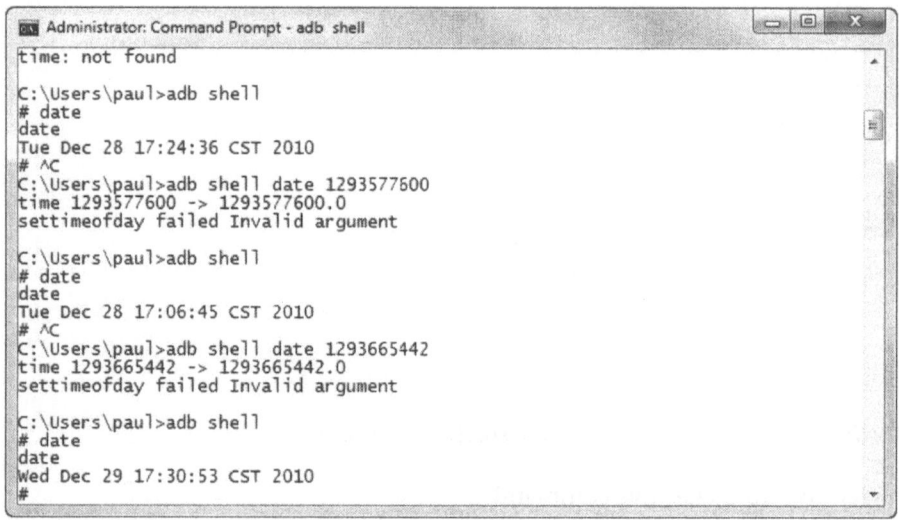

Figure 3-15. *Setting the emulator date with the shell command*

You can launch any application on the emulator using the command-line interface to the ActivityManager, as follows:

`adb shell am start command`

Figure 3-16 shows the output of the help given when you type in **am** at the telnet prompt.

Figure 3-16. *Launching activities on the emulator with the shell am command*

To launch a web browser, you would use this command:

`adb shell am start 'http://www.google.com'`

The command **adb shell dumpsys** provides insight into virtually everything about the current state of any attached Android device. If you run this command against the emulator, you'll get a list of available subcommands as shown in Table 3-4.

Table 3-4. Listing of Dumpsys Subcommands

SurfaceFlinger	accessibility	account
activity	alarm	appwidget
audio	backup	battery
batteryinfo	clipboard	connectivity
content	cpuinfo	device_policy
devicestoragemonitor	diskstats	dropbox
entropy	hardware	input_method
iphonesubinfo	isms	location
media.audio_flinger	media.audio_policy	media.camera
media.player	meminfo	mount
netstat	network_management	notification
package	permission	phone
power	search	sensor
simphonebook	statusbar	telephony.registry
throttle	uimode	usagestats
vibrator	wallpaper	wifi
window		

For the emulator, the output of the command adb shell dumpsys battery looks like this:

```
Current Battery Service state:
  AC powered: true
  USB powered: false
  status: 2
  health: 2
  present: true
  level: 50
```

```
scale: 100
voltage:0
temperature: 0
technology: Li-ion
```

Another interesting subcommand is `location`. If you look at the output of the command `adb shell dumpsys location` for the emulator, you won't see much. Run the same command on a real device, and you'll see all kinds of information. If you examine the output of the command `adb shell dumpsys activity`, you'll see a long list of information about the current activity state on the device.

You can get a list of information maintained by the `PackageManagerService` with the command `adb shell dumpsys package`. The output of this command has a number of different sections, with the first being the Activity Resolver Table. This section contains lists of MIME types, Non-Data Actions, and MIME Typed Actions complete with the intent used to launch a specific action. Non-Data Actions start an activity that does not require any data to launch. An example of one of these would be `com.android.contacts.action.LIST_ALL_CONTACTS`. The behavior of this intent is fairly obvious from the name, but you can see the results with this command:

```
adb shell am start -a com.android.contacts.action.LIST_ALL_CONTACTS
```

To launch more complex actions through the intent mechanism, you must specify a number of different fields. As seen in Figure 3-16, you have a number of options available including `-a` to specify the action, `-c` for a category, `-d` to specify a Data URI, `-t` for MIME type, and `-e` for extras. You could launch the contacts application to add an entry with this command:

```
adb shell am start -a android.intent.action.INSERT -d 'content://contacts/people' -t↩
 'vnd.android.cursor.dir/person' -c 'android.intent.category.DEFAULT' -e 'name' 'Paul'↩
 -e 'phone' '1112223333'
```

At this point you might want to refer to the Android developer documentation and read up on the Intent topic. Understanding how Intents are used to launch an activity will give you insight into what you would need to provide for your application. While you can launch pretty much any Android activity from the command line using the ADB utility, you can also launch an activity programmatically. Later chapters will use this concept to build scripts to automate multiple activities.

This same technique can be used to launch SL4A to execute a script as follows:

```
am start -a
com.googlecode.android_scripting.action.LAUNCH_FOREGROUND_SCRIPT -n
com.googlecode.android_scripting/.activity.ScriptingLayerServiceLauncher -e
com.googlecode.android_scripting.extra.SCRIPT_PATH
"/sdcard/sl4a/scripts/hello_world.py"
```

I'll show you how to do this in the next chapter on using Eclipse to automatically deploy a solution to either the emulator or a target device and launch it. One last command that I find really useful will launch a private server on the device to enable remote debugging:

```
adb shell am start -a com.googlecode.android_scripting.action.LAUNCH_SERVER -n
com.googlecode.android_scripting/.activity.ScriptingLayerServiceLauncher
```

logcat

`logcat` is the name of the ADB command to dump or cat the current logfile from either an emulator or hardware device. If you type this command either at a command prompt in Windows or a terminal window in Linux or Mac OS X, it will dump the current log and continue displaying new entries until you hit Ctrl+C to stop it. This tool will help you debug applications that unexpectedly stop without error. It is also available from an Eclipse window, as you will see in the next chapter.

Dalvik Debug Monitor Service (DDMS)

The DDMS is a complementary tool to ADB and actually uses the ADB host server-to-device daemon for all communication. This will become painfully obvious if you upgrade from a version of the SDK with the ADB tool in a different directory. Figure 3-17 shows what the DDMS user interface looks like with both an emulator and physical device currently connected.

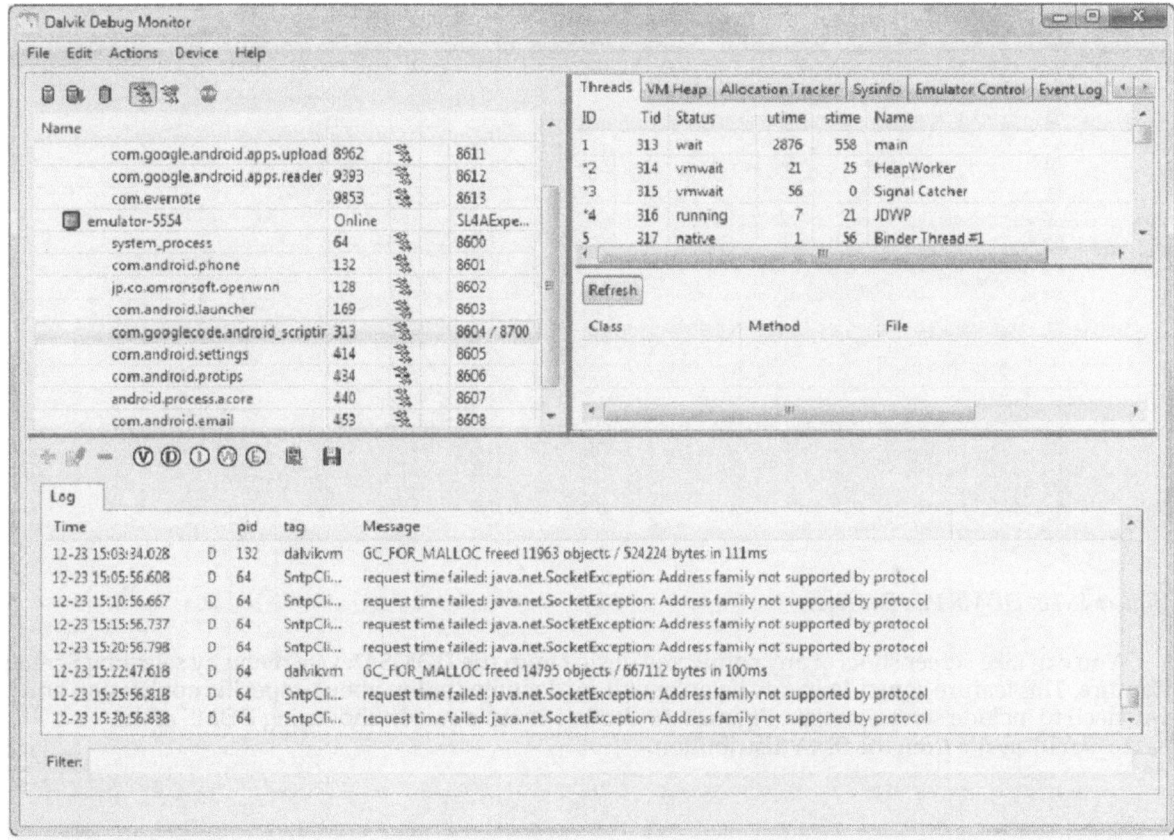

Figure 3-17. *DDMS display*

DDMS has a number of features you will want to learn more about. One is the File Explorer tool available from the Device menu. To browse files on a particular device, select the device in the top-left pane of the DDMS application and then open File Explorer. Be aware that you won't be able to see any of the files in the system area on a normal device because they are protected. You will be able to see those files if the device has been rooted. The term *rooted* means gaining root access to a device by using either a third-party application or by some other nontrival method. Most devices ship with the system file area set to read only, so a user can't make any changes. Full browsing is allowed on an emulated device and will look something like Figure 3-18. Here you can see the contacts database which is actually an SQLite database file.

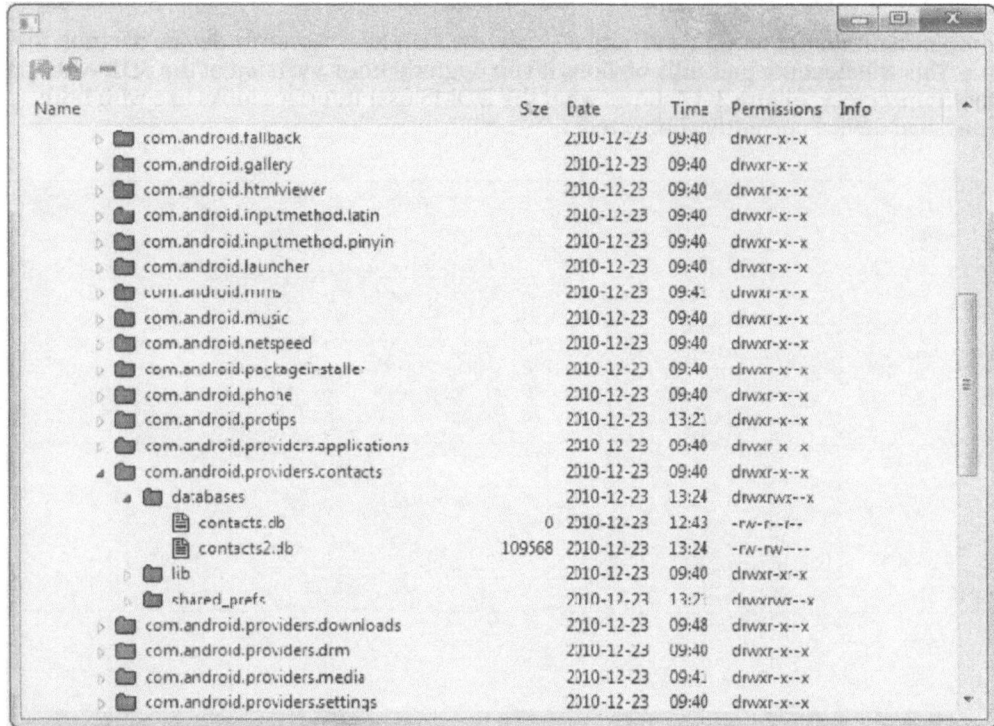

Figure 3-18. DDMS File Explorer

You can take screenshots of any connected device from the DDMS Device menu by selecting Screen Capture. This feature comes in handy if you're writing documentation about a specific application and you need to include screen images. Figure 3-19 shows a sample screen shot using DDMS of the hello_world.py file from the SL4A distribution.

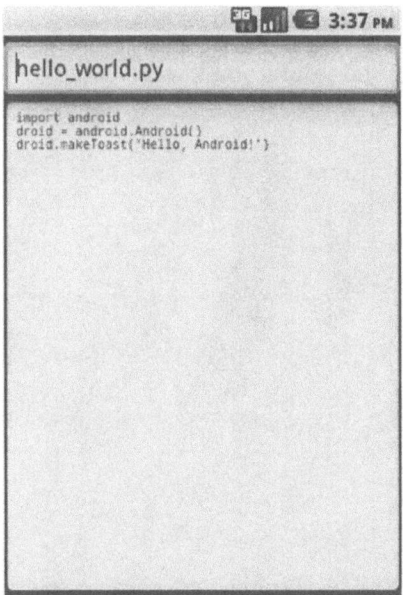

Figure 3-19. *DDMS screen capture example*

In the next chapter I'll show you how these tools integrate directly with Eclipse to provide access to everything you need to code, test, debug and deploy any application for Android.

Summary

This chapter focused on getting the Android SDK fully installed and configured to make it easier to develop and test on both emulated and real devices. Many of the tools and concepts discussed here will be used later to help streamline and, in some cases, automate the development process. The next chapter covers using Eclipse as a primary development platform along with the Android Development Toolkit (ADT).

Here's a list of key take-aways for this chapter:

- **Android SDK**: It's really big and probably has more stuff than you'll ever look at, but it does have a number of tools like ADB, device emulators, and DDMS that are really useful

- **Linux command line**: If you're not comfortable typing in commands at either the Linux command line or a Windows DOS prompt, you might want to take some time to read up on the subject. Many of the tools like ADB use the command line to accomplish tasks, and you might as well learn how to take advantage of them.

- **Use the emulator**: The best thing about an emulator is you can delete it and start over. The emulator should work just fine for many of the things you'll want to try out. Better to test something on an emulator before you try it on a real device. Don't be afraid to delete an emulator and start over if it gets really slow or doesn't seem to work right.

- **Use batch/script files**: One of the first things I did was to write a few batch scripts on Windows to do things like launch a private server on the device and copy files to the right directory. If you're doing any amount of coding and testing you'll want to have some of these scripts around.

CHAPTER 4

Developing with Eclipse

This chapter will walk you through installing, configuring, and developing with Eclipse.

Note While Eclipse will work on Linux, Mac OS X, and Windows, this chapter will use Windows as the primary development environment.

Okay. Let's get started. Here's what I'll cover in this chapter:

- Installing Eclipse on a development machine
- Using Eclipse basics
- Understanding the Android Development Toolkit
- Using Pydev

By using the instructions given here, you will be able to get Eclipse installed and ready for productive work in just a few minutes. I'll walk you through the basic installation steps for Eclipse itself along with a number of other plugins to help us with developing all of the examples in this book.

It's important to point out at this point that Eclipse was developed from the outset as an extensible, integrated development environment (IDE) written in the Java language. Since it's written in Java, it automatically qualifies as a cross-platform application and, in fact, that was the general idea from the beginning. Eclipse has grown into a huge project, and this single point often scares some people off.

Installing Eclipse on a Development Machine

Eclipse comes in many flavors. Choosing the right one for you is, in large part, a matter of taste. If you plan on using it just for completing the exercises in this book, you can go with the "Classic" download. The current version as of the writing of this book is 3.6.1 code named Galileo. For both Linux and Windows you will be offered the choice of a 32-bit or 64-bit download. For the Mac you'll have the option of Mac OS X (Carbon), Mac OS X (Cocoa 32) or Mac OS X (Cocoa 64). Choose the one that matches your operating system. Eclipse requires an installation of Java to work, so if you skipped the section in Chapter 2 on downloading and installing Java you'll need to go back and do that now. Eclipse is distributed in a single `.zip` file, meaning all you have to do to install the program is unpack the contents. On Windows Vista and Windows 7 you can double-click the `.zip` file, and Windows Explorer will open, giving you the option to extract all the files as shown in Figure 4-1.

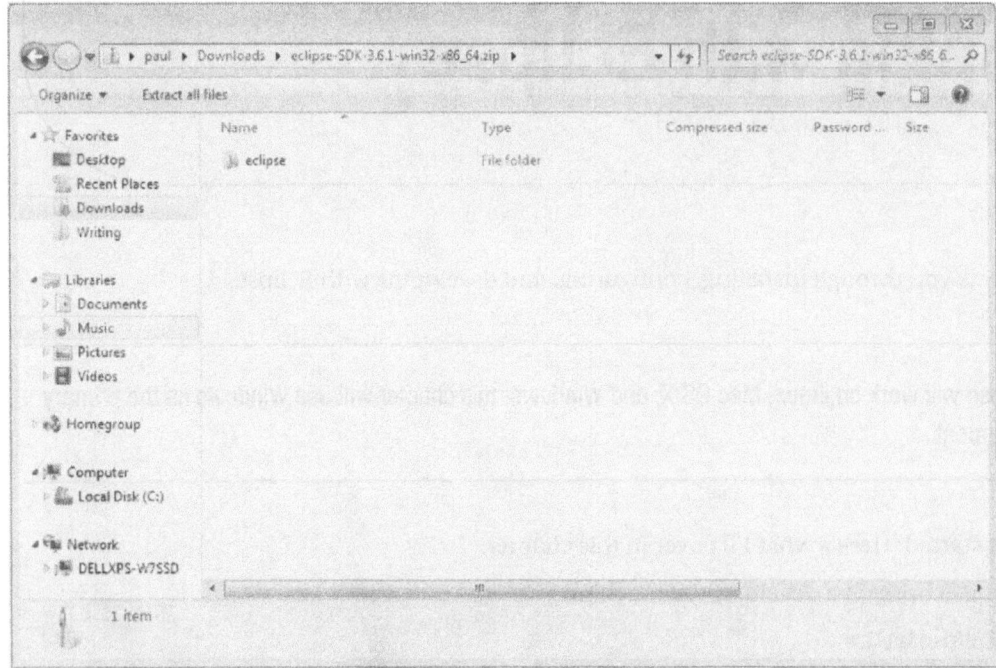

Figure 4-1. *Eclipse SDK installation*

Once you have a directory with all the Eclipse files unpacked, you should be able to start the program in Windows by double-clicking the **Eclipse.exe** file. You probably want to create a shortcut on your desktop since this will be a frequently used application. Remember to use the right-click Create Shortcut Here method to ensure that Eclipse will start properly. The first time you run Eclipse you will see a dialog box screen like the one in Figure 4-2, prompting you to choose where to store your project files. This is called the Workspace in Eclipse. You have the option to select the default, and if you check the box next to Use This As The Default And Do Not Ask Again, it will become the permanent default directory. If you don't select this box, you'll be prompted to select a Workspace every time you start Eclipse.

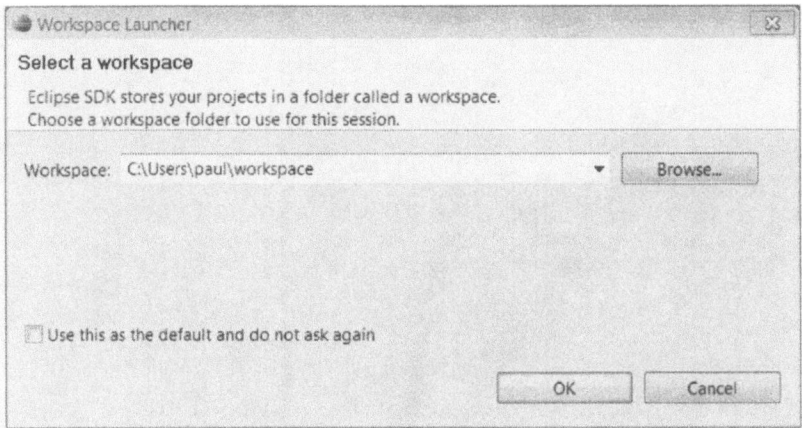

Figure 4-2. Select workspace directory dialog box

Installing plugin modules in Eclipse happens from the Help menu by selecting the Install New Software option. This will open the dialog box shown in Figure 4-3. Each add-on is typically installed from a default repository on the Internet. This makes it easier to keep current with updates and to install the most up-to-date version. To add a new repository, click the Add button next to the text box labeled Work With. You can also just type in the URL in the same text box and the Eclipse installer will go out to that address to look for add-on packages. Figure 4-3 shows the result of entering the URL for the Android Development Tools (ADT) plugin for Eclipse. If you use the Add button, you'll be given the chance to name the repository. The URL for the ADT is

`https://dl-ssl.google.com/android/eclipse`

You must choose either individual options underneath the Developer Tools line or just check the box next to Developer Tools to select them all. Once the download completes, you'll be instructed to restart Eclipse for the changes to take effect. If you can't remember what you have installed, just check the box next to Hide Items That Are Already Installed and all you'll see is new items. If you'd like to see a list of what has been installed, you can click the Already Installed link. There's also a link named Available Software Sites that will take you to a list of predefined add-on sites.

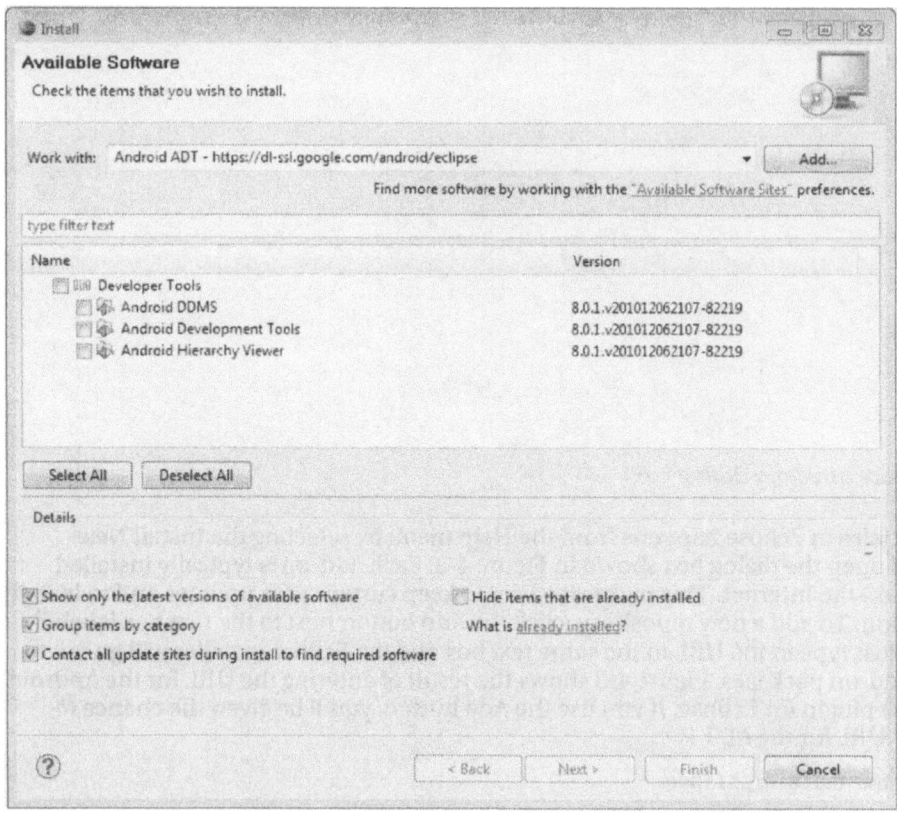

Figure 4-3. *ADT installation dialog box*

The next add-on you'll want to install is Pydev. Writing and debugging Python code using Eclipse and Pydev is a truly integrated development experience. I'll walk you through using Pydev a little later. For now, open the Software update screen from the Help menu again. This time we'll enter another URL for the Pydev update site. It should look like the following:

```
http://Pydev.org/updates
```

Figure 4-4 shows the dialog box you will see after entering the **pydev.org** URL.

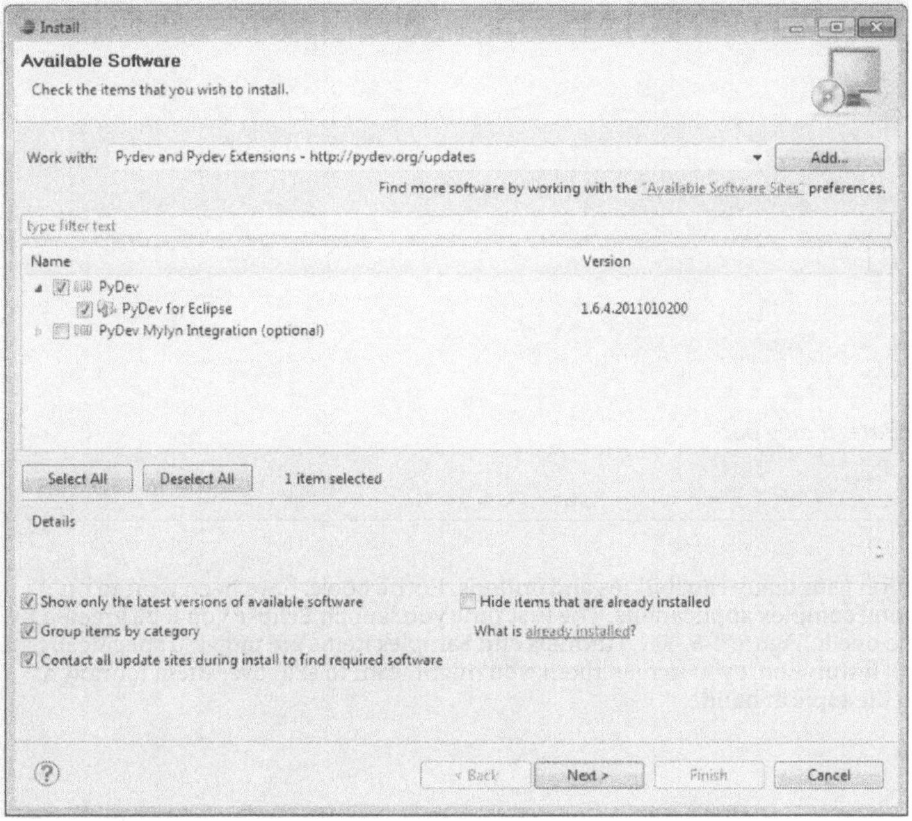

Figure 4-4. *Pydev installation dialog box*

The last Eclipse add-on you'll need for the exercises in this book is Aptana Studio. It shines when it comes to editing HTML, CSS, and JavaScript. Using the same procedure as with ADT and Pydev, enter the following line in the text box beside the label Work with:

`http://download.aptana.com/tools/studio/plugin/install/studio`

This will create a new entry in the list of available sites and display another dialog box in which you can select and download the add-in.

It's a good idea to periodically check for updates to Eclipse and the add-ons. You do this by selecting Check For Updates from the Help menu. You'll see a dialog box like the one in Figure 4-5 if any updates are found. This particular update was for Pydev on an Ubuntu system.

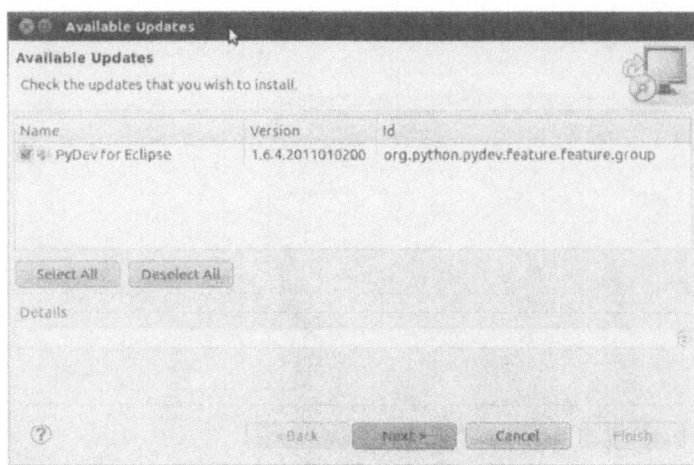

Figure 4-5. *Available Updates dialog box*

Eclipse Basics

Eclipse is a huge application with many capabilities and options. Entire books have been written on using Eclipse for developing complex applications. The first time you launch Eclipse you'll be greeted by a Welcome screen like the one in Figure 4-6. The Tutorials and Samples items are targeted specifically at Java developers. Although it won't hurt you to read them, you might want to skip over them for now as they don't really apply to the topic at hand.

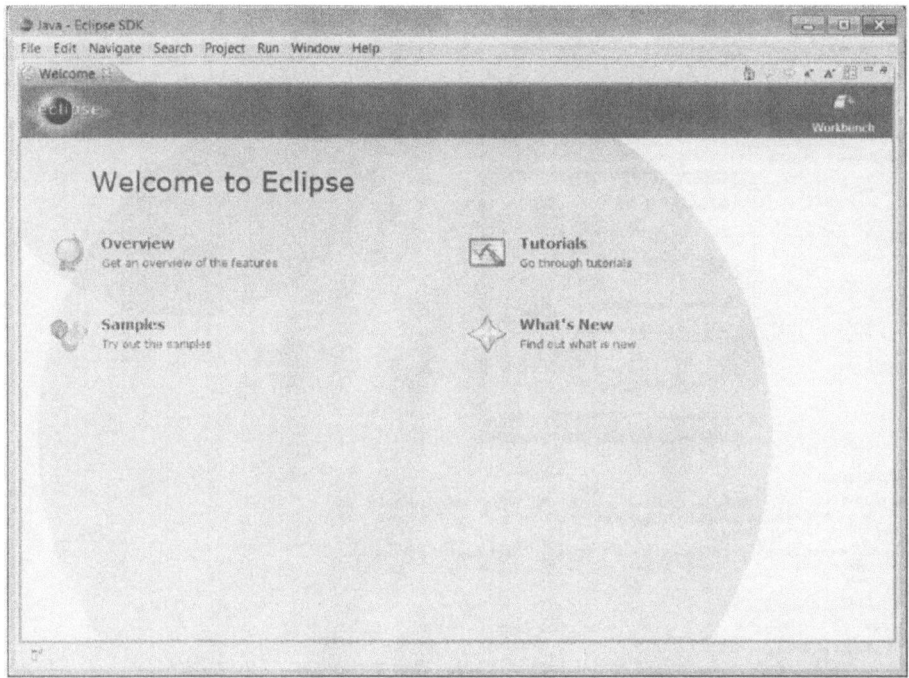

Figure 4-6. *Eclipse welcome screen*

If you click the Overview item, it will open another screen with four topics: Workbench Basics, Java Development, Team Support, and Eclipse Plug-In Development. The only item of any real importance to this book is the Workbench Basics topic. Clicking this item will launch the Eclipse Help system, as shown in Figure 4-7. If you expand the Getting Started section, you'll find a detailed tutorial covering all the basic operations you'll need to know to navigate through Eclipse. It will be well worth your time to explore the tutorial material if you haven't worked with Eclipse before.

Eclipse uses a number of basic concepts and terminology to address different functions and operations of the program. *Workbench* is the term used to identify the overall window of the Eclipse application. The Workbench window will typically contain multiple child windows with editors and views such as the Project Explorer. When you open additional windows, they will hold either an editor or a view. Eclipse also supports multiple tabs within windows, so you can have multiple files open in the same editor window. Use the Help menu to navigate back to the Welcome page at any time.

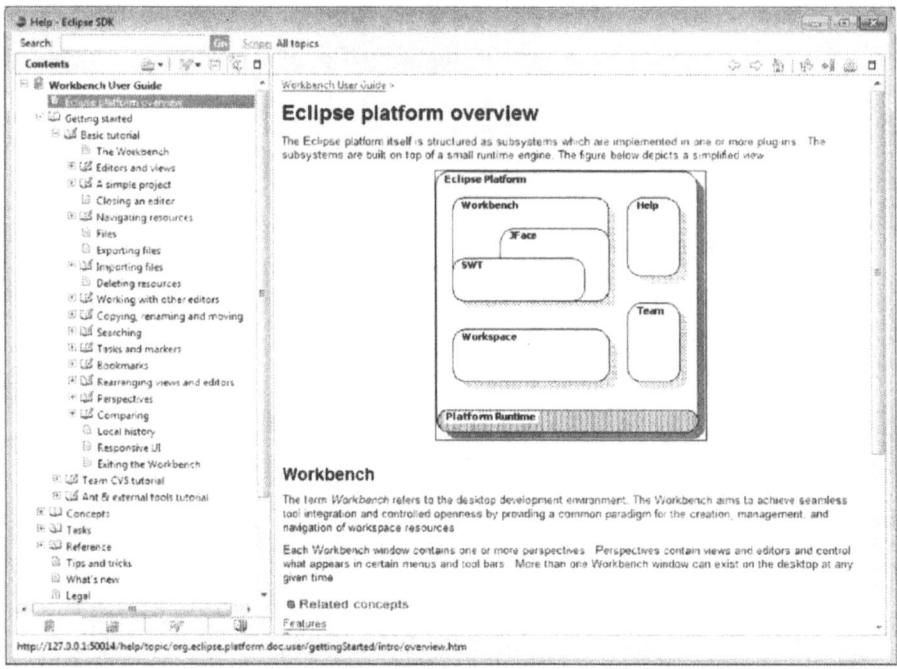

Figure 4-7. *Eclipse Help screen*

Perspectives

The concept of a *perspective* is better understood from the viewpoint of a person using the program. Each person brings his or her own perspective or preferences to any activity. A perspective is really nothing more than personal preferences for which menus and windows are open at any one time. The Eclipse definition of a perspective is "a visual container for a set of views and editors (parts)" (`http://www.eclipse.org/articles/using-perspectives/PerspectiveArticle.html`). Eclipse comes with a number of perspectives already configured for typical usage, such as writing code. You switch to a different perspective when your activity changes, such as when you switch from coding to debugging. Figure 4-8 shows a typical Pydev perspective.

■ **Note** Large-screen monitors at high resolution provide a lot of real estate from which to run Eclipse with multiple windows. You can also run Eclipse with multiple monitors and use the tear-away feature to move an individual window out of the Workspace container and over to a different monitor.

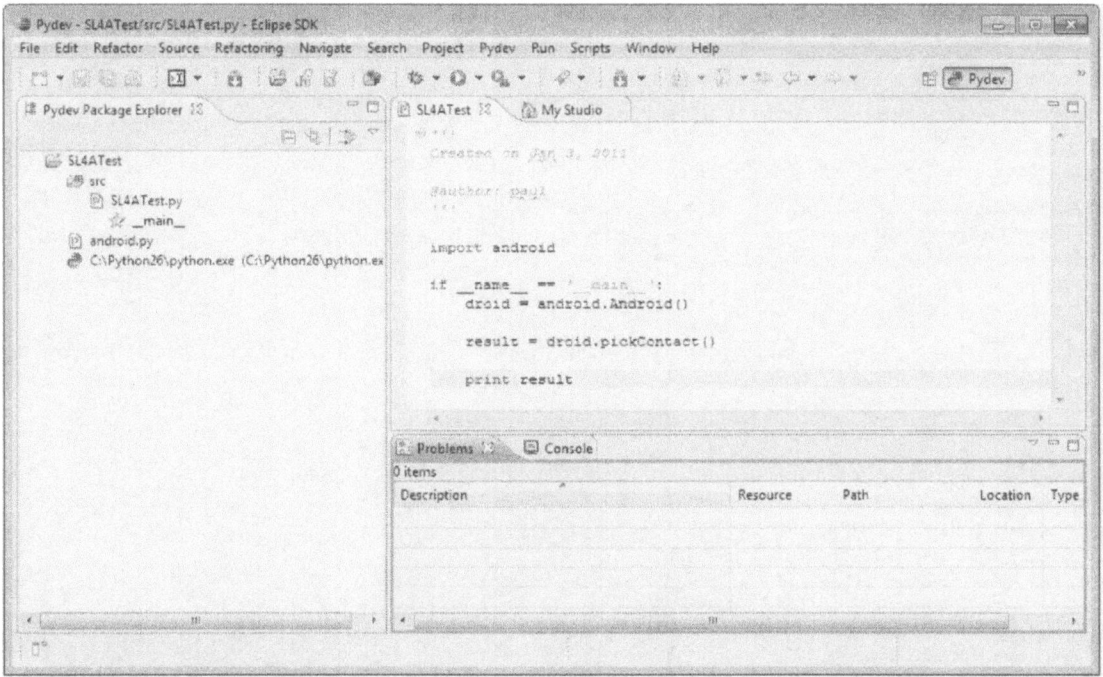

Figure 4-8. *Pydev perspective Workspace*

Perspectives are customizable to the fullest extent. If you don't like a particular toolbar, you can turn it off. Each perspective will load specific windows into default locations on the screen. You can move any of these windows around to arrange them to your liking. To customize the current perspective, right-click the name/icon at the top-right corner of the Workspace and select Customize. You'll be presented with the screen shown in Figure 4-9. Several of the options have been expanded to show the difference between selections.

This dialog box gives you full control over every aspect of the current perspective. If a check box beside an item in this screen has a check, it means every option beneath it is also selected. A blue box filling the check box indicates some of the options beneath this item are selected and some are not. If you expand every item, you will quickly see that Eclipse has a lot of options. The best approach to take at this point is to tweak the things you think will help you be more productive and leave the rest alone.

The additional tabs allow you to customize Tool Bar Visibility, Menu Visibility (or which items appear across the top of your main Workspace window), Command Groups Availability, and which Shortcuts will appear as submenu items. The Filter By Command Group check box will open or close another list of items on the left side of the dialog box, showing options as they appear in the different command groups.

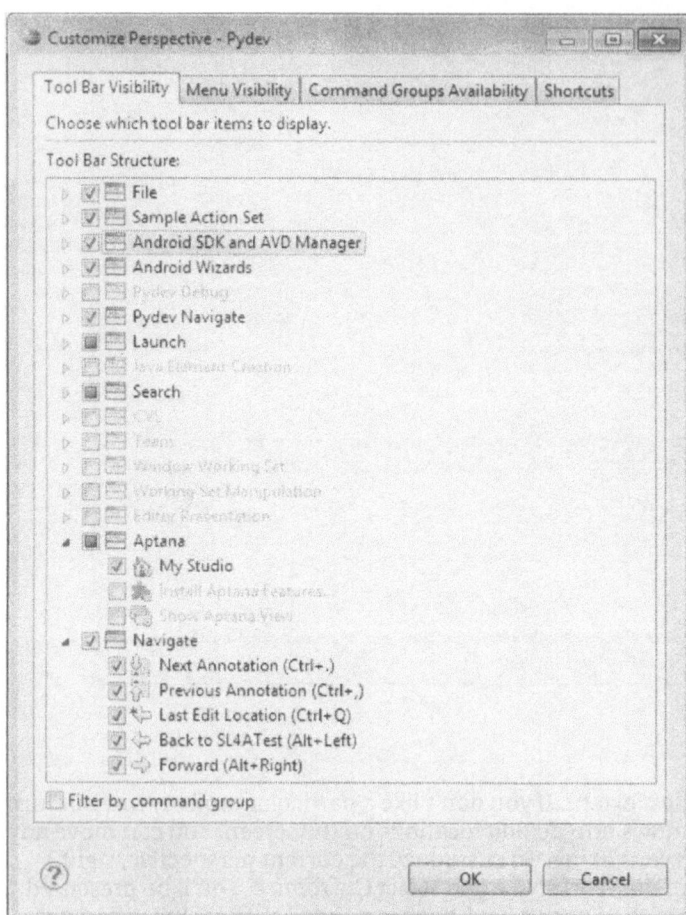

Figure 4-9. *Customize perspective screen*

You can quickly open a new perspective by clicking the small icon that looks like a window with a little plus sign in the top-right corner. It is found next to the current perspective indicator at the top of the screen. (See Figure 4-8.) This brings up the Open Perspective dialog box shown in Figure 4-10 with a list of every available perspective. Clicking any item opens that perspective along with all its windows and views.

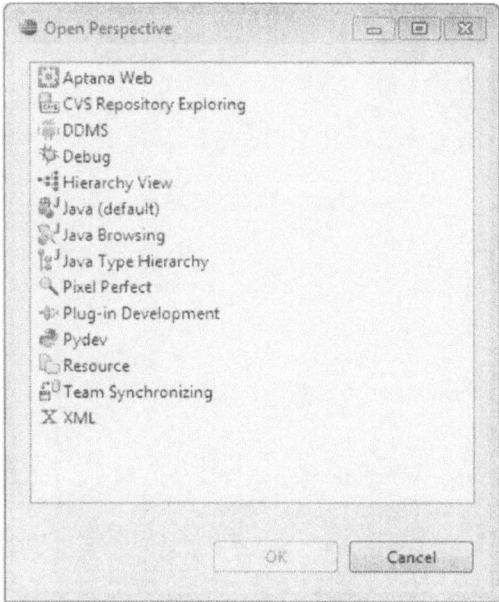

Figure 4-10. *Eclipse Open Perspective dialog box*

You can always change your mind and return to the currently opened perspective by clicking the Cancel button.

Projects

Projects are where all the moving parts of a particular application are collected. A project could be nothing more than a single source file or any number of different files and file types. Creating a new project happens using either File ➤ New Project or with the Alt+Shift+N key combination. On the Mac you would use Command+Shift+N. Either method will launch the New Project Wizard (see Figure 4-11).

Selecting General Project will launch one additional dialog box prompting you to name your project and will then create an empty folder underneath your default workspace directory with that name. We'll cover creating a Pydev project a little later.

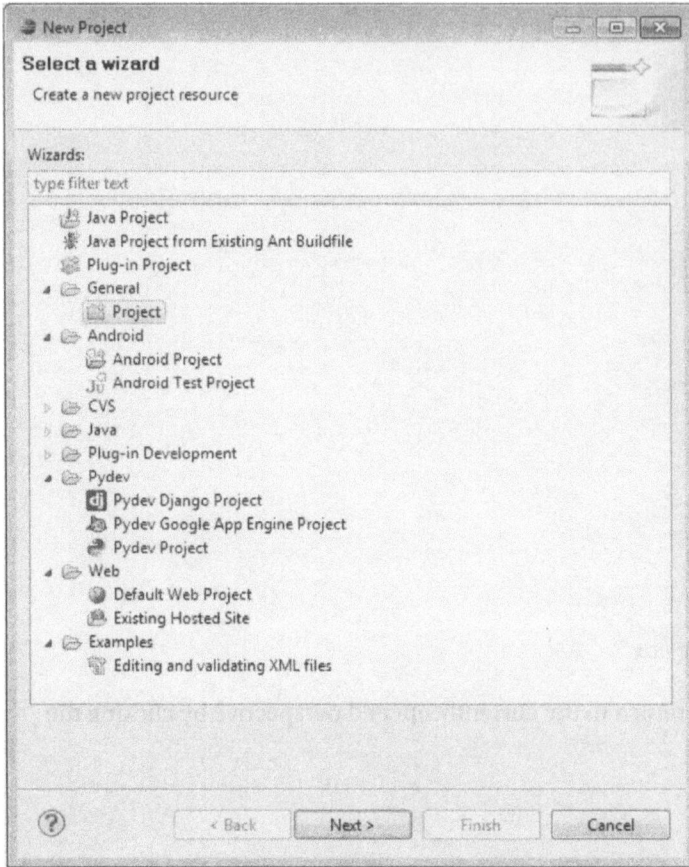

Figure 4-11. *Eclipse New Project wizard*

Android Development Toolkit

Google has made every attempt to simplify the process of developing applications for the Android platform including providing the Android Development Toolkit (ADT) extension for Eclipse. One of the options when creating a new project is Android Project. This is a good way to explore what developing a native application using Java for the Android platform is like. Figure 4-12 shows the New Android Project Wizard creating a new project named MyTestApp based on the sample NotePad app. The ADT ships with a number of sample applications in an effort to demonstrate how to take advantage of the different features of the Android platform.

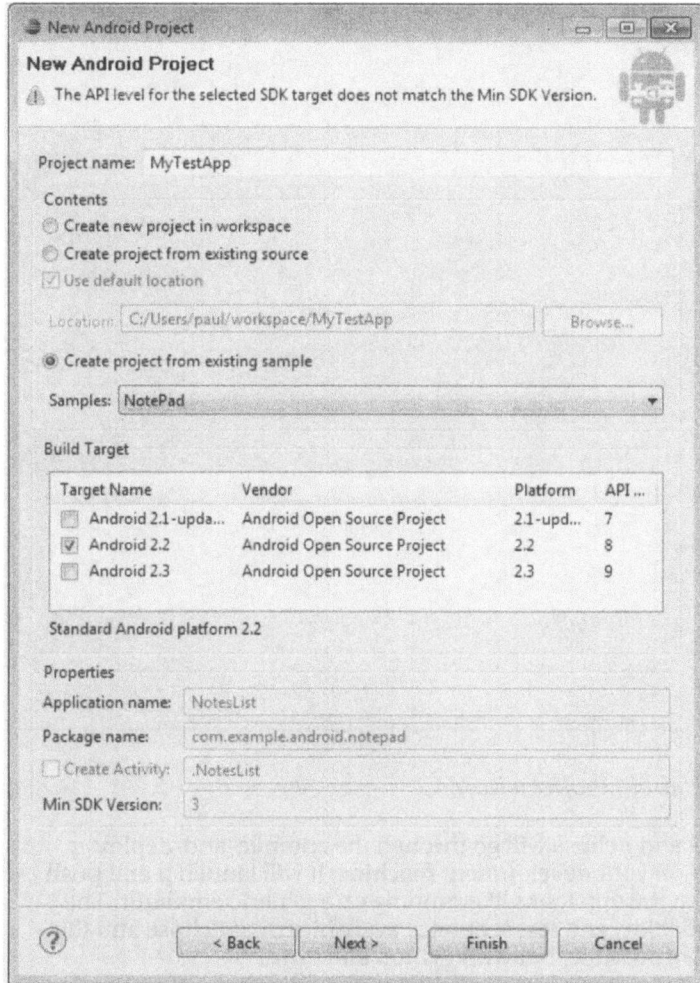

Figure 4-12. *New Android Project wizard*

When you click the Finish button, the wizard creates the new project and copies all the sample source code into the working directory. Figure 4-13 shows shows what this project will look like in the editor.

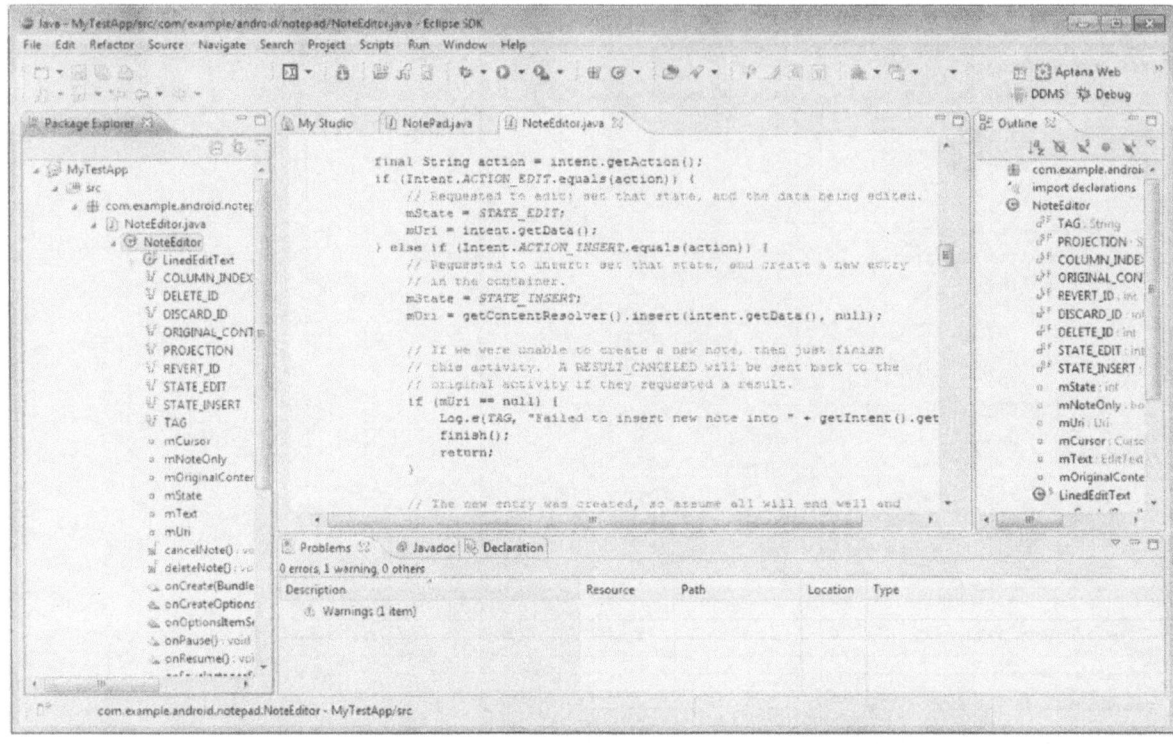

Figure 4-13. *MyTestApp created with New Android Project wizard*

At this point you can click the Run icon, and Eclipse will go through the compile-and-deploy process. If you have configured an emulator on your development machine, it will launch it and push the app to the device. Figure 4-14 shows what the app looks like running on a generic emulator. The beauty of this process is the rapid compile, deploy, and test sequence available using Eclipse and the ADT. The goal is to make the same experience possible, but with Python and SL4A.

■ **Tip**   You have multiple ways to accomplish the same task within Eclipse. If you prefer mouse clicks, you'll find icons for just about any action you need to perform. If you're more of a keyboard person, you'll find those as well. You can explore the different options using the Customize Perspective dialog box mentioned earlier in this chapter.

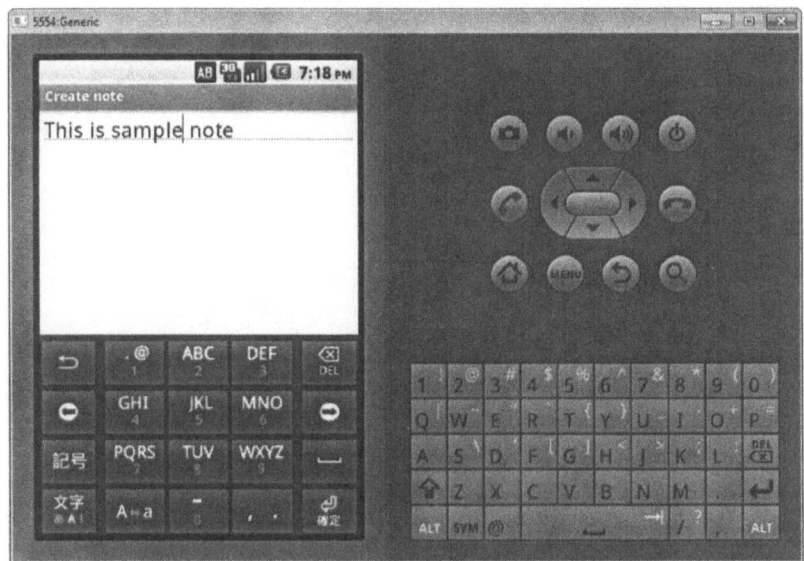

Figure 4-14. *MyTestApp running on a generic emulator*

One of the perspectives available is labeled DDMS. Figure 4-15 shows this perspective with MyTestApp running in the emulator. This perspective gives you access to the complete functionality of the DDMS utility discussed in Chapter 3. Windows opened by this perspective include Devices; Emulator Control; Logcat; and a tabbed window with quick access to Threads, Heap, Allocation Tracker, and File Explorer.

To see the information related to MyTestApp you have to scroll down to the bottom of the Devices window and locate the application. In this case, it's named `com.example.android.notepad`. When you select this line, you'll be able to see everything you ever wanted to know about an Android application—and then some.

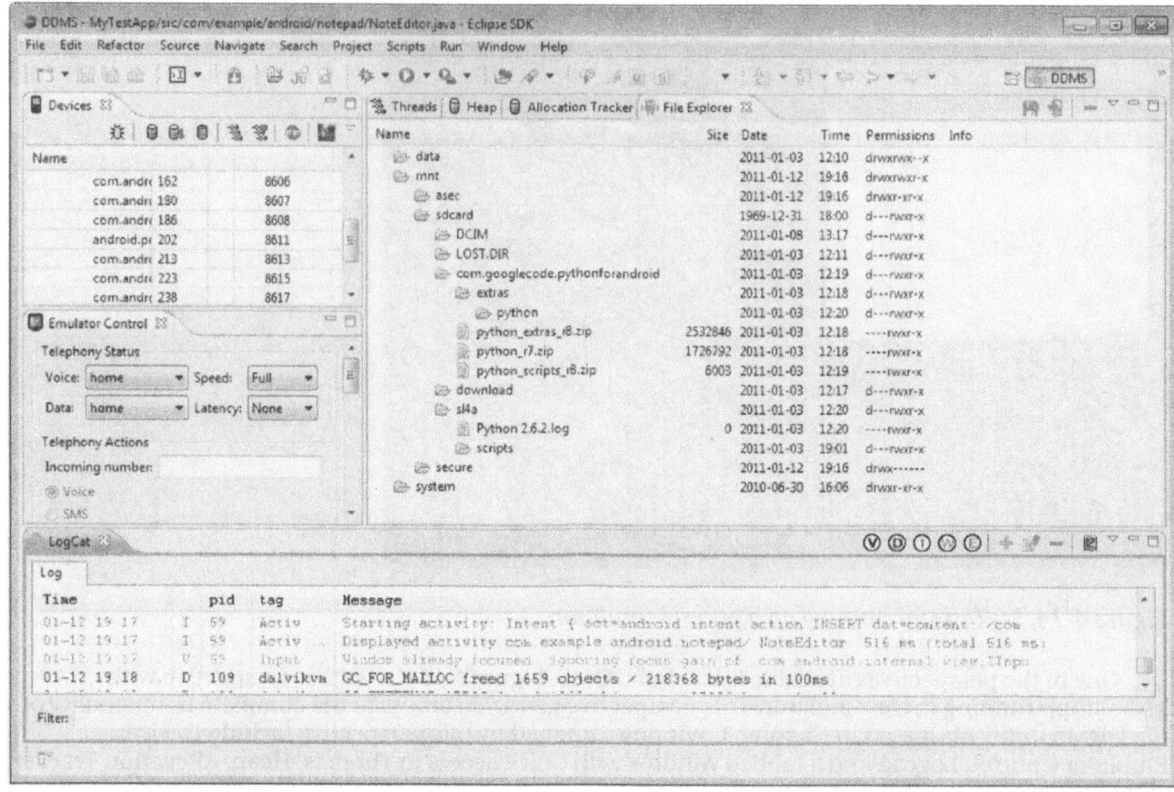

Figure 4-15. *DDMS Perspective with MyTestApp running*

One of the features mentioned earlier when discussing multiple monitors is the ability to "tear off" any window and drag it out of the main Eclipse window. Figure 4-16 shows the Emulator Control Window after it has been moved out on its own. To do this, left-click and hold under the window title; then drag the mouse away from the main Eclipse window. This won't work if the main window is maximized. To close the window, simply click the X at the top-right corner of the window. To re-open the window within Eclipse, open the Window menu; then from Show View, select the window you want to open. If you previously separated it from Eclipse, it will restore undocked from the main window. You can drag it back into the main window using the same technique as when you un-docked it. If you just want to get back to the default settings for any perspective, there's a Reset Perspective option on the Window menu to get you back to the initial starting place.

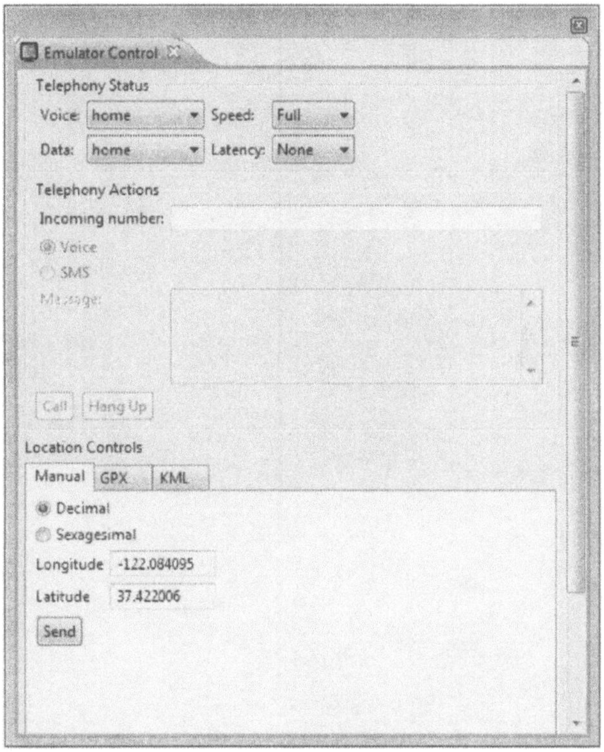

Figure 4-16. Emulator Control window separated from main Eclipse window

Using Pydev

Pydev is an Eclipse plugin created to make life easier for the Python developer. It has many features specifically targeted at the Python language along with shortcuts, templates, and its own default perspective. Probably the most important part of Pydev is that it was created by Python developers for Python developers. If you develop Python code on any platform, this is one of those tools you don't want to leave home without.

One of the things you must do before Pydev will work is configure the location of your Python installation. Figure 4-17 shows the Pydev menu item expanded from the Preferences window. You'll find the Preferences option under the Window menu on the list at the top of the Workspace window. Selecting the Interpreter - Python menu item initially displays a blank window. This needs to be configured to point to your Python 2.6 interpreter installation directory. On Windows, this is typically in the path `C:\Python26`. On Ubuntu 10.10, and most other Debian-based distributions, you'll find the Python executable in `/usr/bin/python`.

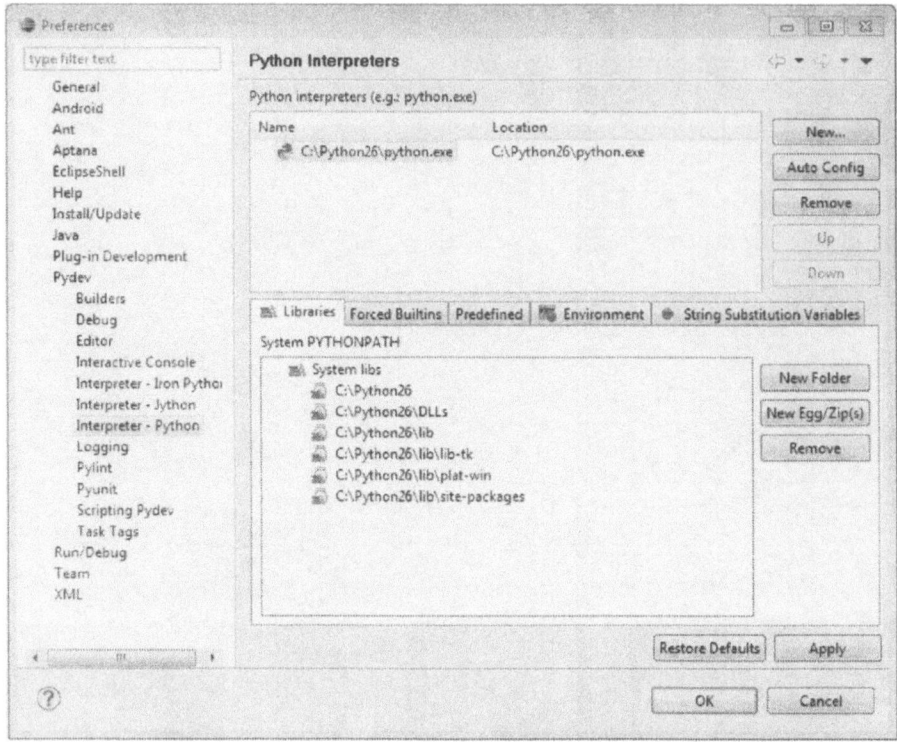

Figure 4-17. *Preferences dialog box for configuring Python interpreter*

With Pydev installed, you are given two options at this point: new Pydev project and new Project. Figure 4-18 shows what the new Pydev project screen looks like. There are a number of items that must be set in this dialog box. At the top of the dialog box you must enter a name for your new project, which will be used as the name of the subdirectory beneath your default workspace area as well as the title that will be displayed in the Project Explorer window. Next, you must change the Grammar Version using the drop-down box and select 2.6. Finally, you should set the Interpreter to point to the Python26 directory just in case you happen to have multiple versions of Python installed.

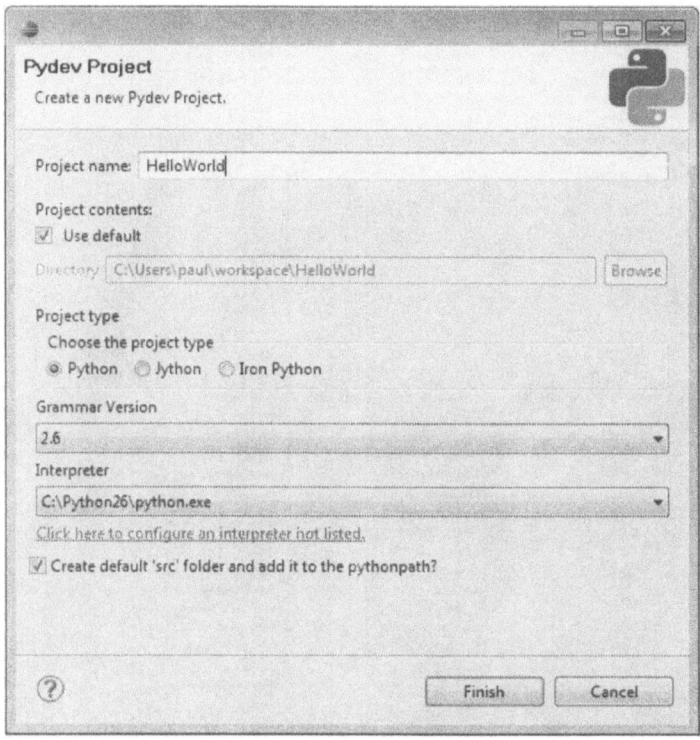

Figure 4-18. *New Pydev Project dialog box*

Once the new project is created you're ready to start entering code. Pydev uses templates to help you quickly build code with predefined sources. You can use any of the provided templates or create your own. This is where you would put some standard header comments including copyright information, your name, and anything else that might be pertinent.

If you want to get a look at all the default keyboard shortcuts, you can press Ctrl+Shift+L. This will bring up a scrollable window of all currently defined shortcuts as shown in Figure 4-19. As with just about everything else in Eclipse, you can define your own shortcut keys from the Preferences dialog box. If you have the shortcut list onscreen, you can jump straight to that page by pressing Ctrl+Shift+L again.

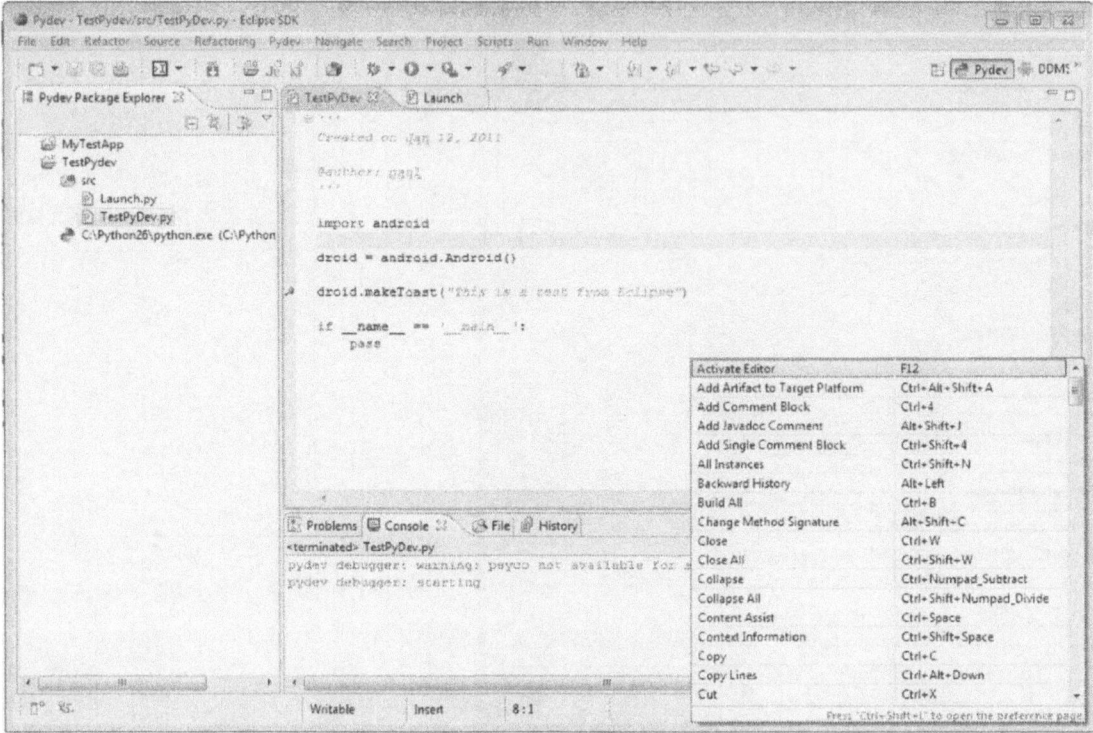

Figure 4-19. *Example of shortcut display window*

Pydev comes with a number of predefined templates available to use when you create a new source file or for quick insertion into your code window. You'll have the chance to use a template file when you use the File ➤ New ➤ Pydev Module procedure to create a new source file. This will open a dialog box like the one shown in Figure 4-20. If you have an editor window open, you can access the templates using the Ctrl+space key combination. This opens a window with a list of potential code snippets for you to insert. Pressing Return with any of the items highlighted will insert the code at that point.

If you press Ctrl+space a second time, you'll see a list of available templates applicable at this point. This will switch the current list to show available templates and, in a second window, a view of the statements that will be inserted if you hit Return. New templates can be created from the config link shown on the Create A New Python Module dialog box. Clicking this link will open up the Preferences dialog box with the Templates option selected.

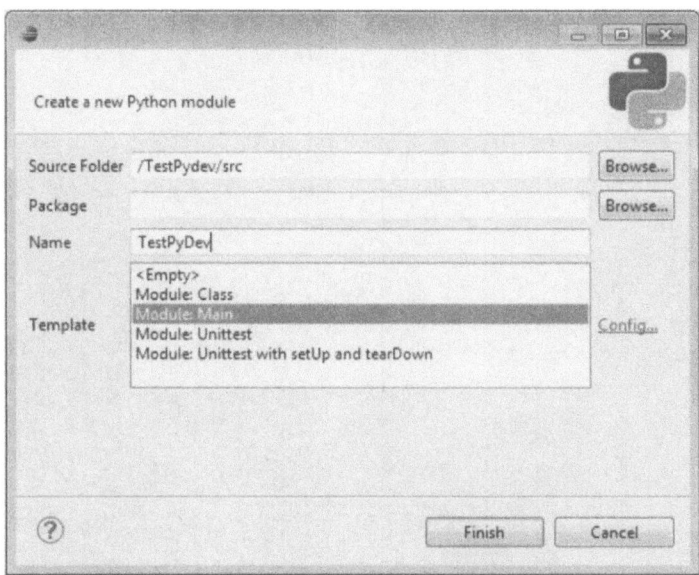

Figure 4-20. *New Pydev module dialog box*

To define a new template, click the New button and complete the dialog box shown in Figure 4-21. This will allow you to save keystrokes when creating the same basic code at the beginning of every Python module. The Insert Variable button lets you insert text based on some variable such as file path, file or module name, date, time, or the currently selected word.

The text in the Pattern window will be inserted when the template is chosen. In this case, you'll see code that will be found at the beginning of virtually every SL4A application. The Android module includes the code to communicate between SL4A applications and the underlying native APIs using a remote procedure call (RPC) mechanism. In this case, the RPC calls are used with a pseudo-proxy to pass information to and from the underlying Android OS. This provides an extra layer of security to keep a rogue application from doing something nefarious on your device.

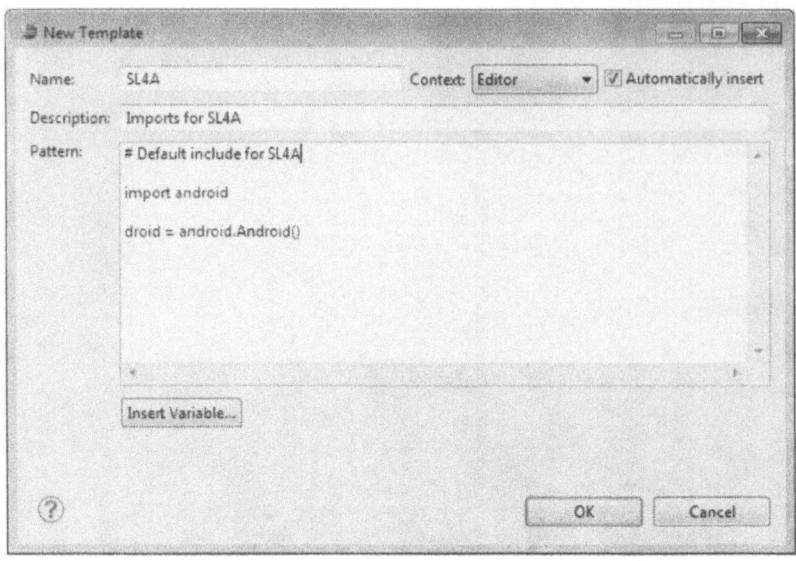

Figure 4-21. *Pydev New Template dialog box*

You must use the ADB tool in order to deploy an SL4A application to either the emulator or a real device. This can be done from the command line, or you could automate the process with a little code:

```python
#!/usr/bin/env python

import subprocess

ADB = r'C:\Program Files (x86)\Android\android-sdk-windows\platform-tools\adb.exe'
APPLICATION = 'hello_world.py'
TARGET = '/sdcard/sl4a/scripts/'

def main():
    # Upload the application.
    subprocess.call([ADB, '-e', 'push', APPLICATION, TARGET + APPLICATION])

    # Launch the application.
    subprocess.call('"%s" -e shell am start \
                -a com.googlecode.android_scripting.action.LAUNCH_BACKGROUND_SCRIPT \
                -n \
                com.googlecode.android_scripting/.activity.ScriptingLayerServiceLauncher \
                -e com.googlecode.android_scripting.extra.SCRIPT_PATH \
                "%s%s"' % (ADB, TARGET, APPLICATION))

if __name__ == '__main__':
    main()
```

If you create a file with this code, include it in your Pydev project, and run it when you get ready to test, it will do the work for you. A good descriptive name such as Launch_app.py will help you identify it when it comes time to use it. Save it to a directory in your workspace area so you'll be able to copy it into each project. The only thing you should have to change is the following line:

```
APPLICATION = 'hello_world.py'
```

This will obviously change for each application and should match the name of the file as stored on disk. Pydev provides a complete debugging facility allowing you to set breakpoints, examine variables, and step through lines of code as shown in Figure 4-22. You can set breakpoints while viewing your code in an editor window using the mouse to right-click Add Breakpoint. Once a breakpoint has been set, you can modify its properties and add conditions. This is invaluable when you have a long loop and you want to break after some number of iterations. Now when you run the application you will be prompted once the breakpoint has been hit and the condition satisfied.

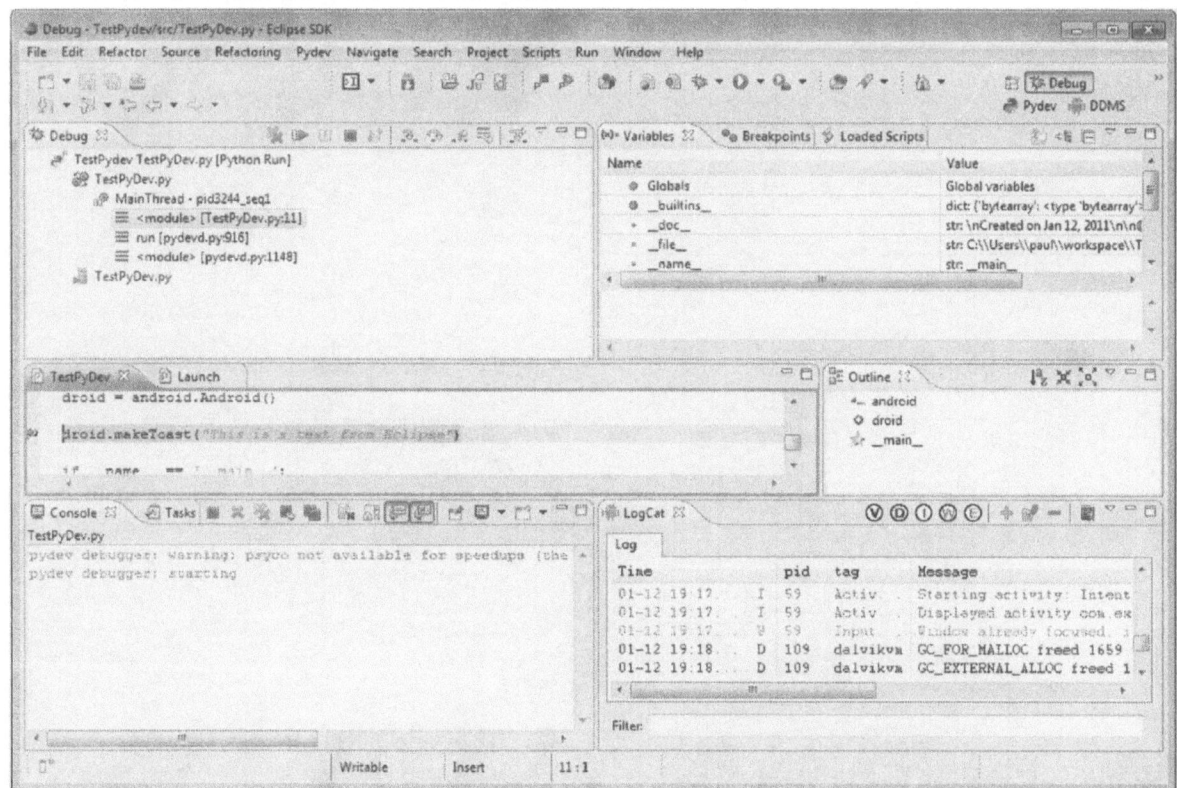

Figure 4-22. Pydev application debugging

Another way to execute code from within Eclipse on either a real or emulated device is to use the ADB utility to establish a proxy to the device. This was covered in Chapter 3, but I'll go through the steps again here to show you how to do it from Eclipse. To make this work with a real device, you will need to connect it using a USB cable and with the appropriate settings configured on the device such as USB

Debugging enabled and something other than Charge Only enabled. Next, you must launch SL4A and start a server from the Interpreters menu. Finally, you must take note of the TCP port assigned to the server from the Notifications page on the device. Last, but not least, you must type the following in a command window with administrator privileges:

```
adb forward tcp:9999 tcp:50681
```

This instructs ADB to forward all TCP traffic from local port 9999 to remote port 50681. With all that accomplished, you should now be able to run your Python code from Eclipse, and all calls to an Android API will be sent via proxy to the device. The nice thing about running from within Eclipse is that you'll be able to see all the debug information in DDMS and all the console output, including any error messages returned from the device.

One of the tools I find invaluable is the file comparison or diff tool. To use it, first select the two files in the navigator pane on the left side of the Workspace window by a single left-click on the first file and then a Shift left-click on the second file. Next, use a right-click mouse action and choose Compare With ➤ Each Other. This will produce a two-pane window with any differences highlighted, as shown in Figure 4-23.

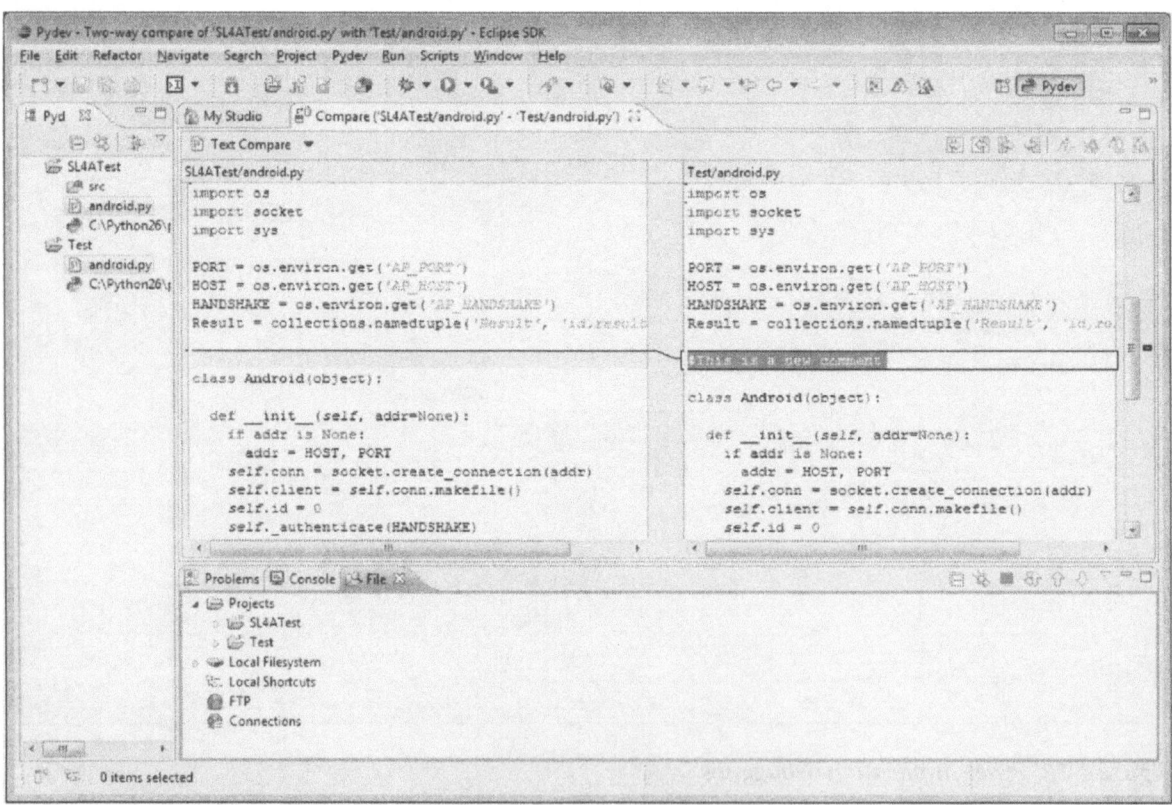

Figure 4-23. *File comparison tool*

Using Multiple File Types in Eclipse

One of the things that Eclipse is really good at is managing complex applications with multiple file types. Chapter 9 will examine the SMS Sender program in great detail, but for now it will serve as an example of how to create a project with a number of different files. This can be done from scratch or from existing files. In this case we'll use existing files and add them to a new Pydev project.

The first thing you have to do is create a new Pydev project. This will create a new folder under your workspace and a single **src** directory. To add files to the project you can either use the Import tool from the File menu or just drag and drop files from a file manager such as Windows Explorer on Windows or Nautilus on Linux into your project. Figure 4-24 shows the dialog box you will see if you choose the Import method.

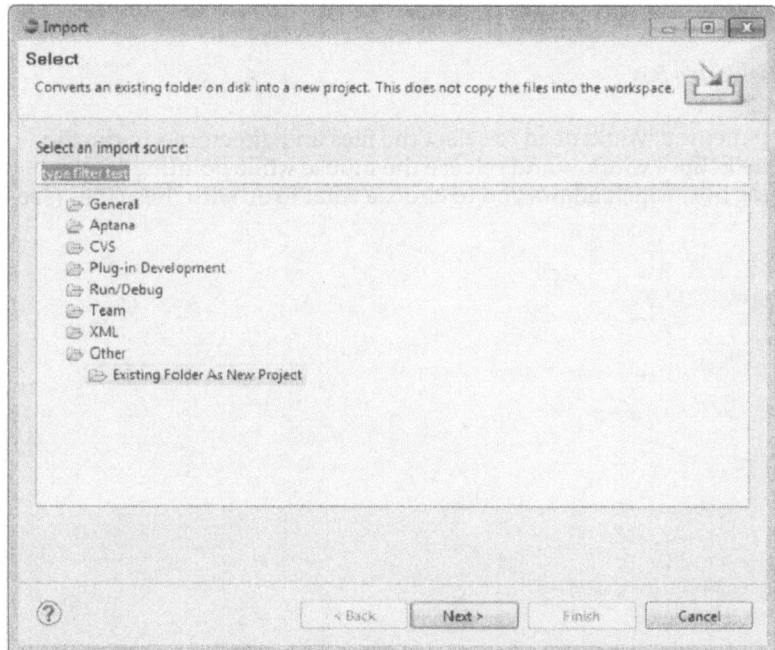

Figure 4-24. *Import files tool*

When you click the next button you'll be presented with another dialog box allowing you to browse for the directory you wish to import (see Figure 4-25). This should be the top or root directory with all files you wish to import in that directory or subdirectories.

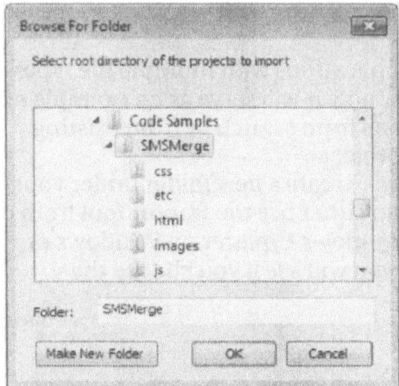

Figure 4-25. *Import directory chooser dialog box*

If you choose the drag-and-drop method, you'll need to select the files and directories in the file manager and then drag them onto the Eclipse window and release the mouse while pointing to the project. This will bring up a new dialog box, which allows you to choose what to do with these files (see Figure 4-26).

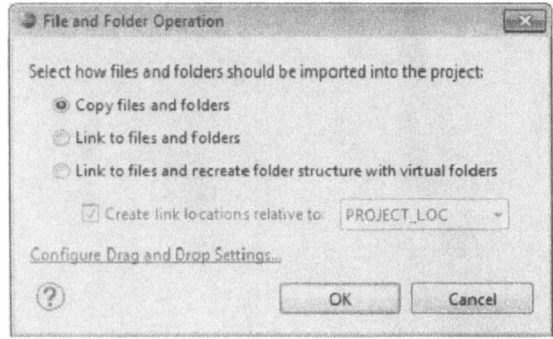

Figure 4-26. *File and Folder Operation dialog box*

Once the import is complete you will have a new Pydev project. Figure 4-27 shows the SMSSender project with files that were included using the drag-and-drop method. The left pane shows a directory tree containing all files associated with this project. You can and should include all files, even those you wouldn't edit with Eclipse such as images, in your project to simplify the deployment process later. Building a package for distribution requires that all files be included in your project so you might as well learn how to do that now. This also includes any library files, such as the JavaScript library, that your project depends on.

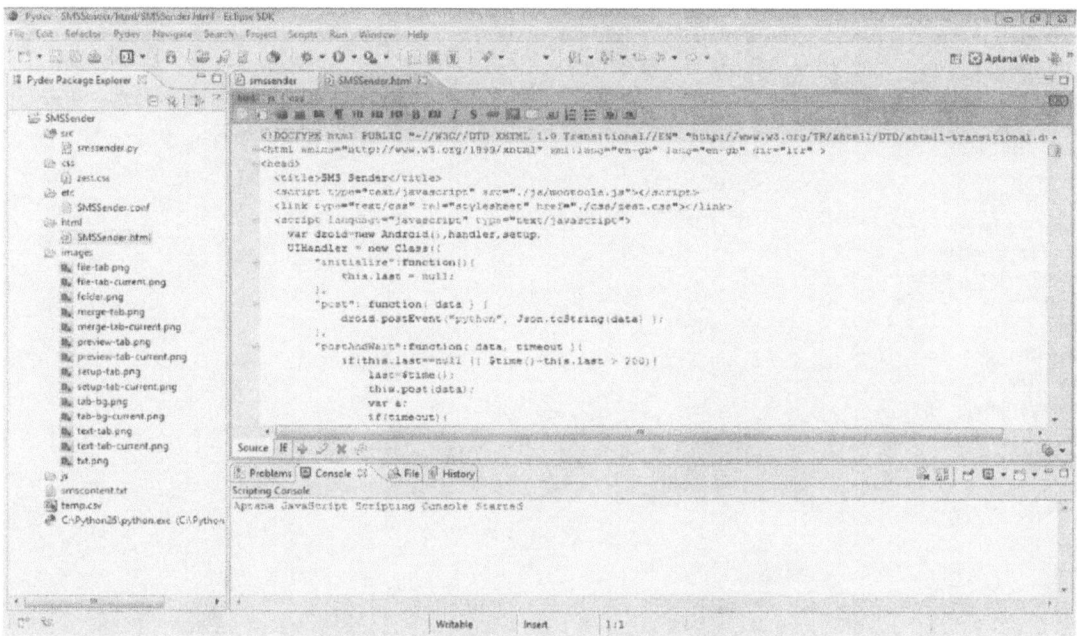

Figure 4-27. *Multifile example created using drag-and-drop method*

If you double-click one of the non-text files in the project Eclipse will attempt to open the file with the default viewer application. If you right-click a file, you will be shown options including Open With. Figure 4-28 shows the open option menu.

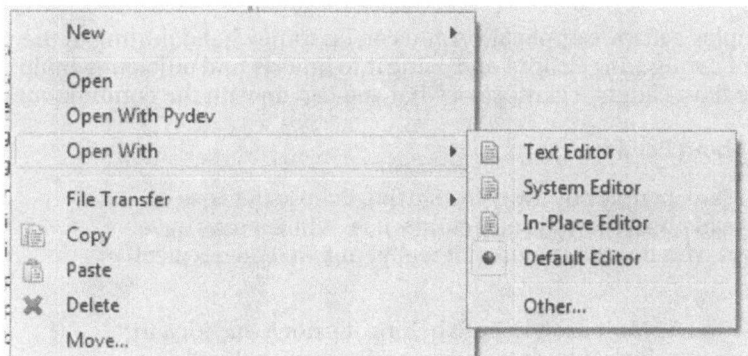

Figure 4-28. *Open file option menu*

The Other option will open another dialog box (see Figure 4-29) with a long list of default editors. If you select the External programs radio button, you'll get a list of every registered mime type on your system.

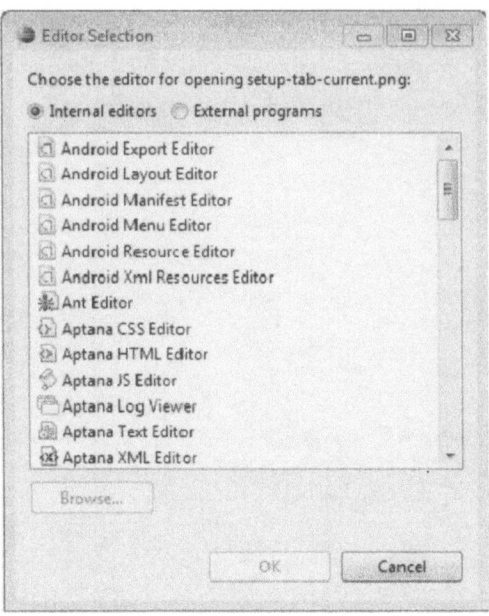

Figure 4-29. *Editor Selection menu*

Eclipse does a great job of providing the right editor for the file type, as you can see from the HTML tags in Figure 4-27.

Summary

Eclipse is a powerful IDE. It's also a complex software application and can be somewhat daunting to the newbie. This chapter hit the highlights of configuring Eclipse and using it to quickly and efficiently build and test your application. Hopefully you have caught a glimpse of what you can do with the combination of Eclipse, Pydev and the ADT.

Here's a list of things to remember about Eclipse:

- **Don't be afraid of Eclipse**: Many people shy away from using Eclipse because of something they've heard or read about how big and clunky it is. While it may have been slow on older computers with limited memory, it really runs well on a typical modern workstation.

- **Read the documentation**: If you haven't used Eclipse before, it's not a bad idea to take a look through the documentation. At least look around for a recent Eclipse tutorial to help get you going quickly.

- **Find your plugins**: There are many plugins besides the ones mentioned in this chapter. Browse the `eclipse.org` site and do a few Google searches if there's something else you think you need. Aptana Studio isn't the only HTML editor so feel free to check out some of the other options.

- **Learn the quick keys**: Learning a few keyboard shortcuts can save you a lot of time and help keep your hands on the keyboard. Every time you have to move your hand to the mouse not only takes time but also potentially increases your fatigue factor.

CHAPTER 5

Exploring the Android API

This chapter will examine the Android application programming interface (API) in depth and show how to use Python to call the different functions.

▓ **Note**   Python cannot access every Android API with the r3 release of SL4A. Other languages such as BeanShell do have this capability and will be used to look at some of the missing functions.

This chapter will rely heavily on a basic understanding of the concepts introduced in Chapter 1. The topics include Android activities and intents, JSON, Python types, and RPC. I'll walk you through each API facade and include examples of how to use them where appropriate. They're all fairly self-explanatory with descriptive names such as `cameraCapturePicture` and `recognizeSpeech`.

All communication in both directions to and from the Android API uses JSON as the underlying structure for passing data. You might want to go back to Chapter 1 and read the section on JSON at this point if you skipped over that portion. JSON is not complicated, but it can be somewhat confusing if you don't know what you're looking at. Python handles JSON quite nicely and even has a built-in procedure, `pprint`, to pretty print a JSON structure. Figure 5-1 shows what the return from the API call `getLaunchableApplications` looks like without using the pretty print routine.

Figure 5-1. Example of JSON return from getLaunchableApplications API call

Figure 5-2 shows the same results, but in a much more readable form using the `pprint` module.

Figure 5-2. *Example of getLaunchableApplications JSON formatted using pprint*

The other concept I'll assume you understand at this point is an Android activity. SL4A provides an interface to launch and forget (or launch and wait) for an Android activity to complete.

Exploring the Android APIs

From Python, all SL4A API calls return an object with three fields:

- **id**: A strictly increasing, numeric ID associated with the API call

- **result**: The return value of the API call, or **null** if there is no return value

- **error**: A description of any error that occurred, or **null** if no error occurred

The android.py file defines an Android class with three methods. Examining the _rpc method gives some insight into how API requests are passed to the underlying operating system using an RPC call and JSON:

```python
def _rpc(self, method, *args):
    data = {'id': self.id,
            'method': method,
            'params': args}
    request = json.dumps(data)
    self.client.write(request+'\n')
    self.client.flush()
    response = self.client.readline()
    self.id += 1
    result = json.loads(response)
    if result['error'] is not None:
        print result['error']
    # namedtuple doesn't work with unicode keys.
    return Result(id=result['id'], result=result['result'],
                  error=result['error'], )
```

The same basic concept applies to other languages as well. In BeanShell the code looks like the following:

```java
call(String method, JSONArray params) {
    JSONObject request = new JSONObject();
    request.put("id", id);
    request.put("method", method);
    request.put("params", params);
    out.write(request.toString() + "\n");
    out.flush();
    String data = in.readLine();
    if (data == null) {
        return null;
    }
    return new JSONObject(data);
}
```

Android Facades

Chapter 1 discussed the basics of the RPC mechanism used by SL4A to pass information to the underlying Android API. Every supported API function has a corresponding interface in each SL4A language, called a *facade*, with the appropriate parameters required by the API. Some of these parameters will be mandatory, and some will be optional. Table 5-1 shows the top-level facades and what functionality they provide access to. Appendix A contains a complete listing of all the SL4A API calls.

Table 5-1. *Android API Facades*

ActivityResultFacade	Sets return values for an activity
AndroidFacade	Common Android functions
ApplicationManagerFacade	Gets information about installed applications
BatteryManagerFacade	Exposes Batterymanager API
BluetoothFacade	Allows access to Bluetooth functions
CameraFacade	All camera-related operations
CommonIntentsFacade	Generic Android intents
ContactsFacade	Provides access to contacts-related functionality
EventFacade	Exposes functionality to read from the event queue as an RPC and functionality to write to the event queue as a pure Java function
EyesFreeFacade	Provides text-to-speech (TTS) services for API 3 or lower
LocationFacade	Exposes the LocationManager-related functionality
MediaPlayerFacade	Exposes basic mediaPlayer functionality
MediaRecorderFacade	Records media
PhoneFacade	Exposes TelephonyManager functionality
PreferencesFacade	Allows access to the Preferences interface
SensorManagerFacade	Exposes the SensorManager-related functionality
SettingsFacade	Exposes phone settings functionality
SignalStrengthFacade	Exposes SignalStrength functionality
SmsFacade	Provides access to SMS-related functionality
SpeechRecognitionFacade	Contains RPC implementations related to the speech-to-text functionality of Android
TextToSpeechFacade	Provides TTS services for API 4 or higher

Continued

ToneGeneratorFacade	Generates DTMF tones
UiFacade	Creates and handles information from dialog boxes
WakeLockFacade	Exposes some of the functionality of the PowerManager (wake locks, in particular)
WebCamFacade	Captures video from the front-facing camera
WifiFacade	Manages all aspects of the WiFi radio

ActivityResultFacade

This facade provides a mechanism to explicitly set how your script will return information as an activity. It's used whenever a script APK is launched using the Android API call startActivityForResult(). Using this method implies that your script will return a result of some kind, and it is important to set the type of the result (resultValue) and either RESULT_CANCELED (0) or RESULT_OK (-1).

AndroidFacade

This facade is somewhat of a catchall and presents a number of functions available from the Android operating system (OS). There are functions to check version numbers of the currently executing package (getPackageVersion and getPackageVersionCode) and the version of SL4A (requiredVersion). The second one provides a nice mechanism to check for a minimum version of SL4A in the event that your code requires some version-specific feature.

There are a few deprecated calls in this façade, including getInput and getPassword. Both have been replaced with newer Android API calls, but are kept around to support older scripts. Figure 5-3 shows what you'll see if you use a deprecated API call.

Figure 5-3. *Notification message for deprecated API call*

SL4A will add a message to your notification window whenever you use a deprecated function. You'll find the functions here to start an Android activity and wait for a result or simply launch and return. Like both Windows and Linux, Android supports the concept of a Clipboard for copying and pasting information between applications. You can do this from a script using the functiongetClipboard and setClipboard functionsfunction.

The log and notify functions provide a way to either display (notify) or save (log) information for viewing with the logcat application. There's also the frequently used makeToast function that simply flashes a message on the screen of the device for a short time period and then removes it. If you want to get the user's attention by vibrating the device, you can use the **vibrate** function. The **sendEmail** function will launch an activity to send an e-mail (the activity will depend on what applications you have loaded on your device that are able to send e-mail) and populate the **recipient**, **subject**, **body**, and **attachment** fields. You will have to use that application to actually send the message. In a later chapter, I'll show you another method for sending an e-mail message that does not require an external activity.

In the introduction I gave an explanation of the Android architecture and how an activity fits into the execution of different applications. Early versions of SL4A included the ability to just start an activity (**startActivity**) and also start an activity and wait for the result (**startActivityForResult**). SL4A r4 introduced two additional functions allowing you to start an activity using an intent (**startActivityIntent**) and start an activity for a result intent (**startActivityForResultIntent**). Another new function call in SLA r4 is **makeIntent**. This function is needed to create an intent to be used by either of the **startActivity** calls requiring an intent. The return of this function is an object representing an intent.

SL4A r4 also introduced the **getConstants** function in the Android facade to help you determine what constants are available from a specific Android class. This function can come in really handy when you want to query a content provider, but don't have a clue what's available. Here's a single line of code demonstrating the use of this call to show the constants available from the contacts provider:

```
res=droid.getConstants("android.provider.ContactsContract$CommonDataKinds$Phone").result
```

Android 2.2 will return a total of 99 constants available from the contacts provider. Here's a short list showing some of those constants:

```
{u'AGGREGATION_MODE': u'aggregation_mode',
 u'AVAILABLE': 5,
 u'AWAY': 2,
 u'CONTACT_ID': u'contact_id',
 u'CONTACT_PRESENCE': u'contact_presence',
 u'CONTACT_STATUS': u'contact_status',
 u'CONTACT_STATUS_ICON': u'contact_status_icon',
 u'CONTACT_STATUS_LABEL': u'contact_status_label',
 u'CONTACT_STATUS_RES_PACKAGE': u'contact_status_res_package',
 u'CONTACT_STATUS_TIMESTAMP': u'contact_status_ts',
 u'CONTENT_FILTER_URI': u'content://com.android.contacts/data/phones/filter',
 u'CONTENT_ITEM_TYPE': u'vnd.android.cursor.item/phone_v2',
 u'CONTENT_TYPE': u'vnd.android.cursor.dir/phone_v2',
 u'CONTENT_URI': u'content://com.android.contacts/data/phones',
 u'CUSTOM_RINGTONE': u'custom_ringtone',
 u'DATA': u'data1',
 u'DATA1': u'data1',
 u'DATA2': u'data2',
 u'DATA_VERSION': u'data_version',
 u'DELETED': u'deleted',
 u'DISPLAY_NAME': u'display_name',
 u'DISPLAY_NAME_ALTERNATIVE': u'display_name_alt',
 u'DISPLAY_NAME_PRIMARY': u'display_name',
 u'DISPLAY_NAME_SOURCE': u'display_name_source',
 u'DO_NOT_DISTURB': 4,
 u'HAS_PHONE_NUMBER': u'has_phone_number',
 u'IDLE': 3,
 u'INVISIBLE': 1,
 u'IN_VISIBLE_GROUP': u'in_visible_group',
```

```
u'IS_PRIMARY': u'is_primary',
u'LAST_TIME_CONTACTED': u'last_time_contacted',
u'LOOKUP_KEY': u'lookup',
u'MIMETYPE': u'mimetype',
u'NAME_RAW_CONTACT_ID': u'name_raw_contact_id',
u'NAME_VERIFIED': u'name_verified',
u'NUMBER': u'data1',
u'_COUNT': u'_count',
u'_ID': u'_id'}
```

The same getConstants function can be used to get a list of all the available constants in android.content.Intent. This will include all the standard Android intents. Here's a short code snippet that will print the list to the console:

```
import android
droid = android.Android()
myconst = droid.getConstants("android.content.Intent").result
for c in myconst:
    print c,"=",myconst[c]
```

The result of running this code will produce a nice formatted list that will look something like the following:

```
ACTION_AIRPLANE_MODE_CHANGED = android.intent.action.AIRPLANE_MODE
ACTION_ALARM_CHANGED = android.intent.action.ALARM_CHANGED
ACTION_ALL_APPS = android.intent.action.ALL_APPS
ACTION_ANSWER = android.intent.action.ANSWER
ACTION_APP_ERROR = android.intent.action.APP_ERROR
ACTION_ATTACH_DATA = android.intent.action.ATTACH_DATA
ACTION_BATTERY_CHANGED = android.intent.action.BATTERY_CHANGED
ACTION_BATTERY_LOW = android.intent.action.BATTERY_LOW
ACTION_BATTERY_OKAY = android.intent.action.BATTERY_OKAY
ACTION_BOOT_COMPLETED = android.intent.action.BOOT_COMPLETED
ACTION_BROADCAST_KEYEVENT = android.intent.action.BROADCAST_KEYEVENT
ACTION_BROADCAST_MOTIONEVENT = android.intent.action.BROADCAST_MOTIONEVENT
ACTION_BROADCAST_TRACKBALLEVENT = android.intent.action.BROADCAST_TRACKBALLEVENT
ACTION_BUG_REPORT = android.intent.action.BUG_REPORT
ACTION_CALL = android.intent.action.CALL
ACTION_CALL_BUTTON = android.intent.action.CALL_BUTTON
ACTION_CALL_EMERGENCY = android.intent.action.CALL_EMERGENCY
ACTION_CALL_PRIVILEGED = android.intent.action.CALL_PRIVILEGED
ACTION_CAMERA_BUTTON = android.intent.action.CAMERA_BUTTON
ACTION_CHECK_CONTACT_DB_CORRUPT = android.intent.action.ACTION_CHECK_CONTACT_DB_CORRUPT
ACTION_CHOOSER = android.intent.action.CHOOSER
ACTION_CLOSE_SYSTEM_DIALOGS = android.intent.action.CLOSE_SYSTEM_DIALOGS
ACTION_CONFIGURATION_CHANGED = android.intent.action.CONFIGURATION_CHANGED
ACTION_CONTACTS_CHANGE = anddroid.intent.action.CONTACTS_CHANGE
ACTION_CONTACTS_DB_READY = android.intent.action.CONTACTS_DB_READY
ACTION_CONTACT_DATABASE_CORRUPT = android.intent.action.CONTACT_DB_CORRUPT
ACTION_CREATE_SHORTCUT = android.intent.action.CREATE_SHORTCUT
ACTION_DATE_CHANGED = android.intent.action.DATE_CHANGED
ACTION_DEFAULT = android.intent.action.VIEW
ACTION_DELETE = android.intent.action.DELETE
```

```
ACTION_DELETE_THREAD_MSG = android.intent.action.DELETE_THREAD_MSG
ACTION_DEVICE_STORAGE_LOW = android.intent.action.DEVICE_STORAGE_LOW
ACTION_DEVICE_STORAGE_OK = android.intent.action.DEVICE_STORAGE_OK
ACTION_DIAL = android.intent.action.DIAL
ACTION_DIALER_NEED_CHANGE = android.intent.action.DIALER_NEED_CHANGE
ACTION_DOCK_EVENT = android.intent.action.DOCK_EVENT
ACTION_EDIT = android.intent.action.EDIT
```

With this information you can then use the makeIntent function and startActivityForResultIntent to access virtually any functionality buried in the depths of the Android operating system. Here's a short snippet that uses this technique to display your call log:

```
import android
droid = android.Android()
myconst = droid.getConstants("android.provider.CallLog$Calls").result
calls=droid.queryContent(myconst["CONTENT_URI"],["name","number","duration"]).result
for call in calls:
    print call
```

Notice that this code first uses the getConstants function to determine the value for CONTENT_URI and then uses the queryContent (part of the ContactsFacade) call to actually return the results.

ApplicationManagerFacade

The four functions in this facade make it possible to list all available and all running packages, launch an activity, or force-stop a package. You could use these calls to write your own task manager or terminate a specific set of packages. Be aware that the getLaunchableApplications call could take a little while to return a result depending on the number of applications you have loaded on the device. Figure 5-1 shows a partial list of applications in raw JSON form, whereas Figure 5-2 shows the same list formatted using the pprint function.

BatteryManagerFacade

Anything and everything having to do with your device's battery is here. This facade is a good place to talk about the concept of monitoring. There are a number of other cases where you must start and stop monitoring for some type of information in order to gather meaningful data. Figure 5-4 shows an example of what you might see in an interactive session using some of these API calls.

This is also a good place to point out some of the differences in the information returned by each API call. The Python IDLE tool makes it really easy to explore the different calls from the comfort of your workstation keyboard. That is assuming you've already launched SL4A on the device, started a server, and connected to it using ADB (see Chapter 2 if none of this makes sense). In the examples that follow, you'll see three arrows, as in >>>, indicating a prompt from IDLE. Don't type those in if you want to try out the code for yourself.

As mentioned in Chapter 1, everything in Python is an object. Every return from an API call is a result object. If you examine the last line from the _rpc method, you'll see the following:

```
return Result(id=result['id'], result=result['result'],
              error=result['error'], )
```

To access just the result of a call from Python, you could assign it to a variable and then evaluate the result, as in the following:

```
>>> apps = droid.getLaunchableApplications()
>>> pprint.pprint(apps.result)
```

To determine the type of an object in Python, you can use the **type()** function, as follows:

```
>>> type(apps)
<class 'android.Result'>
>>> type(apps.result)
<type 'dict'>
```

This says that **apps** is an object derived from the class **android.Result**. The following line shows that **apps.result** is of type **dict**, which in Python is essentially a key/value pair. In Java this would be represented as a **Map** object. Figure 5-4 shows what you will see upon examining the results returned by different battery management API calls.

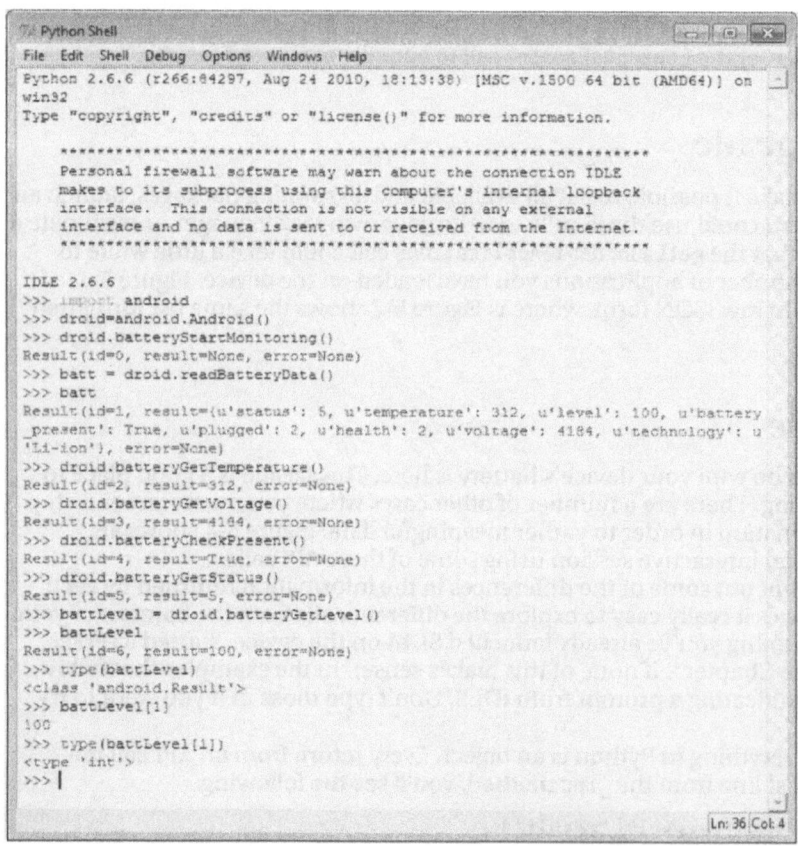

Figure 5-4. *Example of battery management API calls*

BluetoothFacade

Android devices have a wide range of Bluetooth capabilities you probably wouldn't expect on a mobile device. The BluetoothFacade provides access to all these functions, from the basic connection features to sending and receiving both ASCII and binary data. At the simplest level are bluetoothAccept, bluetoothConnect, bluetoothMakeDiscoverable, and bluetoothStop for controlling connectivity. You can also use checkBluetoothState and toggleBluetoothState to simply turn the Bluetooth radio on and off or just check to see what state it's in. Although the toggleBluetoothState function sounds like it simply flips the current state of the Bluetooth radio, it will actually set it to the state you desire with an optional parameter. By default, this will cause a pop-up screen on the device asking for permission, as shown in Figure 5-5.

Figure 5-5. *Bluetooth API prompting for permission*

BluetoothFacade also provides support for transferring data both to and from the device. Options here include bluetoothRead and bluetoothWrite to send / receive ASCII characters. There's also a bluetoothReadLine to read an entire line of text. For sending and receiving binary data there's bluetoothWriteBinary and bluetoothReadBinary. These two functions make it possible to transfer binary files to/from your device using Bluetooth.

CameraFacade

You basically have two options when it comes to taking a picture from a script. Either you snap a picture of whatever the camera is currently looking at (cameraCapturePicture) or you launch the image-capture application (`cameraInteractiveCapturePicture`). This is strictly for using the lens on the rear of the device. For devices with a front-facing camera, there is `WebCamFacade`. It should be noted that both of these API calls require you to pass a path on the device to store the image. You should take some time to browse your device if you aren't familiar with how to get to the different directories. On most devices, there will be a removable device typically named `sdcard`. The Android camera app stores pictures in `/sdcard/DCIM/100Media`.

As a side note, you should be aware that Android has a media scanner application that looks for specific file types, such as `.jpg` for pictures, and adds those images to the browse list for the default application such as Gallery. If you don't want that to happen, you can use a hidden directory with a leading period such as `/sdcard/.donotscan`. You can also add a file named `.nomedia,` and Android should ignore the media files in that directory.

CommonIntentsFacade

Version 2.x of the Android OS has a set of common intents available through `CommonIntentsFacade`. For scanning barcodes, there's the `scanBarcode` function. The underlying code will attempt to interpret what you're scanning and then present it as a result. To test this function, I used a few lines of Python code to launch the barcode scanner and then pointed it at the SL4A home page with its QR code for downloading the `.apk` file. Here's what I got:

```
>>> import android
>>> droid = android.Android()
>>> res = droid.scanBarcode()
>>> res.result
{u'extras': {u'SCAN_RESULT': u'http://android-scripting.googlecode.com/files/sl4a_r3.apk', ↩
 u'SCAN_RESULT_FORMAT': u'QR_CODE'}}
```

Next up is the `search` API function. You can call this API function with a generic string, as follows:

```
>>> search('pizza')
```

What happens next depends on how many different applications on your device are capable of performing a search. Figure 5-6 shows just a few of the options on a typical Android phone. You could pick one app and make it the default, but it might not give you the results you want. Calling the `pick` function displays content to be picked based on the Uniform Resource Identifier (URI) passed as an argument. You could use this to display a list of contacts with this code:

```
>>> import android
>>> droid = android.Android()
>>> droid.pick('u'content://contacts/people')
```

The `view` API function starts a view action based on a URI passed as an argument. This function also takes two optional arguments: `type` is a string representing the MIME type of the URI, and `extras` is a JSON object containing a map of any extra information needed by the intent. Understanding how to use the API call requires some understanding of intents and URIs. The basics were covered in Chapter 2, although it wouldn't hurt to revisit the Google Android developer site.

If you simply want to launch the contacts app, then use `viewContacts`. This function uses the launch activity call to simply start the application and then return to the caller. If you happen to have any HTML content stored locally on your device, you can use the `viewHtml` function to display it. It requires a full path to the file as a single argument. To search for something on a map, use the `viewMap` function with a string argument containing what you're looking for. This will launch the maps application with the search bar containing your search string.

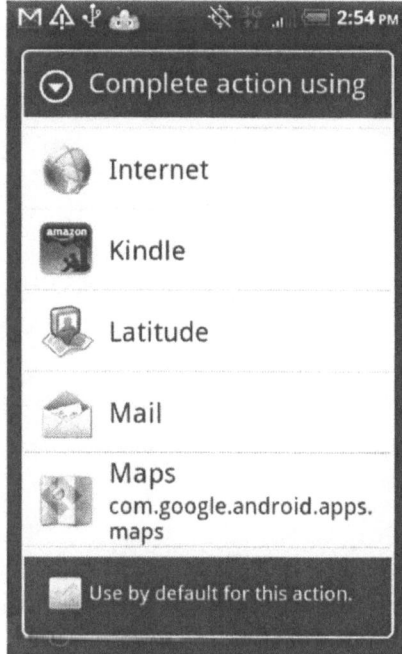

Figure 5-6. *Results of the search API function*

ContactsFacade

This facade gives you access to anything and everything having to do with contacts. If you just want to get one big list of all the contacts on your device, use contactsGet. You might want to use the contactsGetAttributes call first to figure out what information is available for each contact. This list could change over time as Google enhances their products. Another call you might want to use before retrieving the entire list is contactsGetCount. This simply returns the total number of contacts stored on the device.

If you need to select a specific contact for use in some other action, use the pickContact function. This will launch the People application with the search box and keyboard displayed. Be aware that it returns an intent pointing to the contact chosen. If you just need a phone number for one of your contacts, you'll want to use the pickPhone function. This will display the list of contacts as before, but only give you the associated phone numbers after you choose a name. This function returns the phone number chosen as a part of the result. The last two functions here are contactsGetById and contactsGetIds. These two go together and allow you to pick a specific contact using only the ID. Figure 5-7 shows some of these functions in action.

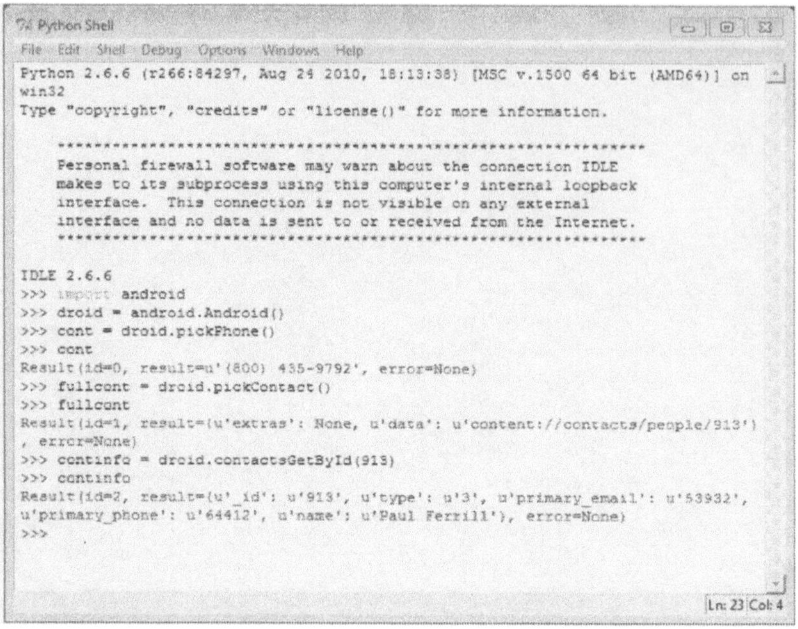

Figure 5-7. *Results of different Contacts API functions*

SL4A r4 introduced a new **queryContent** function to the contacts facade. This function has a total of five parameters you need to pass it in order to fully define what you wish your query to return. The first parameter is the URI of the content provider you wish to query. For the contacts database this would be **content://com.android.contacts/data/phones**. The remaining parameters are optional but you must pass the keyword '**None**' if you wish to use the default. Parameter two is a list of columns from the database you wish returned. Parameter three is a selection filter to choose specific rows to return from the database. The final two parameters are **selectionArgs** and **order**.

Here's a short snippet showing how you might use this function:

```
import android
droid = android.Android()
contacts = droid.queryContent('content://com.android.contacts/data/phones',\
        ['display_name','data1'],None,None,None).result
for c in contacts:
  print c
```

You'll also need to have installed at least **PythonForAndroid_r6.apk** for this example to work. With that said, you should see an output from this snippet that looks something like the following:

```
[{u'data1': u'321-555-1212', u'display_name': u'John Doe'},
 {u'data1': u'321-555-1212', u'display_name': u'Jane Doe'},
 {u'data1': u'321-555-1212', u'display_name': u'Jed Doe'},
 {u'data1': u'321-555-1234', u'display_name': u'John Smith'},
 {u'data1': u'321-555-1234', u'display_name': u'Jane Smith'},
 {u'data1': u'321-555-1234', u'display_name': u'Jill Smith'},
 {u'data1': u'800-555-1212', u'display_name': u'Toll Free'}]
```

EventFacade

The Android OS keeps an event queue for passing information between applications asynchronously. This facade gives you access to functions to manipulate Android events. If you simply want to clear the event buffer, just call **eventClearBuffer**. To add or remove an event to the queue, you should use **eventPost** or **eventPoll**. To wait for an event, use **eventWaitFor** with a parameter of **eventName**, but be aware that this will block further execution until the named event occurs.

One example of events can be seen using example code from the SL4A API wiki. I updated the code to use the SL4A r4 functions as shown here:

```
import android, time
droid = android.Android()
droid.startSensingTimed(1,1000)
e = droid.eventPoll(1).result
event_entry_number = 0
x = e[event_entry_number]['data']['xforce']
```

The **eventPost** function is one way to implement a modal dialog box that I'll demonstrate in a later chapter. It also works as a cross-thread communication medium if you're building a multithreaded application.

EyesFreeFacade

This facade provides TTS services for API 3 or lower. The only function here is **ttsSpeak**, which outputs the passed string using the TTS capability.

LocationFacade

LocationFacade functions make it possible to know where you are at any point in time, either by GPS or by using information about the cell tower you're currently using. If you use the **getLastKnownLocation** function, you'll get information that may or may not be the most current available. To make sure you get relevant information, you must invoke the **startLocating** call. Follow that with a **readLocation** call, and you should see a result like the following:

```
Result(id=6, result={u'network': {u'altitude': 0, u'provider': u'network', u'longitude':↵
 -84.480000000000004, u'time': 1296595452577L, u'latitude': 31.392499999999998, u'speed':↵
 0, u'accuracy': 1000}}, error=None)
```

startLocating will only use currently enabled location resources. That means you won't get a GPS fix unless you already have GPS enabled. Use the **stopLocating** call to stop collecting location data. The last function available in this facade is **geocode**, which you can use in conjunction with either **readLocation** or **getLastKnownLocation** to get a list of addresses for the given latitude and longitude.

Feeding the previous location into **geocode** returns the following:

```
Result(id=7, result=[{u'locality': u'Milford', u'sub_admin_area': u'Baker', u'admin_area':↵
 u'Georgia', u'feature_name': u'Milford', u'country_code': u'US', u'country_name':↵
 u'United States'}], error=None)
```

Keep in mind that this feature requires an active Internet connection to do the actual lookup.

MediaPlayerFacade

This is the facade to use if you want to play music or video content. SL4A r4 made this function an official part of the API. The functions available provide a way to open, close, play, pause, and seek to a position in a media file. The functions mediaIsPlaying, mediaPlayInfo, and mediaPlayList provide information about the current state of the media player. Keep in mind that these functions do not actually manipulate the media player application; they launch a media player service. There is a way to launch the media player using **startActivity** if that's what you want to do.

Function names are pretty obvious: mediaPlay, mediaPlayClose, mediaPlayPause, mediaPlaySeek, and MediaPlayStart. You will need to use mediaPlay to actually load a media resource specified by a URL. The function mediaPlaySetLooping is the last function that you might find handy if you're creating something like a background noise player.

MediaRecorderFacade

The MediaRecorder facade gives you access to both audio and video recording capabilities. You must provide a valid path for the output file or the call will fail. If you simply want to launch the video capture application, use the startInteractiveVideoRecording function. To start an audio recording, use the recorderStartMicrophone function. For a video recording, use recorderCaptureVideo function. If you use either of these, you must explicitly call **recorderStop** to end a previously started recording.

PhoneFacade

Every Android cell phone makes basic phone operations available programmatically. This facade also includes a number of network-specific capabilities. Some functions simply return with no information if it's not available on the device. One example of this behavior is the getCellLocation call. If you try this call on a CDMA phone, you'll get nothing in the result. If you want to monitor the state of the phone, you must first call the startTrackingPhoneState function. The readPhoneState function returns the current state along with the incoming phone number for any incoming call.

There are two basic ways to place a phone call. First are the phoneCallNumber and phoneDialNumber functions. These take a phone number as a string as the only argument. The difference between the two is that the phoneCallNumber function will actually place the call; phoneDialNumber will open the phone dialer with the number you pass it, entered as if you typed it on the keypad.

You can also use either the phoneCall or phoneDial functions to dial with a URI string. You could pass the intent returned by the pickContact function, and it will call the primary number for that contact. To do this in Python, you need to extract just the intent as returned by the pickContact function. In Python this would look like this:

```
cont = droid.pickContact()
droid.phoneDial(cont[1]['data'])
```

PreferencesFacade

If you're looking to build an application with its own set of preferences, you'll need this facade. There are three functions supported in the SL4A r4 release: prefGetAll, prefGetValue, and prefPutValue. By default, all three operate on the Shared Preferences store, which contains the usage tracking preference. Here's what you will see from IDLE:

```
>>> import android
>>> droid = android.Android()
>>> pref = droid.prefGetAll()
>>> pref
Result(id=0, result={u'usagetracking': False, u'present_usagetracking': False}, error=None)
```

To create your own preferences file, you need to add a filename as an argument to pass to the Get and Put routines like this:

```
>>> droid.prefPutValue('GPSTracking', True, 'myprefs')
Result(id=7, result=None, error=None)
>>> droid.prefGetValue('GPSTracking','myprefs')
Result(id=9, result=True, error=None)
```

SensorManagerFacade

Every Android device has one or more sensors available to applications. At a minimum, there's an accelerometer to determine the orientation of the screen. The SensorManager facade provides access to all the sensors currently supported by Android. It's also another one of the facade types requiring you to start and stop the process of sensing because this happens in the background. To start and stop sensing, use the startSensing and stopSensing function calls. Data will be available once you have started sensing and waited some amount of time to allow sensor data to be collected.

At the highest level is the readSensors function call. The following example shows the data returned by this function:

```
>>> res = droid.readSensors()
>>> import pprint
>>> pprint.pprint(res.result)
{u'accuracy': 3,
 u'azimuth': -2.734636402130127,
 u'pitch': -1.0204463958740235,
 u'roll': 0.034272377938032152,
 u'time': 1296683466.802,
 u'xforce': -0.14982382999999999,
 u'xmag': 13.75,
 u'yforce': 8.6625409999999992,
 u'ymag': -38.4375,
 u'zforce': 5.3664170000000002,
 u'zmag': 15.375}
```

There are individual function calls to return specific information: sensorsGetAccuracy, sensorsGetLight, sensorsReadAccelerometer, sensorsReadMagnetometer, and sensorsReadOrientation. The results of calling these functions are shown here:

```
>>> droid.sensorsGetAccuracy()
Result(id=7, result=3, error=None)
>>> droid.sensorsGetLight()
Result(id=8, result=None, error=None)
>>> droid.sensorsReadAccelerometer()
Result(id=9, result=[-0.14982382999999999, 8.7306430000000006, 5.4345189999999999],↵
 error=None)
>>> droid.sensorsReadMagnetometer()
```

```
Result(id=10, result=[11.25, -37.6875, 13.3125], error=None)
>>> droid.sensorsReadOrientation()
Result(id=11, result=[-2.7596172332763671, -1.0129913330078124, 0.035179258137941358], ⏎
error=None)
```

The accelerometer and magnetometer functions return values as a list of X, Y, and Z. Orientation returns a list of azimuth, pitch, and roll. In SL4A r4 the startSensing function has been deprecated and replaced with startSensingThreshold and startSensingTimed. In many cases when you need to use the sensors you either want to detect motion based on time or when the device crosses some threshold of movement. The startSensingThreshold function allows you to record sensor events into the event queue when a specific threshold has been exceeded in orientation, movement (accelerometer), direction (magnetometer), or light. If you wish to use multiple sensors you must make multiple calls to startSensingThreshold to enable a specific threshold for each. The startSensingTimed function takes two parameters to determine which sensor to record (1 = all, 2 = accelerometer, 3 = magnetometer, and 4 = light) along with a delayTime (specified in milliseconds) parameter to specify the amount of time between readings.

SettingsFacade

This façade gives you access to all the different settings on your phone: ringer volume, screen brightness, and more. It's probably one of the more useful facades when you think about scripting your device. Later chapters will use these function calls to demonstrate the power of SL4A. For now, let's just take a look at what's available.

There are three function calls that simply check the status of something. These include checkAirplaneMode, checkRingerSilentMode, and checkScreenOn. All three simply return a Boolean indicating whether the mode is on (True) or off (False). Be aware that checkScreenOn requires at least API level 7 or higher (Android 2.1). To change either AirplaneMode or RingerSilentMode, you can use toggleAirplaneMode or toggleRingerSilentMode. These functions are similar to other toggle functions in that you can explicitly set a mode by passing an optional parameter. The result returned will reflect the current state of the device. There's also a toggleVibrateMode to set the device to vibrate only if the ringer is enabled and to vibrate on a new notification otherwise.

The remaining functions either get a particular setting or set a value for a setting. For getting a value, you use getMaxMediaVolume, getMaxRingerVolume, getMediaVolume, getRingerVolume, getScreenBrightness, getScreenTimeout, and getVibrateMode. To set values, you should use setMediaVolume, setRingerVolume, setScreenBrightness, and setScreenTimeout.

SignalStrengthFacade

If you want to know or display how good your signal is, you should use this facade. First, you must call the startTrackingSignalStrengths function to start gathering data. Next, you should call readSignalStrengths to actually read the data. It will return something like this:

```
>>> droid.readSignalStrengths().result
{u'cdma_ecio': -70, u'evdo_dbm': -98, u'cdma_dbm': -97, u'evdo_ecio': -1515,⏎
 u'gsm_signal_strength': 99, u'gsm_bit_error_rate': -1}
```

Once you're done, you should issue stopTrackingSignalStrengths to shut the process down.

SmsFacade

This facade lets you manipulate the store of SMS messages stored on the phone. It has a number of functions for deleting, reading, marking, and sending SMS messages. SMS messages are another area where Google decided to make the attributes flexible. The smsGetAttributes function returns a list of available attributes as currently defined. Using Python and the pprint function will show the following:

```
>>> pprint.pprint(droid.smsGetAttributes().result)
[u'_id',
 u'thread_id',
 u'toa',
 u'address',
 u'person',
 u'date',
 u'protocol',
 u'read',
 u'status',
 u'type',
 u'reply_path_present',
 u'subject',
 u'body',
 u'sc_toa',
 u'report_date',
 u'service_center',
 u'locked',
 u'index_on_sim',
 u'callback_number',
 u'priority',
 u'htc_category',
 u'cs_timestamp',
 u'cs_id',
 u'cs_synced',
 u'error_code',
 u'seen']
```

If you want to know how many SMS messages are currently stored on the device, use smsGetMessageCount. This function has a required Boolean argument to indicate whether you want a count of just the unread messages or everything. If you don't pass it an argument, you'll get an error message like this:

```
>>> droid.smsGetMessageCount()
com.googlecode.android_scripting.rpc.RpcError: Argument 1 is not present
Result(id=24, result=None, error=u'com.googlecode.android_scripting.rpc.RpcError: Argument 1↵
 is not present')
```

Calling it with either True or False as the argument will return an integer count, as follows:

```
>>> droid.smsGetMessageCount(True).result
0
>>> droid.smsGetMessageCount(False).result
228
```

Manipulating individual messages is done by ID. Calling smsGetMessageIds will return either a list of all message IDs or just unread messages, depending on the Boolean argument passed. This just returns a list of numbers so you'll have to get all the messages if you really want to do anything with them. You can do this one of two ways. Either make a call to smsGetMessages and get everything, or iterate over the list of message IDs returned by smsGetMessageIds and then use smsGetMessageById to get each one individually.

If you want to work with only unread messages, you can set the Boolean passed to any of the GetMessage calls. Then you could use either smsMarkMessageRead or smsDeleteMessage to deal with each message. Finally, there's smsSend for actually sending an SMS message. This function has two parameters: a destination address, which is typically a phone number, and the actual text of the message.

SpeechRecognitionFacade

You can use this facade to add speech recognition to your script. It has only one function call named recognizeSpeech. There are three optional arguments including a prompt string, a language string to inform the recognizer to expect speech in a language different than the default, and a language Model string to tell the recognizer which speech model to prefer. It returns a string representing the best effort to convert the speech to text. If it can't interpret it, you'll get an empty string. Here's what I get when I call this function and say, "The rain in Spain falls mainly on the plain":

```
>>> droid.recognizeSpeech()
Result(id=2, result=u'the rain in spain falls mainly on the plane', error=None)
```

TextToSpeechFacade

These functions provide TTS services for API4 and later. To have the device "speak" a phrase you would use the ttsSpeak function, passing it a string containing the phrase. Control is immediately passed back to the calling script once you issue this call. You must use the function ttsIsSpeaking to determine whether the speech function has completed.

ToneGeneratorFacade

If you need to generate DTMF tones for a specific function, such as interacting with an interactive voice response application, this call is for you. To use it you must call generateDtmfTones, passing in a string representing the numbers you wish to have generated. An optional integer argument allows you to alter the duration of each tone, with the default being 100 milliseconds.

UiFacade

This facade provides all the functions you'll need for creating user interface elements such as text boxes, check boxes, date pickers, and more. Some of these functions are *single-action,* meaning you need to call them only once to actually get a response. These functions also block or wait for the user to complete the action and close the dialog box. The two single-action, input–related dialog boxes are dialogGetInput and dialogGetPassword. Both have optional parameters to set the title, prompt message, and default input. Figure 5-8 shows the result of the following code:

```
>>> droid.dialogGetInput(u'My Title', u'My Message')
```

Figure 5-8. *Example of dialogGetInput*

There are a number of functions in this façade that require two calls to actually show the dialog box and a third to get the response. The process involves setting up the dialog box with one call and then presenting it with a call to `dialogShow`. Figure 5-9 shows an example of `dialogCreateAlert`.

Figure 5-9. *Example of dialogCreate Alert*

This particular dialog box is meant to present some type of alert information to the user, which requires an acknowledgment before doing anything else on the device. It does not return any information and does not block any further program execution. You can close the dialog box either by pressing one of the hardware buttons or programmatically with a call to `dialogDismiss`.

For other UI elements with information to return, you'll need to call **dialogGetResponse** to actually get the data. The sequencing here is important because **dialogGetResponse** actually blocks until the user closes the dialog box. You should check the result variable to determine whether the user actually entered data or pressed the Cancel button instead. To prompt for and actually get a time with the **dialogCreateTimePicker**, do the following:

```
>>> droid.dialogCreateTimePicker()
Result(id=22, result=None, error=None)
>>> droid.dialogShow()
Result(id=23, result=None, error=None)
>>> droid.dialogGetResponse()
Result(id=24, result={u'hour': 15, u'minute': 53, u'which': u'positive'}, error=None)
```

You can see the result of the call to **dialogGetResponse** when using Python and IDLE because the prompt will go away until you close the dialog box. If the user clicks the Cancel button, you'll get a positive return in the **'which'** parameter, as follows:

```
>>> droid.dialogGetResponse()
Result(id=26, result={u'hour': 0, u'minute': 0, u'which': u'negative'}, error=None)
```

There are three function calls that allow you to set the text of the buttons displayed in the alert box. Here's a short Python routine to demonstrate the usage of **dialogSetPositiveButtonText**, **dialogSetNegativeButtonText**, and **dialogSetNeutralButtonText**. Figure 5-10 shows the actual dialog box.

```
import android

droid = android.Android()

title = 'Alert'
message = ('This alert box has 3 buttons '
           'and waits for you to press one.')
droid.dialogCreateAlert(title, message)
droid.dialogSetPositiveButtonText('Yes')
droid.dialogSetNegativeButtonText('No')
droid.dialogSetNeutralButtonText('Cancel')
droid.dialogShow()
response = droid.dialogGetResponse().result

print ['which'] in ('positive', 'negative', 'neutral')
```

Figure 5-10. *Example of multibutton alert dialog box*

The next set of dialog box functions contain multiple elements that must be set before you present them. These elements include a list of items to choose from in either a single- or multiple choice fashion. Figure 5-11 shows the use of `dialogSetItems` to create the list. Here's a short piece of Python code to set a list of items:

```
droid.dialogCreateAlert(title)
droid.dialogSetItems(['one', 'two', 'three'])
droid.dialogShow()
response = droid.dialogGetResponse().result
```

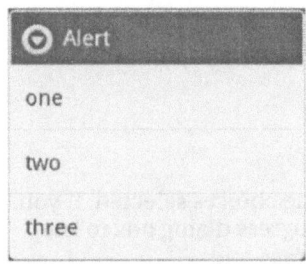

Figure 5-11. *Example of multioption alert dialog box*

A slight variation on this theme is to use `dialogSetSingleChoiceItems` or `dialogSetMultiChoiceItems` to create a list of items with either a radio button or a check box to select the items. The only real difference between using `dialogSetItems` and `dialogSetSingleChoiceItems` is the visual display with the radio buttons and the button to acknowledge the choice and return. Here's the code for using `dialogSetSingleChoiceItems`:

```
droid.dialogCreateAlert(title)
droid.dialogSetSingleChoiceItems(['One', 'Two', 'Three'])
droid.dialogSetPositiveButtonText('Done')
droid.dialogShow()
```

For the multiple choice option, you need one more function call to get the selected items: `dialogGetSelectedItems`. The order of operations does matter in this example as well. You have to wait for the user to actually choose the items and close the dialog box before you try to read them. As a result, you must insert the call to `dialogGetSelectedItems` after the call to `dialogGetResponse`. Figure 5-12 shows what the dialog box will look like. Here's the code snippet showing how you would use this call to create the dialog box and get the response:

```
droid.dialogCreateAlert(title)
droid.dialogSetMultiChoiceItems(['One', 'Two', 'Three'])
droid.dialogSetPositiveButtonText('Done')
droid.dialogShow()
droid.dialogGetResponse()
ans = droid.dialogGetSelectedItems()
```

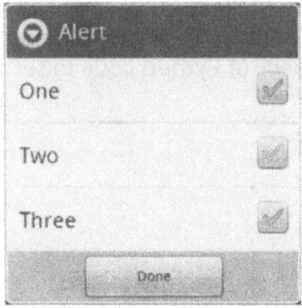

Figure 5-12. *Example of multiple choice alert dialog box*

The result from picking options One and Three is the following:

```
Result(id=5, result=[0, 2], error=None)
```

In Python, the result is actually a list of values (zero-based) representing the choices selected. If you have any script code that will take some time to complete, you should use a progress dialog box to keep the user informed. The two options available are **dialogCreateHorizontalProgress** and **dialogCreateSpinnerProgress**. To update the progress settings, you must call **dialogSetCurrentProgress**. There's also **dialogSetMaxProgress** to define the end point. Figure 5-13 shows a horizontal progress bar generated with the following code:

```
import android
import time

droid = android.Android()

title = 'Horizontal'
message = 'This is simple horizontal progress.'
droid.dialogCreateHorizontalProgress(title, message, 100)
droid.dialogShow()
for x in range(0, 99):
  time.sleep(0.1)
  droid.dialogSetCurrentProgress(x)
droid.dialogDismiss()
```

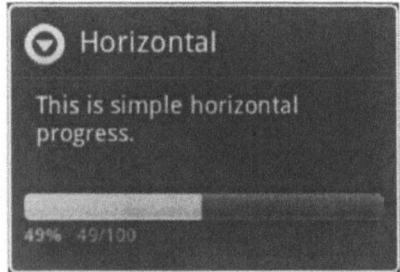

Figure 5-13. *Example of horizontal progress dialog box*

Notice that you must make a call to `dialogDismiss` to actually make the progress dialog box go away. The spinner progress dialog box is created with `dialogCreateSpinnerProgress` and is intended for displaying something moving to let the user know that processing is happening. As with the horizontal progress dialog box, you must make a call to `dialogDismiss` to actually close the spinner dialog box.

Android provides two types of menus for applications to use: context and options. A *context menu* is analogous to what you see when you right-click your mouse in a desktop operating system. The *options menu* is what you see when you press the device Menu button while a script is running. The user can then set preferences or even exit a script in a relatively standard Android way. You add items to either of these menus using `addContextMenuItem` or `addOptionsMenuItem`. To clear either menu, use `clearContextMenu` or `clearOptionsMenu`.

The final UI dialog box element is `webViewShow`. This dialog box opens up the world of HTML forms to SL4A scripts and will be used in a later chapter to build a full-featured application. For now, let's just say it will display a WebView using the URL passed to it. An optional `wait` Boolean parameter will cause the script to block until the user exits the WebView if set to `True`. Chapter 8 uses this facade to build a number of dialog box–based user interface examples.

WakeLockFacade

In the world of mobile device applications there is the concept of locking a device in the wake state to allow for some critical process to complete. This can be potentially dangerous to your battery life and should only be used for short periods of time. It could also be used in the case of an application like a video player to keep the normal screen shutdown from occurring. Function calls provided to create a wake lock include `wakeLockAcquireBright`, `wakeLockAcquireDim`, `wakeLockAcquireFull`, and `wakeLockAcquirePartial`. Each one affects the screen brightness and CPU state. When your application has no more need for the wake lock, it calls the `wakeLockRelease` function to turn it off.

WebCamFacade

The web cam on an Android device is the front-facing camera. To start or stop the web cam, you use `webcamStart` or `webcamStop`. When you start the web cam, you can either use the default settings for resolution, quality, and port number, or pass them in as options. There's also a separate function, `webcamAdjustQuality`, used to adjust the quality while streaming video.

WifiFacade

With `WifiFacade`, you can completely control the WiFi radio on your device. Basic operations are `checkWifiState` and `toggleWifiState`. These operate in much the same way as other similarly named functions, meaning you can pass a Boolean value to `toggleWifiState` to implicitly enable or disable the WiFi radio. Calls to `wifiDisconnect`, `wifiReconnect`, and `wifiReassociate` do what their names imply. To retrieve information about the currently active access point, use `wifiGetConnectionInfo`.

You could use the remaining function calls to build a WiFi scanning application. Available function calls include `wifiStartScan`, `wifiGetScanResults`, `wifiLockAcquireFull`, `wifiLockAcquireScanOnly`, and `wifiLockRelease`. If you want exclusive access to the WiFi radio, you should make a call to either `wifiLockAcquireFull` or `wifiLockAcquireScanOnly`. Make sure you call `wifiLockRelease` when you're done, or else other applications won't be able to get to the WiFi connection.

Summary

This chapter focused on getting you acquainted with the Android APIs as presented by SL4A. Examples given all used Python and the IDLE application running on Windows. You should be able to repeat the examples on Linux or Mac OS X by using the same basic approach. In the next chapter, I'll start actually creating real scripts you can put to use right away.

Here's a list of things you want to remember from this chapter.

- **Things change**: The SL4A project is a dynamic one, and new releases often bring changes to the API. If a particular function has been replaced you'll get a notification about it.

- **Know your facades**: SL4A uses the concept of a facade to mimic the native Android API calls. It will help you to have some understanding of how the native calls work, especially for things such as startActivity and makeIntent.

- **Don't be afraid to experiment**: The emulator is a great place to try out many of the API calls. Unfortunately, not all the functionality will work in the emulator. Sensors, cameras, WiFi, and web cams work only on real devices. You can't really hurt anything testing these features on a device. so go ahead and give it a shot.

- **Read the documentation**: I know how hard it is sometimes to just read the documentation. In the case of working with Android and SL4A, it can save you time and frustration if you'll just do a little reading. Google search can be your friend here as well.

CHAPTER 6

Background Scripting with Python

This chapter will take a look at creating scripts that use Scripting Layer for Android (SL4A) with no user interface and are meant to be run in the background.

Here are the main topics for this chapter:

- Writing scripts that perform specific tasks in the background

- Demonstrating different functional aspects of SL4A

Python has a reputation as a language for developing scripts to do basic functional tasks quickly and efficiently. This chapter will show you how to build scripts that perform specific operations with essentially no intervention. So the scripts in this chapter will have no user interface to speak of. While there might be some status information if you launch the script in a terminal window, there won't be anything for the user to do other than start the script.

Background Tasks

With the latest version of SL4A (r4 as of this writing) you can launch any script either in a terminal or in the background. To launch it in the background, choose the icon that looks like a little cog wheel, as shown in Figure 6-1.

Figure 6-1. SL4A script launch options

When the script runs, it places an entry on the Notifications page that identifies the application and gives you a way to shut it down, if necessary. There's also an application specifically written with SL4A in mind if you want a script to launch when your device boots. The application is called Launch On Boot and does pretty much what it says. Figure 6-2 shows what the main screen looks like.

Figure 6-2. *Launch On Boot preferences screen*

This utility will launch a single SL4A script every time your device boots. If you want to launch multiple scripts, you'll need to create a master script that will, in turn, launch other scripts. That brings up the obvious question: How do you launch another SL4A script from Python? To answer that question we need to take a look at the makeIntent function. Here's what the documentation has for makeIntent:

```
makeIntent(
    String action,
    String uri[optional],
    String type[optional]: MIME type/subtype of the URI,
    JSONObject extras[optional]: a Map of extras to add to the Intent,
    JSONArray categories[optional]: a List of categories to add to the Intent,
    String packagename[optional]: name of package. If used, requires classname to be useful,
    String classname[optional]: name of class. If used, requires packagename to be useful,
    Integer flags[optional]: Intent flags)
```

The key is that this is an explicit intent, meaning you don't need a URI. For the purpose of launching another SL4A script you must fully qualify the packagename and the componentname. The resulting call would then look like this:

```
intent=droid.makeIntent("com.googlecode.android_scripting.action.LAUNCH_BACKGROUND_SCRIPT",\
None, \
None, \
{"com.googlecode.android_scripting.extra.SCRIPT_PATH" : "/sdcard/sl4a/scripts/hello_world.py"}, \
None, \
"com.googlecode.android_scripting", \
"com.googlecode.android_scripting.activity.ScriptingLayerServiceLauncher").result
```

We can make that much easier to read with a just a few extra lines of code as follows:

```
import android
droid = android.Android()
action = "com.googlecode.android_scripting.action.LAUNCH_BACKGROUND_SCRIPT"
clsname = "com.googlecode.android_scripting"
pkgname = "com.googlecode.android_scripting.activity.ScriptingLayerServiceLauncher"
extras = {"com.googlecode.android_scripting.extra.SCRIPT_PATH":
        "/sdcard/sl4a/scripts/hello_world.py"}
myintent = droid.makeIntent(action, None, None, extras, None, clsname, pkgname).result
droid.startActivityIntent(myintent)
```

Triggers

SL4A has a provision for implementing triggers. I want to mention them here briefly, but be aware that as of this writing they are still somewhat buggy. The basic concept is to provide a mechanism to trigger some functionality based on some condition or event that happens on your device. Figure 6-3 shows the menu you will see if you press the Menu button when viewing the list of scripts and then select Triggers.

Figure 6-3. *Trigger menu*

Any existing triggers will be displayed in this screen. You can cancel all triggers with the Cancel All button or select individual triggers by long-pressing on the one you want to remove to bring up a Remove button (see Figure 6-4). To add a new trigger, press the Add button shown in Figure 6-3. This will display the contents of the /sdcard/sl4a/scripts directory and allow you to choose a script to run. Once you choose a script, you will see a popup menu like the one in Figure 6-5. This is where you choose what will trigger your script to run. The list of options includes battery, location, phone, sensors, and signal strength.

The bad news is that triggers are not fully functional, so use them at your own risk. On the bright side, there is a way to achieve some of the same functionality using a slightly different approach.

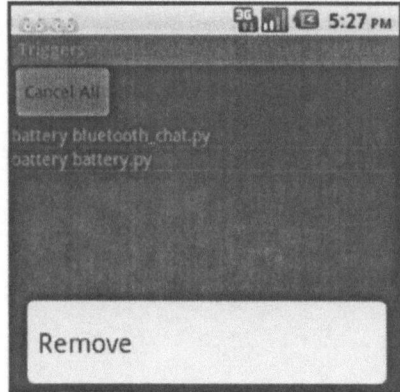

Figure 6-4. Remove Trigger Button

Be warned that if you start an application that crashes, you can get into an infinite loop in which every time SL4A launches it tries to start your triggered script and then it just crashes again. If you can get to the notification screen and bring up the SL4A triggers, you should be able to press the Cancel All button and remove the offending script. The only other way to get around this is to uninstall and then reinstall SL4A.

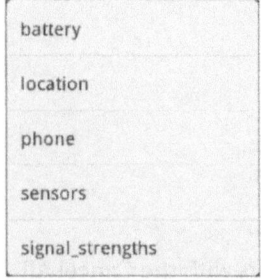

Figure 6-5. Trigger activation menu

Orientation-based Actions

Here's a handy script that will place your phone in silent mode if you set it face down on a flat surface. The code uses the **startSensingTimed** API call to determine orientation and movement. If it determines that the device is still and essentially horizontal, it will set the ringer to be silent using the **toggleRingerSilentMode** call. Here's what the code looks like:

```python
import android, time
droid = android.Android()

droid.startSensingTimed(1, 5)
silent = False
while True:
    e = droid.eventPoll(1)

    facedown = e.result and 'data' in e.result[0] and \
                e.result[0]['data']['zforce'] and e.result[0]['data']['zforce'] < -5
    if facedown and not silent:
        droid.vibrate(100)
        droid.toggleRingerSilentMode(True)
        silent = True
    elif not facedown and silent:
        droid.toggleRingerSilentMode(False)
        silent = False

    time.sleep(5)
```

Another way to detect that the phone has been placed face down is to use the light sensor. Here's a short snippet that will use the text-to-speech (TTS) function to let you know when the phone is face down:

```python
import android, time

droid = android.Android()
droid.startSensing()

while True:
    result = droid.sensorsGetLight().result
    if result is not None and result <= 10:
        droid.ttsSpeak('I can\'t see!')
    time.sleep(5)
```

This is probably a good place to talk about logging. One of the biggest challenges of writing a program with no user interface is debugging. There are a number of ways to debug "silent" code—from inserting print statements to using the DDMS tool from the Android SDK. Most Linux system applications generate a log of some type expressly for the purpose of monitoring execution and to record error information. The Android platform provides a logging tool called logcat. There's an API function named **log** that will write any string message you'd like to the **logcat** file. Alternatively, you can write to your own log file.

In Chapter 9, I'll go over a complex application in detail that uses logging to record information. Here's what some of the log entries look like:

```
{"task":"loadconfig"} <type 'unicode'>
ok... {u'task': u'loadconfig'}
loadconfig
{"sections": {"locale": [{"name": "prefix", "value": "+60", "description": "International
prefix. Used to clean up phone numbers before sending.\nThis will only affect numbers that do
not yet have an international code.\nExamples (assuming prefix is +60):\n0123456789 will
become +60123456789\n60123456789 will become +60123456789\n+49332211225 remains unchanged"}],
```

```
"merger": [{"name": "informeveryratio", "value": "10", "description": "Use TTS to inform you
every total / n messages. Set to 1 if you do not wish to use this feature.\nExample\nIf you
are sending 200 messages and set this value to 5, you will be informed by TTS of the status
every 200 / 5 = 40 messages."}, {"name": "informevery", "value": "0", "description": "Use TTS
to inform you every n messages. Set to 0 if you do not wish to use this feature."}],
"application": [{"name": "showonlycsvfiles", "value": "0", "description": "While importing the
CSV file, only files with the extension .csv will be shown if this is set to 1."}, {"name":
"showonlytextfiles", "value": "1", "description": "While importing template text from a file,
only files with the extension .txt will be shown if this is set to 1."}, {"name":
"showhiddendirectories", "value": "0", "description": "While browsing, hidden directories
(stating with '.') will not be shown if this is set to 1."}]}}
Had to wait cause process was only 0.005585 second
{"task":"listdir","path":"/sdcard","type":"csv"} <type 'unicode'>
ok... {u'path': u'/sdcard', u'task': u'listdir', u'type': u'csv'}
listdir
Loading directory content
{"files": [".._.Trashes", "handcent1.log"], "folders": ["accelerometervalues", "Aldiko",
"amazonmp3", "Android", "astrid", "com.coupons.GroceryIQ", "com.foxnews.android",
"com.googlecode.bshforandroid", "com.googlecode.pythonforandroid", "data", "DCIM", "Digital
Editions", "documents", "download", "Downloads", "droidscript", "dropbox", "eBooks",
"Evernote", "gameloft", "gReader", "Grooveshark", "handcent", "HTC Sync", "ItchingThumb",
"jsword", "logs", "LOST.DIR", "Mail Attachments", "media", "mspot", "Music", "My Documents",
"pulse", "rfsignaldata", "rosie_scroll", "rssreader", "Sample Photo", "skifta", "sl4a",
"StudyDroid", "swiftkey", "tmp", "TunnyBrowser", "twc-cache"]}
{"task":"listdir","path":"/sdcard/sl4a","type":"csv"} <type 'unicode'>
ok... {u'path': u'/sdcard/sl4a', u'task': u'listdir', u'type': u'csv'}
listdir
Loading directory content
{"files": ["battery.py.log", "BeanShell 2.0b4.log", "DockProfile.py.log", "downloader.py.log",
"downloaderv2.py.log", "DroidTrack.py.log", "geostatus.py.log", "getIPaddr.py.log",
"hello_world.bsh.log", "httpd.py.log", "netip.py.log", "null.log", "Python 2.6.2.log",
"Shell.log", "simpleHTTP2.py.log", "smssender.py.log", "speak.py.log", "ssid2key.py.log",
"test.py.log", "trackmylocation.py.log", "weather.py.log", "wifi.py.log",
"wifi_scanner.py.log"], "folders": ["extras", "scripts"]}
Had to wait cause process was only 0.025512 second
{"task":"listdir","path":"/sdcard/sl4a/scripts","type":"csv"} <type 'unicode'>
ok... {u'path': u'/sdcard/sl4a/scripts', u'task': u'listdir', u'type': u'csv'}
listdir
```

If you look closely, you'll notice a number of different types of entries. There are informational entries to identify when a particular section of code has been executed, such as loadconfig. Other entries dump the contents of a Python variable such as this line:

```
{u'path': u'/sdcard/sl4a/scripts', u'task': u'listdir', u'type': u'csv'}
```

The curly braces identify this object as a Python dictionary containing a total of three key/value pairs. You have a lot of flexibility about what goes in a log file. Here's the code from the Chapter 9 SMSSender application to open a log file:

```
# Prepare a log file
# TODO: Would be better thing to use the python logger instead
LOG = "../SMSSender.py.log"
if os.path.exists(LOG) is False:
        f = open(LOG, "w")
        f.close()
LOG = open(LOG, "a")
```

To write entries, you can simply use LOG.write(message) to write the string message to the log file.
The SMSSender app uses a function to write messages both to the terminal and to the log file. Here's
the code:

```
def log(self, message):
    """ Log and print messages

    message -- Message to log
    """
    LOG.write(message)
    print message
```

With the log function defined, you can then use a statement like this:

```
self.log("Selected filename %s " % filename)
```

Logging is an important tool to keep in your toolbox when creating any kind of service application.
It will come in really handy later when your program stops working and you need to see what was going
on at the time. Maybe you write perfect code that never breaks, but that's not always the case for me.

Location-based Actions

There are probably some locations you frequent that you definitely want your phone silenced when
you're there. Church might be one of those locations or maybe a nursing home, hospital, or library. You
can create a script much like the sensor-based actions that will detect your location and take specific
action. What you'll need to know will be the GPS coordinates of the location.

To make this script work, we'll need a few helper functions to calculate distance from present
location to the "special" location. For this search, you might want to give the http://stackoverflow.com
site a try. This site has a large number of coding questions asked and answered. Here's a code snippet
found on http://stackoverflow.com for using the Haversine formula to compute the distance between
two GPS points:

```
from math import *

def haversine(lon1, lat1, lon2, lat2):
    """
    Calculate the great circle distance between two points
    on the earth (specified in decimal degrees)
    """
    # convert decimal degrees to radians
    lon1, lat1, lon2, lat2 = map(radians, [lon1, lat1, lon2, lat2])
    # haversine formula
    dlon = lon2 - lon1
    dlat = lat2 - lat1
```

```
a = sin(dlat/2)**2 + cos(lat1) * cos(lat2) * sin(dlon/2)**2
c = 2 * atan2(sqrt(a), sqrt(1-a))
km = 6367 * c
return km
```

With that in hand, we now just need to write a short script to grab our current location and then call the Haversine function using our fixed location. If we're within a fixed distance (for example, less than 1,000 feet), we'll turn the phone's silent mode on.

```python
import android, time
droid = android.Android()

lat1 = 33.111111
lon1 = 90.000000

droid.startLocating()

time.sleep(15)
while True:
    loc = droid.readLocation().result
    if loc = {}:
        loc = getLastKnownLocation().result
    if loc != {}:
        try:
            n = loc['gps']
        except KeyError:
            n = loc['network']
    la = n['latitude']
    lo = n['longitude']

    if haversine(la, lo, lat1, lon1) < 1:
        droid.toggleRingerSilentMode(True)
    else:
        droid.toggleRingerSilentMode(False)
```

Time-based Actions

Here's a handy script to set your phone to silent at a specific time of day and then turn the ringer back on at another time. Think of it as your do-not-disturb-while-I'm-sleeping script.

```python
""" Silences the phone between set hours

Meant for use on Android phones with the SL4A application
"""

# Created by Christian Blades (christian.blades@docblades.com) - Mon Mar 08, 2010

import android
import datetime
from time import sleep
```

```python
# MIN_HOUR and MAX_HOUR take an integer value between 0 and 23
# 12am == 0 and 1pm == 13
MIN_HOUR = 23
MAX_HOUR = 6

if MIN_HOUR > 23 or MIN_HOUR < 0 or MAX_HOUR > 23 or MAX_HOUR < 0:
    # If the min and max values are out of range, raise an error
    raise ValueError("0 <= (MIN_HOUR|MAX_HOUR) <= 23")

d_now = datetime.datetime.now

d_min = d_now().replace(hour=MIN_HOUR, minute=0, second=0)
d_max = d_now().replace(hour=MAX_HOUR, minute=0, second=0)

a_day = datetime.timedelta(days=1)

droid = android.Android()

def td_to_seconds(td):
    """ Convert a timedelta to seconds """
    return td.seconds + (td.days * 24 * 60 * 60)

def advance_times():
    """ Advance for the following day """
    d_min = d_min + a_day
    d_max = d_max + a_day
    return

def wait_for(dt):
    """ Wait until dt """
    sleep(td_to_seconds(dt - d_now()))

def main_loop():
    """
    Infinite loop that silences and unsilences the phone on schedule

    1. Wait for silent time
    2. Silence the phone
    3. Wait for awake time
    4. Turn on the ringer
    5. Advance the min and max to the following day
    6. Repeat

    NOTE: Must start during a loud period
    """
    while True:
        wait_for(d_min)
        droid.makeToast("Goodnight")
        droid.setRingerSilent(True)
        wait_for(d_max)
```

```python
        droid.makeToast("Good morning")
        droid.setRingerSilent(False)
        advance_times()

t_now = d_now()

if MAX_HOUR < MIN_HOUR:
    # Do a little extra processing if we're going from
    # a larger hour to a smaller (ie: 2300 to 0600)
    if t_now.hour <= d_min.hour and t_now.hour < d_max.hour:
        # If it's, say, 0200 currently and we're going from 2300 to 0600
        # Make the 2300 minimum for the previous night
        d_min = d_min - a_day
    elif t_now.hour >= d_min.hour and t_now.hour > d_max.hour:
        # In this case, it's 0900 and we're going from 2300 to 0600
        # Make the maximum for the next morning
        d_max = d_max + a_day

print "Now: " + t_now.ctime()
print "Min: " + d_min.ctime()
print "Max: " + d_max.ctime()

if t_now >= d_min and t_now < d_max:
    # Is it silent time now?
    # If so, do the silent stuff, then enter the loop
    droid.makeToast("Goodnight")
    droid.setRingerSilent(True)
    wait_for(d_max)
    droid.setRingerSilent(False)
    advance_times()

main_loop()
```

Elapsed Time-based Triggers

Creating scripts that trigger after an elapsed amount of time or at a specific time is pretty simple. Here's a code snippet that simply prints a message every ten seconds:

```python
import android, time

droid = android.Android()

# make Toast every ten seconds.
while True:
    droid.makeToast('New Toast')
    time.sleep(10)
```

With that idea as a starting point, you can build all kinds of scripts. What if you want to build a few scripts that set a fixed timer to go off after an hour or maybe a chime to go off on the hour? There are a few things you need to do before you get too far here. First, you'll need a sound to play for your alarm. A quick Google search for alarm sounds turns up all kinds of results. I found a good collection at the soundjax.com web site. Many of these were in the .wav format. Fortunately, your Android device will play .wav files with no problems.

We'll use the mediaPlay API function to actually play the sound. You can test this out on the emulator if you want. First, you need to create a directory to hold your sound files and then push the sound file to the device with the adb push command as follows:

```
adb shell mkdir /sdcard/sounds
adb push alarm.wav /sdcard/sounds/
```

From there, the script is pretty simple as it just uses the Python Standard Library time.sleep routine to go to sleep for an hour and then play the sound. Here's the script:

```
import android
from time import sleep

droid = android.Android()

# This script will simply sleep for an hour and then play an alarm
droid.makeToast('Alarm set for 1 hour from now')
time.sleep(3600)
droid.mediaPlay('file:///sdcard/sounds/alarm.wav')
```

A slight variation on the elapsed time theme is to perform an action at fixed intervals, such as send an SMS containing current location information at the top and bottom of every hour. This could be useful for tracking someone's whereabouts without the need for an expensive service. Sending an SMS requires a single line of code, as in the following:

```
droid.smsSend('8005551234','Test from Android')
```

To add code to get the present location, you first have to call the startLocating function to begin gathering location information. Next, you call readLocation to actually read in your present position, and finally call stopLocating to turn the location function off. We'll add in a 15-second delay to give the GPS a little time to settle if it's turned on. If we don't have GPS signal, we'll use the current position based on information from the network. Here's what the code looks like:

```
droid = android.Android()
droid.startLocating()
time.sleep(15)
loc = droid.readLocation()
droid.stopLocating()

if 'gps' in loc.result:
    lat = str(loc.result['gps']['latitude'])
    lon = str(loc.result['gps']['longitude'])
else:
    lat = str(loc.result['network']['latitude'])
    lon = str(loc.result['network']['longitude'])
```

```
now = str(datetime.datetime.now())
outString = 'I am here: ' + now + ' ' + lat + ' ' + lon

droid.smsSend('8005551234', outstring)
```

FTP File Sync Tool

Keeping files or directories in sync between two or more machines is one of those tasks that you can't do without once you start using it. There are many ways to accomplish this task using any number of commercial programs. One way to sync files using SL4A is to use an FTP server. Getting an FTP server installed and configured on Linux, Mac OS X, and Windows is pretty straightforward. I'll outline the steps for you here.

On Mac OS X, you'll need to open the System Preferences utility by clicking the Apple symbol in the upper-right corner of the screen and selecting Preferences. You should see a window like the one in Figure 6-6.

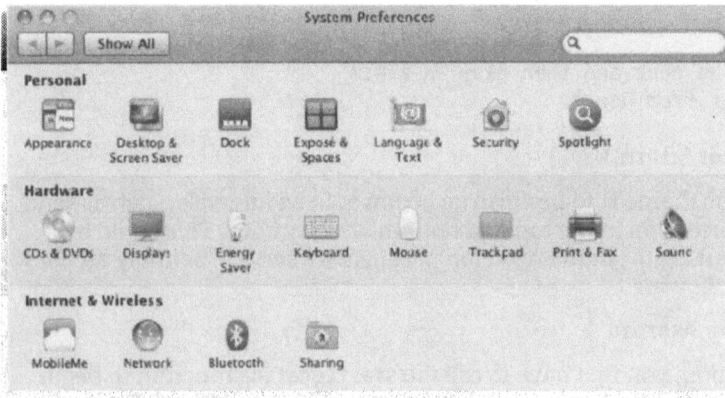

Figure 6-6. *Mac OS X System Preferences screen*

FTP services are a part of the Sharing preferences, so open up that folder by clicking the icon. You will see another window, as shown in Figure 6-7.

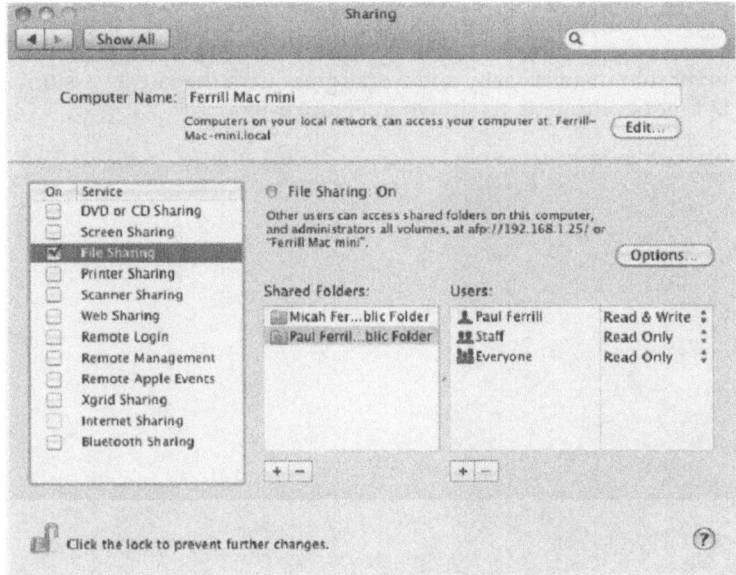

Figure 6-7. *Mac OS X file sharing preferences*

Next, find the File Sharing entry in the Service list and make sure that the On check box is selected (refer to Figure 6-7). Finally, click the Options button above the list of users to bring up the File Sharing Options window, as shown in Figure 6-8.

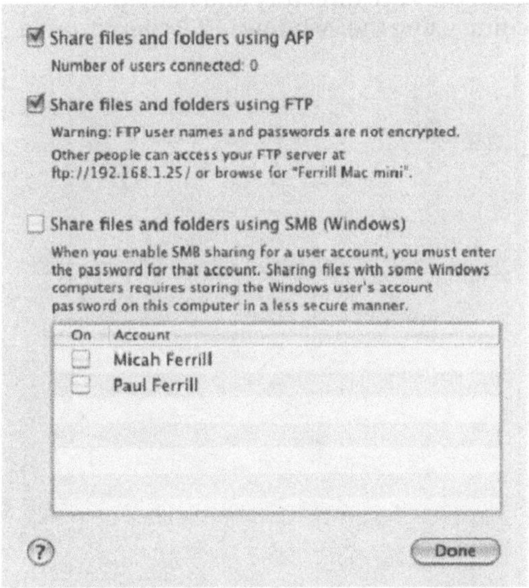

Figure 6-8. *Mac OS X file sharing preferences*

Clicking Share Files and Folders Using FTP will actually start the FTP server. You'll need a user account on the Mac machine in order to access the FTP server remotely. On Linux, I use a program called vsftpd. It's a freely available FTP server that installs easily and works great with the latest version of Ubuntu. To install it, you use a single **apt-get** command, as shown in Figure 6-9.

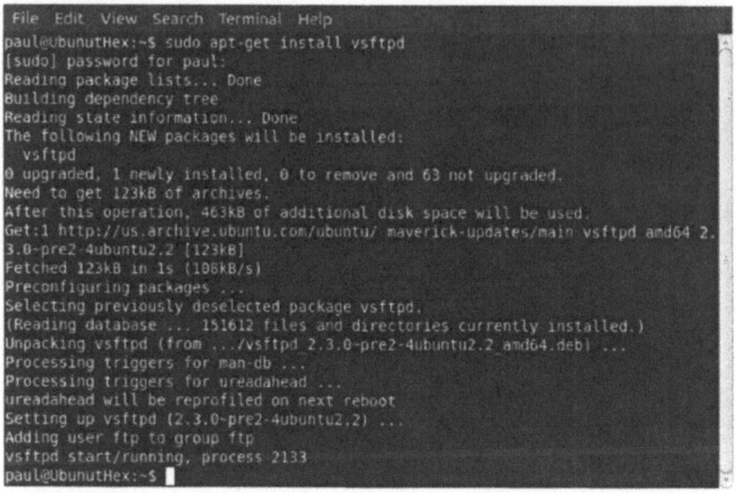

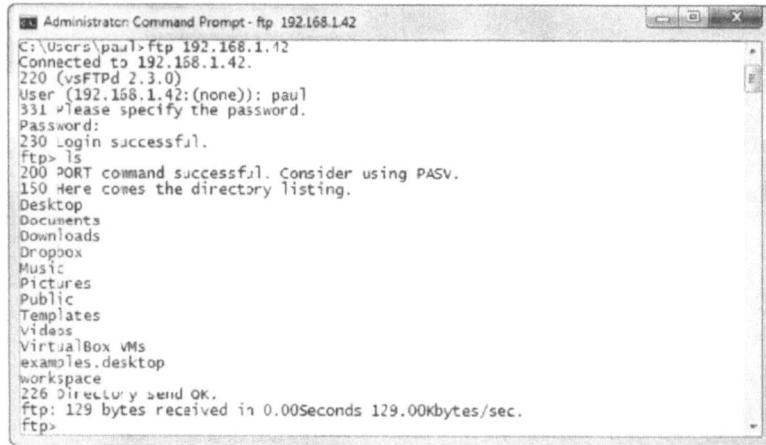

Figure 6-9. *Installation of vsftpd from Terminal window in Ubuntu 10.11*

The program will start automatically once the download finishes. You shouldn't have to change anything with the configuration because things like anonymous connections are disabled by default. If you should want to examine the configuration file, it's located in the **/etc** directory and named **vsftpd.conf**. Figure 6-10 shows connecting to the Linux machine using the Windows FTP client from a command prompt.

Figure 6-10. *Connecting to vsftp from a Windows command prompt*

On Windows, enable the FTP server from the Windows Features screen. The easiest way to get to that screen is to press the Windows icon key on your keyboard and type the words windows features into the search box. The first entry you should see under Control Panel is the line Turn Windows Features On Or Off. Clicking on this line will open the Windows Features panel, as seen in Figure 6-11.

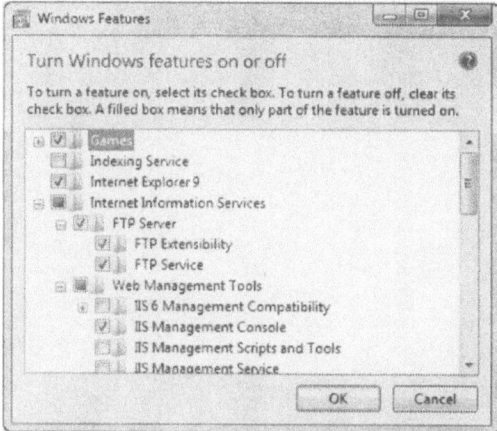

Figure 6-11. *Enabling the Windows FTP server from the Windows Features Control Panel tool*

With the Windows Feature screen open, you need to check two things to get your FTP server running: the FTP Service must be enabled, and you'll need the IIS Management Console in order to manage the FTP Service. When the install finishes, you should be able to launch the IIS Management Console and configure your FTP service.

For this, we'll use the same technique of pressing the Windows icon key on the keyboard and typing Internet into the search box. This will display several options, including Internet Explorer and Internet Information Services (IIS) Manager (see Figure 6-12). Next, you want to launch IIS Manger and to examine the current settings of the FTP service.

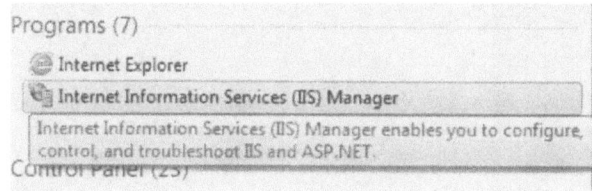

Figure 6-12. *Internet Information Services (IIS) Manager from Quick Launch menu*

Windows 7 has all the default settings set similar to `vsftpd` on Linux with anonymous logins disabled. There are a number of other configuration settings that you can adjust from the IIS Manager console, as shown in Figure 6-13.

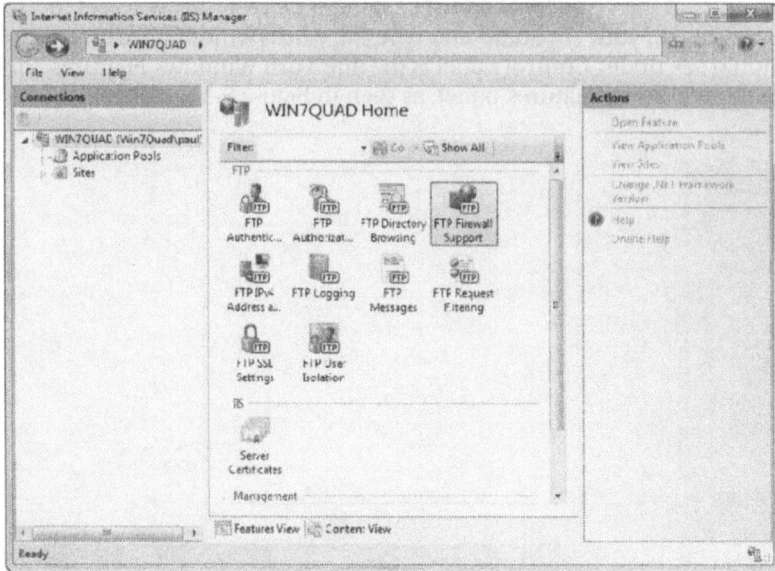

Figure 6-13. *Internet Information Services (IIS) Manager screen*

Once you have the server software enabled, you'll need to actually create a site for the FTP service to use. This is done by either right-clicking on the Sites folder in the left pane or by selecting the Sites folder and clicking on the Add Ftp Site line in the Actions pane. You'll see several dialog boxes to guide you through setting up a new FTP site. The first dialog box prompts for a name and physical location for the files (see Figure 6-14).

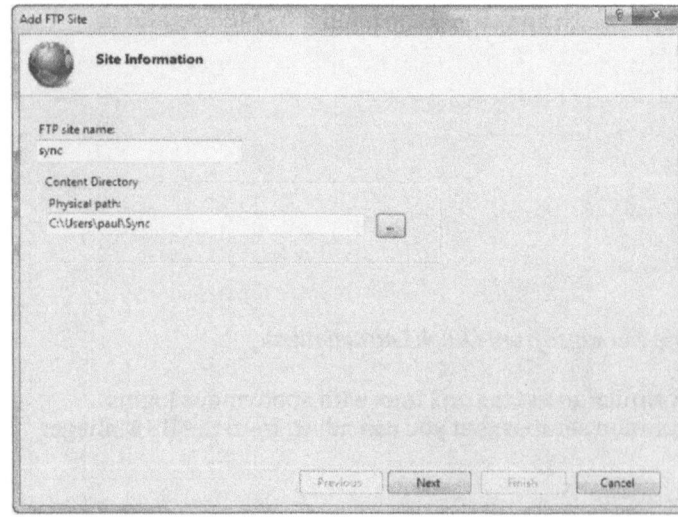

Figure 6-14. *FTP Site Information dialog box*

When you click Next, you'll see a dialog box like the one in Figure 6-15. This is where you assign the FTP server to a specific IP address (in this case, the IP address of the machine) and set the SSL settings. We won't need SSL encryption because this will run only on a local network.

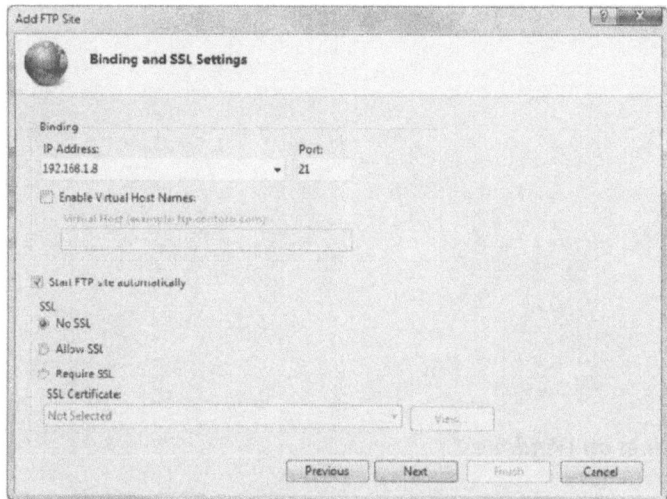

Figure 6-15. *FTP Site Bindings and SSL Settings*

Clicking Next again will take you to a final dialog box, in which you must configure the authentication rules. Because you will require a login, give full access to any authenticated user, as shown in Figure 6-16.

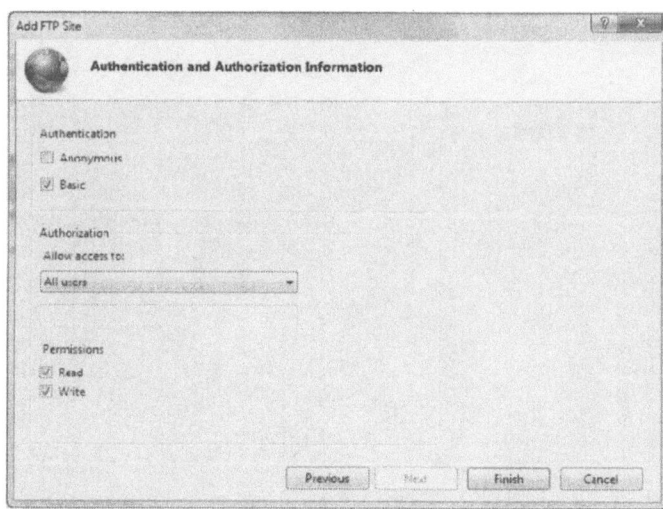

Figure 6-16. *FTP Site authentication settings*

The last thing you'll need to do in Windows 7 is change your firewall settings to allow FTP connections. This can be done in a command window with administrator privileges, as shown in Figure 6-17.

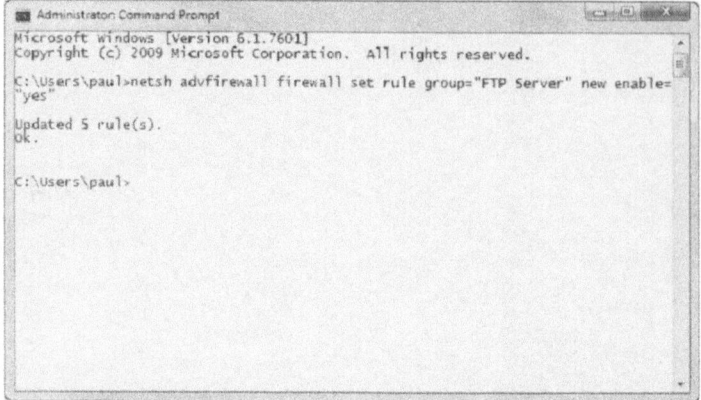

Figure 6-17. *Command to modify firewall settings on Windows 7*

Getting an FTP server configured on Windows is obviously a little more tedious than with Linux or Mac OS X. There are other third-party FTP server programs you can use, but I wanted to show you how to get it working with the basic OS. If you've done everything right, you should see your FTP site in the IIS Manager screen with a status of Started, as shown in Figure 6-18.

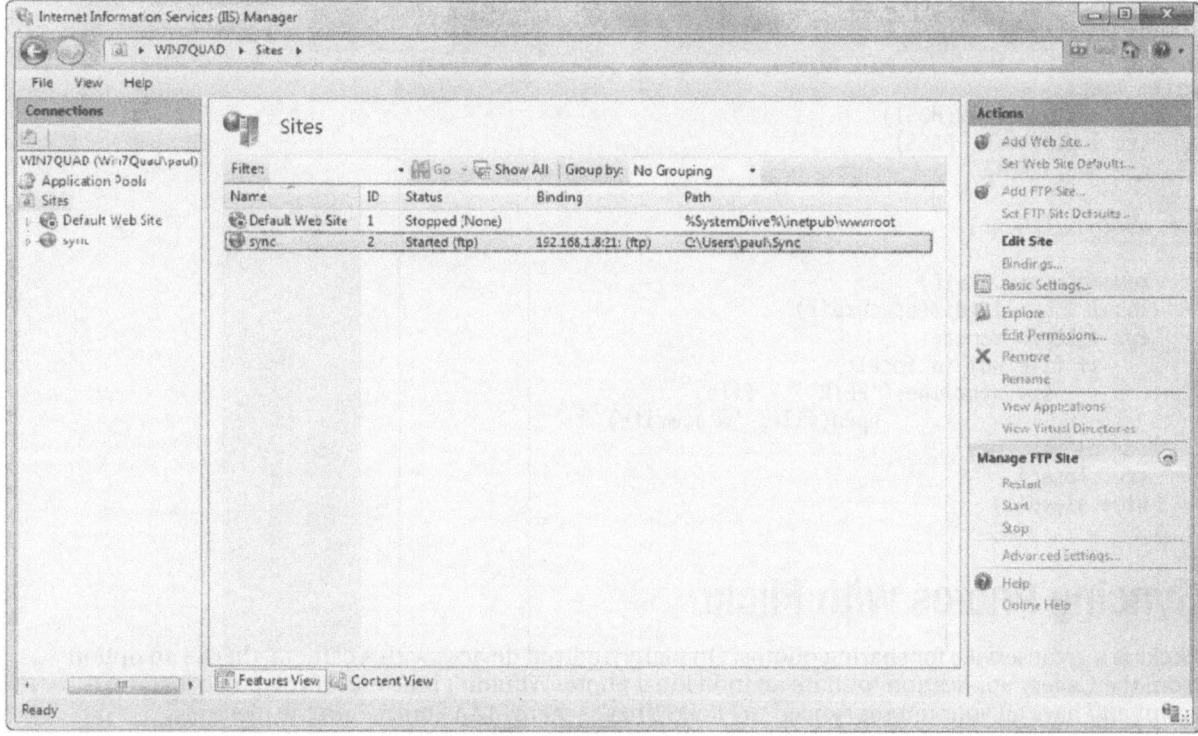

Figure 6-18. IIS Manager showing sync FTP site started

Now that we have the server portion out of the way, we can proceed with building a little client tool using SL4A. The good news is that the Python Standard Library provides an **ftplib** module for building client-side code, so you don't have to go looking for anything. Using the **ftplib** module is very straightforward, consisting mainly of identifying a target system (**HOST**) and the user credentials needed to log in. The meat of the code keeps two directories in sync by comparing the listings of files in each. As written, the sync is one way from the device to the remote server, but you could modify that without a lot of extra coding.

Here's the script:

```
import ftplib
import time
import os

import android
droid = android.Android()

HOST = '192.168.1.81'
USER = 'user'
PASS = 'pass'
REMOTE = 'phone-sync'
LOCAL = '/sdcard/sl4a/scripts/ftp-sync'
```

```python
if not os.path.exists(LOCAL):
    os.makedirs(LOCAL)

while True:
    srv = ftplib.FTP(HOST)
    srv.login(USER, PASS)
    srv.cwd(REMOTE)

    os.chdir(LOCAL)

    remote = srv.nlst()
    local = os.listdir(os.curdir)
    for file in remote:
        if file not in local:
            srv.storlines('RETR ' + file,
                          open(file, 'w').write)

    srv.close()
    time.sleep(1)
```

Syncing Photos with Flickr

Flickr is a great service for sharing photos. On many Android devices with a camera, there's an option from the Gallery application to share an individual photo. Wouldn't it be nice if you could just run a script and have all your photos synced to Flickr? That's where SL4A comes into the picture.

Finding code to do the hard work is another simple Google search away. While there are a number of options out there, I settled on one named uploader.py. It's been around for awhile and was referenced by several blog posts. If you choose to use this code, you'll also need a file named xmltramp.py. This code provides a number of XML functions used by uploader.py. It's not a bad idea to test out the code on your desktop before you try to use it on your Android device. This is a good idea mainly for going through the process of authorizing your application with Flickr.

The first time you actually run the code, you'll be presented with a Yahoo login screen, as shown in Figure 6-19.

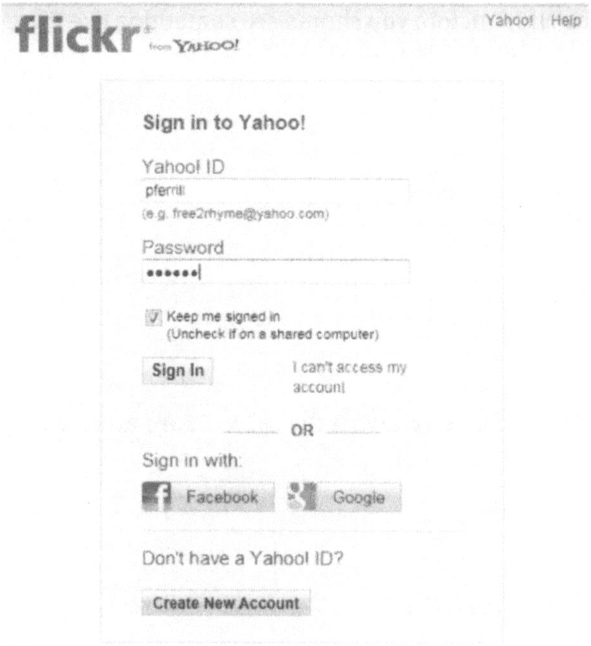

Figure 6-19. Yahoo Flickr login screen

Next, you'll be presented with a page asking you to authorize the uploader.py program to communicate with your Flickr account. That screen will look something like Figure 6-20.

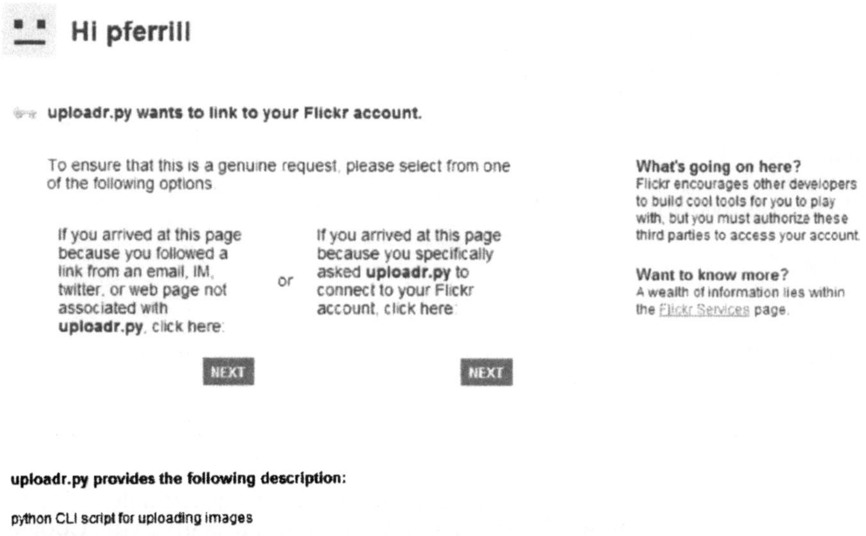

Hi pferrill

uploadr.py wants to link to your Flickr account.

To ensure that this is a genuine request, please select from one of the following options

If you arrived at this page because you followed a link from an email, IM, twitter, or web page not associated with **uploadr.py**, click here:

or

If you arrived at this page because you specifically asked **uploadr.py** to connect to your Flickr account, click here:

NEXT   NEXT

What's going on here?
Flickr encourages other developers to build cool tools for you to play with, but you must authorize these third parties to access your account.

Want to know more?
A wealth of information lies within the Flickr Services page.

uploadr.py provides the following description:

python CLI script for uploading images

Figure 6-20. Flickr authorization screen

You'll have at least one more screen after clicking NEXT before you should see something like Figure 6-21, letting you know that your application has been authorized to connect with Flickr.

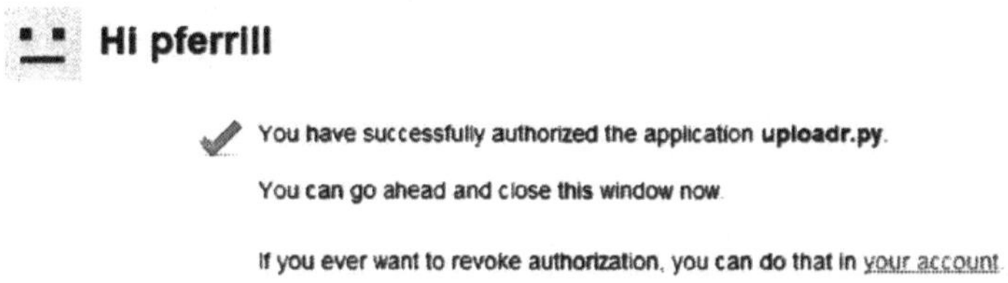

⚈⚈ Hi pferrill

✔ You have successfully authorized the application **uploadr.py**.

You can go ahead and close this window now.

If you ever want to revoke authorization, you can do that in your account.

Figure 6-21. *Successful authorization screen*

The code that actually uploads the image is pretty simple. Here's what the **uploadImage** function looks like:

```python
def uploadImage( self, image ):
    if ( not self.uploaded.has_key( image ) ):
        print "Uploading ", image , "...",
        try:
            photo = ('photo', image, open(image,'rb').read())
            d = {
                api.token    : str(self.token),
                api.perms    : str(self.perms),
                "tags"       : str( FLICKR["tags"] ),
                "is_public"  : str( FLICKR["is_public"] ),
                "is_friend"  : str( FLICKR["is_friend"] ),
                "is_family"  : str( FLICKR["is_family"] )
            }
            sig = self.signCall( d )
            d[ api.sig ] = sig
            d[ api.key ] = FLICKR[ api.key ]
            url = self.build_request(api.upload, d, (photo,))
            xml = urllib2.urlopen( url ).read()
            res = xmltramp.parse(xml)
            if ( self.isGood( res ) ):
                print "successful."
                self.logUpload( res.photoid, image )
            else :
                print "problem.."
                self.reportError( res )
        except:
            print str(sys.exc_info())
```

Syncing with Google Docs

Google Docs is a great way to create spreadsheets or word processing documents from virtually anywhere you have Internet access and a web browser. One idea for a background task involving Google Docs and Python is an automatic call log sync tool. This tool would run once a day and update a spreadsheet in Google Docs with your activity of the day. We'll use a few new techniques here to access an account on Google Docs and do the spreadsheet append by first downloading the current month's spreadsheet and then appending the entries for the current day. Finally, the new spreadsheet will be uploaded back to Google Docs.

To start, we'll use the script from Chapter 5 to get a copy of today's calls. Here's what that snippet looks like:

```
myconst = droid.getConstants("android.provider.CallLog$Calls").result
calls=droid.queryContent(myconst["CONTENT_URI"],["name","number","duration"]).result
for call in calls:
```

This code snippet will insert a new line into your Google Docs spreadsheet:

```
import time
import gdata.spreadsheet.service
email = 'youraccount@gmail.com'
password = 'yourpassword'
weight = '180'
spreadsheet_key = 'pRoiw3us3wh1FyEip46wYtW'
# All spreadsheets have worksheets. I think worksheet #1 by default always
# has a value of 'od6'
worksheet_id = 'od6'
spr_client = gdata.spreadsheet.service.SpreadsheetsService()
spr_client.email = email
spr_client.password = password
spr_client.source = 'Example Spreadsheet Writing Application'
spr_client.ProgrammaticLogin()
# Prepare the dictionary to write
dict = {}
dict['date'] = time.strftime('%m/%d/%Y')
dict['time'] = time.strftime('%H:%M:%S')
dict['weight'] = weight
print dict
entry = spr_client.InsertRow(dict, spreadsheet_key, worksheet_id)
if isinstance(entry, gdata.spreadsheet.SpreadsheetsList):
  print "Insert row succeeded."
else:
  print "Insert row failed."

>>> millis = int(msgs.result[0]['date'])/1000
>>> strtime = datetime.datetime.fromtimestamp(millis)
>>> strtime
```

Figure 6-22 shows what our document looks like in Google docs.

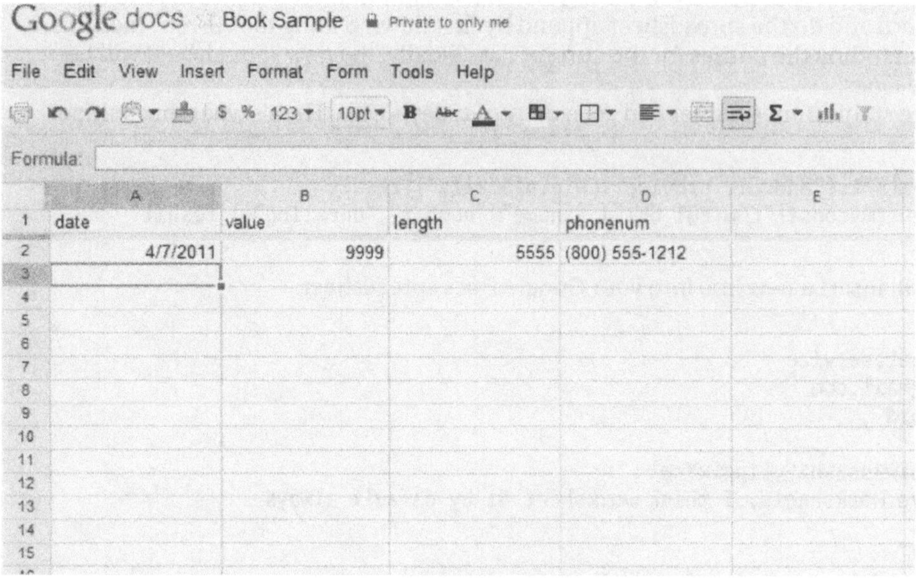

Figure 6-22. *Google Docs spreadsheet with call log data*

A Startup Launcher

Now that I've given you plenty of ideas for little service scripts, let's finish up the chapter with a launcher app that will combine some of the ideas such as logging and launching background scripts to bring it all together. You could use this script to launch other non-SL4A applications as well if you know the intent or activity name.

Here's the final script:

```
import android

STARTUP_SCRIPTS = (
    'facedown.py',
    'logGPS.py',
    'silentnight.py'
)

droid = android.Android()

LOG = "../logtest.py.log"
if os.path.exists(LOG) is False:
        f = open(LOG, "w")
        f.close()
LOG = open(LOG, "a")
```

```
for script in STARTUP_SCRIPTS:
    extras = {"com.googlecode.android_scripting.extra.SCRIPT_PATH":
            "/sdcard/sl4a/scripts/%s" % script}
    myintent = droid.makeIntent(
            "com.googlecode.android_scripting.action.LAUNCH_BACKGROUND_SCRIPT",
            None, None, extras, None,
            "com.googlecode.android_scripting",
            "com.googlecode.android_scripting.activity.ScriptingLayerServiceLauncher").result
    droid.startActivityIntent(myintent)
    LOG.write("Starting %s\n" % script)
```

The last thing we'll add to the script launcher will be an additional script that will open a text file and read from a list of events that need to be alarmed. It's pretty simple and will be one of the scripts that our startup launcher will load.

Here's the code:

```
import time

import android

droid = android.Android()

SCHEDULE = '/sdcard/sl4a/scripts/schedule.txt'

# Parse the schedule into a dict.
alerts = dict()
for line in open(SCHEDULE, 'r').readlines():
    line = line.strip()
    if not line: continue
    t, msg = line.split(' ', 1)

    alerts[t] = msg

# Check the time periodically and handle alarms.
while True:
    t = time.strftime('%H:%M')
    if t in alerts:
        droid.vibrate()
        droid.makeToast(alerts[t])
        del alerts[t]

    time.sleep(5)
```

The schedule.txt text file will contain any number of lines with a time and a message string. Here's a sample of what that might look like:

```
17:00 Time to head home!
21:00 Put the trash out
22:00 Set the alarm
```

Notice that all times must use the 24-hour format. Now we have a way to launch any number of different scripts at startup to turn your Android device into a powerful notification tool.

Summary

This chapter walks you through a number of examples demonstrating how to automate tasks that run in the background using SL4A and Python.

Here's a list of takeaways for this chapter:

- **Launching scripts on boot:** With the new OnBoot application, you can set any SL4A script to start every time your device boots. Use this function only after you've thoroughly tested your script.

- **Taking action based on sensors**: Any running script has access to the full sensory capability of the Android device, and you can take actions based on any sensor input.

- **Time-based actions**: You can use the standard Python timer functions to create time-based scripts. This one's really a no-brainer as long as you don't set up an infinite timer. Remember that you can kill any SL4A script from the notifications screen if you do create an "infinite looping" application.

CHAPTER 7

Python Scripting Utilities

This chapter will take a look at how to use Python to accomplish different utility tasks with SL4A. On a typical PC, these would fall into the command-line utility class of programs.

Note The version of SL4A used when writing this chapter was based on Python 2.6.2. All examples in this chapter were tested with Python 2.6.4 on a Windows 7 64-bit machine and on an Android 2.2–based emulator.

Time to dive in. Here's a list of what this chapter will examine:

- Python libraries and how to use them
- E-mail–based applications
- Location-based applications
- Web servers for transferring files

Python Libraries

There are an enormous number of libraries available for the Python language to accomplish everything from manipulating MP3 ID3 tags to reading and writing EXIF data inside JPEG images. The trick to using these on your SL4A project is to get them installed on your target device. If the library is written entirely in Python, you should be able to use it without any issues. Things become a little more difficult if the library is actually a wrapper around a binary module, as is the case with any MP3 tool based on the open source Lame project. While there is a way to get a binary module recompiled and targeted for the ARM architecture, it's not a trivial task.

Other challenges to using existing libraries come from the way they are typically distributed. There may be additional dependencies needed as well. For most, you'll find a setup.py file that you run from a terminal window with a command like this one:

```
python setup.py install
```

This command will typically install the library into the Python site-packages directory. The only problem with this approach on an Android device is that the site-packages directory is read-only on a nonrooted device. There are a fair number of libraries that are self-contained in a single .py file. If that's the case, then all you have to do is copy the file to the device and into the correct directory.

This is probably a good point to talk about what's in the .zip files that are downloaded when you install Python on your device. If you paid attention when the Python interpreter was installing, you would have seen three files go by. If you missed that, you can still see the files with an adb command like the one shown in Figure 7-1.

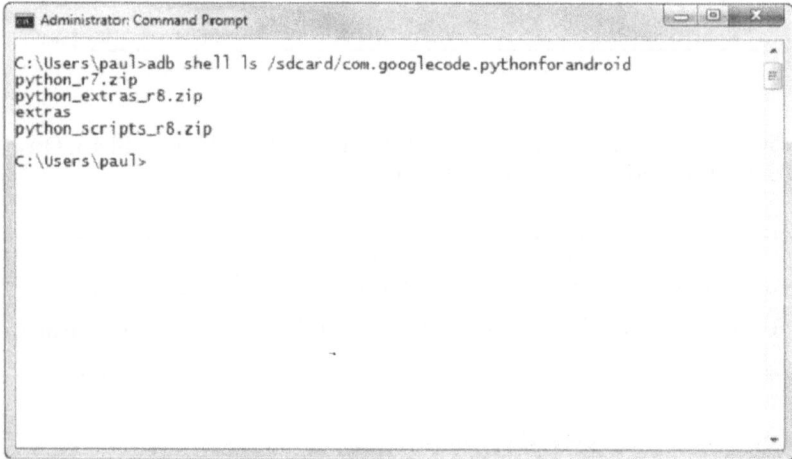

Figure 7-1. *Contents of Python directory on device*

The **python_r7.zip** file contains the basic Python files needed to execute the interpreter. You'll find ten sample programs in the **python_scripts_r8.zip** file that you can use for your learning. The **test.py** file is a good place to start because it comprises a test suite for the different dialog calls. Finally, the **python_extras_r8.zip** file contains a number of helper functions and libraries the project maintainers felt would be helpful to Python developers.

You can download a copy of the **python_extras_r8.zip** file to your development workstation with this command:

```
adb pull /sdcard/com.googlecode.pythonforandroid/python_extras_r8.zip
```

This file holds the contents of what you would expect to find in the site-packages directory of a typical Python installation. If you open up the zip file, you'll see a list of files and directories similar to Figure 7-2.

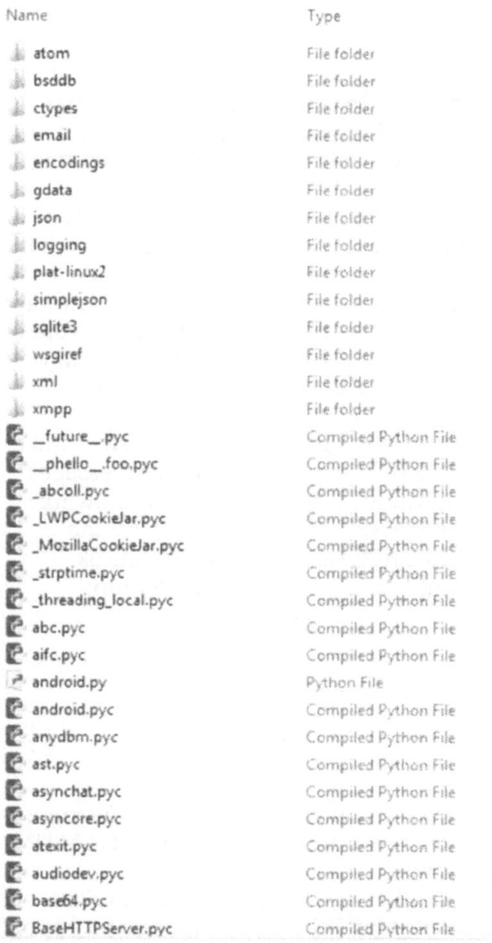

Name	Type
atom	File folder
bsddb	File folder
ctypes	File folder
email	File folder
encodings	File folder
gdata	File folder
json	File folder
logging	File folder
plat-linux2	File folder
simplejson	File folder
sqlite3	File folder
wsgiref	File folder
xml	File folder
xmpp	File folder
__future__.pyc	Compiled Python File
__phello__.foo.pyc	Compiled Python File
_abcoll.pyc	Compiled Python File
_LWPCookieJar.pyc	Compiled Python File
_MozillaCookieJar.pyc	Compiled Python File
_strptime.pyc	Compiled Python File
_threading_local.pyc	Compiled Python File
abc.pyc	Compiled Python File
aifc.pyc	Compiled Python File
android.py	Python File
android.pyc	Compiled Python File
anydbm.pyc	Compiled Python File
ast.pyc	Compiled Python File
asynchat.pyc	Compiled Python File
asyncore.pyc	Compiled Python File
atexit.pyc	Compiled Python File
audiodev.pyc	Compiled Python File
base64.pyc	Compiled Python File
BaseHTTPServer.pyc	Compiled Python File

Figure 7-2. Contents of Python extras .zip file

If you're using Windows for your development machine, you will find the equivalent directory in C:\Python26\Lib\site-packages. There is a way, when using Python on an Android device, to add a local path to the PYTHONPATH variable. This requires two lines of code, thus:

```
import sys
sys.path.append('/sdcard/sl4a/mylib')
```

In this example, the directory /sdcard/sl4a/mylib contains the files you wish to make available to Python on your device. The absolute easiest way to use a Python library comes in the form of an egg. Python supports a zip-compressed file format for libraries using .egg as the file extension. It's similar in concept to .jar files in Java. All you have to do to use a Python .egg file is copy it to the appropriate directory on the device. This can be accomplished with the adb push command like this:

```
adb push library.egg /sdcard/com.googlecode.pythonforandroid/extras/python
```

E-mail–Based Applications

Sending an e-mail message is something most of us just take for granted. In the world of mobile e-mail, we probably have the Blackberry device to thank for bringing it to you wherever you may be. Android devices have e-mail by default and tight integration with Google's Gmail. This makes the idea of writing utility scripts that send e-mail messages very appealing.

There is a sendEmail API call available through the SL4A Android facade. This function takes three parameters: to_address, which is a comma-separated list of recipients, title, and message. From there it passes the information off to the default e-mail application. You must then use that application to actually send the message. If you happen to have more than one application registered on your device as handling e-mail, you'll also be prompted to choose which one to use. While that method certainly works, it really doesn't accomplish the task at hand. By that I mean you could use the built-in e-mail program but it would be tedious and what I really want is an automated way to send an e-mail. That's where Python comes to our rescue.

The library we'll use for this task is smtplib. It's part of the Python standard library so you don't have to do anything special to use it. We'll also take advantage of Gmail's SMTP service to send our messages through. In addition, we'll use the email library, which contains a number of helper functions allowing us to construct our message in the correct form. Last, we'll use the mimetypes library to help with the encoding of our message. The email library provides something called MIMEMultipart, which lets us define the different parts of an e-mail message. Here's how you would create a message in Python:

```
# Create an SMTP formatted message
msg = MIMEMultipart()
msg['Subject'] = 'Our Subject'
msg['To'] = 'receiver@host.net'
msg['From'] = 'sender@gmail.com'
msg.attach(MIMEText(body, 'plain'))
```

Most of the data used in the msg structure is of type string so it's a simple matter to create the main body of our message. Since Google requires authentication in order to send messages through its SMTP server, you will need to have a Gmail account in order to use this script.

Here's what communicating with the Google SMTP server looks like from the command line. To launch Python, you need to have a terminal window open on Linux or Mac OS X or a command prompt in Windows. From there you should be able to just type Python:

```
>>> smtpObj = smtplib.SMTP(smtp_server,smtp_port)
>>> smtpObj.starttls()
(220, '2.0.0 Ready to start TLS')
>>> smtpObj.ehlo()
(250, 'mx.google.com at your service, [72.148.19.136]\nSIZE 35651584\n8BITMIME\nAUTH↵
 LOGIN PLAIN XOAUTH\nENHANCEDSTATUSCODES')
>>> smtpObj.login(username,password)
(235, '2.7.0 Accepted')
>>> smtpObj.sendmail(username,to_addr,msg.as_string())
>>> smtpObj.close()
```

If you count the lines of code, you only need five to set up the message and six to send it. That's not bad in terms of code efficiency. You'll want to add some error-checking to the final script, but it shouldn't take many more lines to write a useful e-mail–sending tool. Now that we have the basis of creating a generic e-mail sender, what would be really useful to send? Why not all your SMS messages?

The SMS facade provides easy access to SMS messages either in bulk or one at a time. If you want to get everything, you should use **smsGetMessages**. Before we get too deep here, we should investigate what information is available for each SMS message. The first thing you can do is use the **smsGetAttributes** function to see what data you can retrieve. Here's what that looks like running on the emulator:

```
>>> pprint.pprint(droid.smsGetAttributes().result)
[u'_id',
 u'thread_id',
 u'address',
 u'person',
 u'date',
 u'protocol',
 u'read',
 u'status',
 u'type',
 u'reply_path_present',
 u'subject',
 u'body',
 u'service_center',
 u'locked',
 u'error_code',
 u'seen']
```

Now that we know what's available we can use the **smsGetMessages** function to create a list and then iterate over that list, extracting only the information we're interested in. First, we need to create a few messages on the emulator for our use. This requires a little command-line magic using the ADB tool covered in Chapter 3. On Windows you must open a command window and type **telnet localhost 5554**. Figure 7-3 shows the telnet screen and the commands required to generate a few SMS messages.

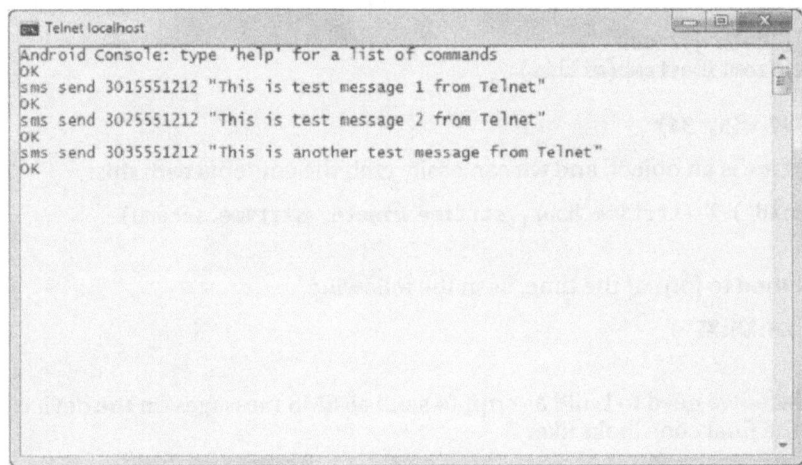

Figure 7-3. *Using telnet to send SMS messages to the emulator*

Now we can use the `smsGetMessages` function to read all the messages by passing in a `False` parameter to indicate we don't want just the unread messages. In reality, it doesn't matter in this case since all these messages were just received, and we'll get the same result either way.

```
>>> msgs = droid.smsGetMessages(False)
>>> pprint.pprint(msgs.result)
[{u'_id': u'3',
  u'address': u'3035551212',
  u'body': u'"This is a another test message from Telnet"',
  u'date': u'1297814134176',
  u'read': u'0'},
 {u'_id': u'2',
  u'address': u'3025551212',
  u'body': u'"This is test message 2 from Telnet"',
  u'date': u'1297814117225',
  u'read': u'0'},
 {u'_id': u'1',
  u'address': u'3015551212',
  u'body': u'"This is test message 1 from Telnet"',
  u'date': u'1297814100976',
  u'read': u'0'}]
```

It's worth noting at this point that the messages are exported in reverse chronological order. Another item worth noticing is the content of the messages. Even though the `smsGetAttributes` function showed us more possible fields, we only get **_id**, **address**, **body**, **date**, and **read** here. For SMS messages, the address is actually a phone number. The **date** field may look a little strange unless you know what you're looking at.

Here's where the Python **datetime** library comes to our aid. As it turns out, the **date** field is actually milliseconds since January 1. So, all we have to do is divide the **date** field by 1000 and pass that number to **datetime** like thus:

```
>>> millis = int(msgs.result[0]['date'])/1000
>>> strtime = datetime.datetime.fromtimestamp(millis)
>>> strtime
datetime.datetime(2011, 2, 15, 17, 55, 34)
```

The cool thing here is that `strtime` is an object, and we can easily grab the contents with this:

```
>>> print('Message time = %d:%d:%d') % (strtime.hour, strtime.minute, strtime.second)
Message time = 17:55:34
```

Even easier is the `strftime` method to format the time, as in the following:

```
>>> strtime.strftime("%m/%d/%y %H:%M:%S")
'02/15/11 17:55:34'
```

Now we should have all the pieces we need to build a script to send all SMS messages on the device to an e-mail address. Here's what the final code looks like:

```
import android, datetime, smtplib
from email.mime.multipart import MIMEMultipart
from email.mime.text import MIMEText

droid = android.Android()
```

```
smtp_server = 'smtp.gmail.com'
smtp_port = 587
mailto = 'paul'
mailfrom = 'paul'
password = 'password'

# Build our SMTP compatible message
msg = MIMEMultipart()
msg['Subject'] = 'SMS Message Export'
msg['To'] = mailto
msg['From'] = mailfrom

# Walk throu the SMS messages and add them to the message body
SMSmsgs = droid.smsGetMessages(False).result

body = ''
for message in SMSmsgs:
  millis = int(message['date'])/1000
  strtime = datetime.datetime.fromtimestamp(millis)
  body += strtime.strftime("%m/%d/%y %H:%M:%S") + ',' + message['address'] + ',' +↵
 message['body'] + '\n'

msg.attach(MIMEText(body, 'plain'))
smtpObj = smtplib.SMTP(smtp_server,smtp_port)
smtpObj.starttls()
smtpObj.login(mailfrom,password)
smtpObj.sendmail(mailfrom,mailto,msg.as_string())
smtpObj.close()
```

Figure 7-4 shows what the received message looks like in the Gmail web interface.

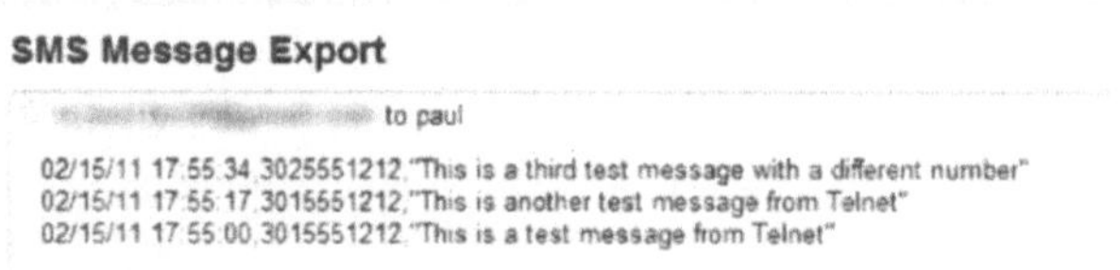

SMS Message Export

to paul

02/15/11 17:55:34,3025551212,"This is a third test message with a different number"
02/15/11 17:55:17,3015551212,"This is another test message from Telnet"
02/15/11 17:55:00,3015551212,"This is a test message from Telnet"

Figure 7-4. *E-mail message with SMS messages*

There are lots of other uses for a generic e-mail tool. The example shows you how to build up a message and then send it using smtpObj. The last thing we really should do for our sample script is add the option to delete all SMS messages once the e-mail has been sent. Here's a five-line script that will delete all SMS messages. Use it with care as it won't ask for any confirmation before it deletes them all:

```
import android
droid = android.Android()
msgids = droid.smsGetMessageIds(False).result
for id in msgids:
    droid.smsDeleteMessage(id)
```

Location-Aware Applications

One of the distinct advantages of mobile devices is the ability to know where you are. SL4A provides a location facade with a number of functions that work with or without a functioning GPS. This opens up a number of possibilities for applications that take advantage of this information. I'll take a look at several of these that you might find interesting, including a tweet of my location to track my travel.

Tweet My Location

This application will require a few external libraries to get the job done. We'll discuss the Twitter library later. The first thing we need to do is examine the data structure returned by the **readLocation** API call. Figure 7-5 shows an example of calling **readLocation** after a call to **startLocating**.

A few things need to be pointed out about the location information available from this call. The first thing you notice when you look at Figure 7-5 is that there are two types of location information available. **readLocation** returns a result object that uses a dictionary to encapsulate the position information. This dictionary object has two keys whose values are, in turn, dictionaries that have multiple key/value pairs containing the position information. To access the GPS-based latitude and longitude, therefore, you would use something like this:

```
lat = result.result['gps']['latitude']
lon = result.result['gps']['longitude']
```

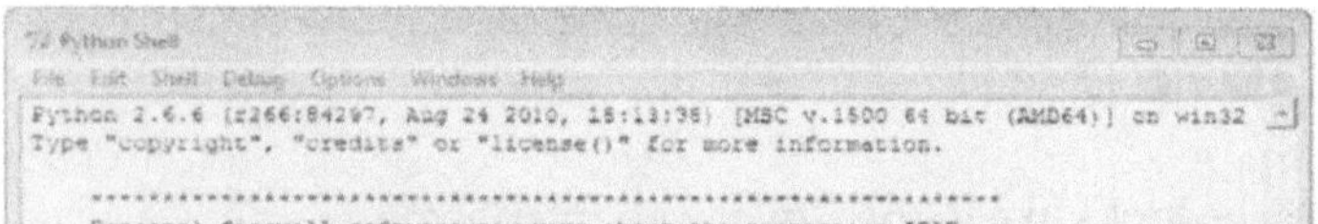

***Figure 7-5.** Example of readLocation API call*

The other key point here is that your device may not return a GPS location if GPS isn't currently enabled. In fact, if you try this code on the emulator, the result object will be empty. So, if you tried to read the GPS location with the preceding code and GPS was off, you'd get an error that would look something like this:

```
>>> lat = droid.readLocation().result['gps']
Traceback (most recent call last):
  File "<stdin>", line 1, in <module>
KeyError: 'gps'
```

In Python, you can check to see what keys are available in a dictionary using the keys method. The readLocation result with GPS off would look like the following:

```
>>> droid.readLocation().result.keys()
[u'network']
```

You can also use the keys method in a conditional, like so:

```
>>> if 'gps' in droid.readLocation().result:
        print 'gps'
    else:
        print 'network'
```

The next thing we need to investigate is communicating with Twitter. When you install the Python interpreter in SL4A, you get a number of libraries installed for you, including twitter.py. The bad news is that Twitter has started requiring a stronger authentication method for connecting to its API.

If you don't know what OAuth is, then you should probably find out. OAuth is an open protocol for secure API authorization. It basically involves multiple keys and a multistep authentication process. There's a community web site at oauth.net where you'll find a copy of the OAuth specification, documentation, and lots of sample code. Many public services, including Google, have begun to adopt and use OAuth as either the primary method of authentication, or at least an alternative.

If you've ever used a third-party Twitter application, you've probably already experienced the steps you must go through when authorizing that application. For this reason, we're going to use another library, tweepy, which is available from http://code.google.com/p/tweepy.

I'll assume at this point you already have a Twitter account and won't take you through the process of signing up. If you don't, just head on over to twitter.com and follow the instructions there. Once you have an account you'll be able to register a new application (http://twitter.com/apps/new). Figure 7-6 shows a screenshot of the registration page.

Register an Application

Application Icon:

Maximum size of 700k. JPG, GIF, PNG.

Browse...

Application Name: Apress Book Sample

Description: This will be a sample application for my upcoming Apress SL4A book.

Application Website: http://my.sampleapp.com

Where's your application's home page, where users can go to download or use it?

Organization:

Website:

The home page of your company or organization.

Application Type: ⦿ Client ◯ Browser

Does your application run in a Web Browser or a Desktop Client?

- Browser uses a Callback URL to return to your App after successfully authentication.

- Client prompts your user to return to your application after approving access.

Default Access type: ⦿ Read & Write ◯ Read-only

What type of access does your application need?
Note: @Anywhere applications require read & write access.

Use Twitter for login: ☑ Yes, use Twitter for login

Does your application intend to use Twitter for authentication?

Figure 7-6. Twitter application registration

At the bottom of the page there's a CAPTCHA box that you must enter correctly to get your app registered. There are a few caveats you should know about. First, you can't use Twitter in the name of your application. Second, you must enter a valid URL in the Application Website box. It doesn't have to be a real URL, but it does have to be in the proper format. With the form properly filled out and the CAPTCHA phrase entered, you're ready to click the Save button.

Once that's done, you'll get a page that looks something like Figure 7-7. You will need to copy and paste the codes you receive in the examples to follow.

Application Details

Apress Book Sample by

This will be a sample application for my upcoming Apress SL4A book.

created by Paul Ferrill - **read and write access by default**

| Edit Application Settings | Reset Consumer Key/Secret |

Consumer key

Consumer secret

Request token URL

http://twitter.com/oauth/request_token

Access token URL

http://twitter.com/oauth/access_token

Authorize URL

http://twitter.com/oauth/authorize

Figure 7-7. Twitter application details

The two things you will need in your application are the Consumer key and the Consumer secret. You can copy these fields and then paste them into another document for future reference. I just open Notepad on Windows and create a text file for saving this information. Now that we have the Consumer key and secret, we're ready to get connected to Twitter.

Our next step is to use the Consumer key and secret to obtain a corresponding Application key and secret. We'll use a little Python code and the IDLE console to obtain the needed Application information as follows:

```
>>> import tweepy
>>> CONSUMER_KEY = 'insert your Consumer key here'
>>> CONSUMER_SECRET = 'insert your Consumer secret here'
>>> auth = tweepy.OAuthHandler(CONSUMER_KEY, CONSUMER_SECRET)
>>> auth_url = auth.get_authorization_url()
>>> print 'Please authorize: ' + auth_url
```

This will display a URL you must copy and paste into a web browser in order to obtain the needed keys. The web page will look something like Figure 7-8.

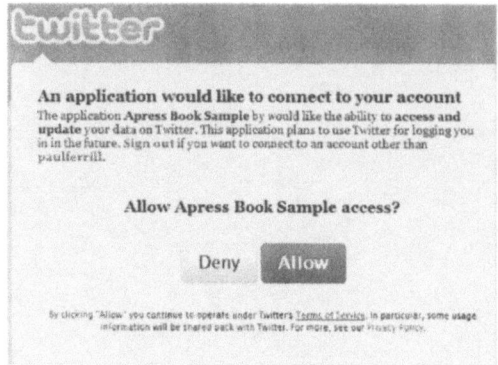

Figure 7-8. *Twitter Application Authorization*

When you click Allow, you'll be taken to the next page, as shown in Figure 7-9.

Figure 7-9. *Twitter PIN authorization code*

Now that we have a PIN code, we have just a few more lines of code to execute. Here's what the next steps would look like in IDLE:

```
>>> auth.get_access_token('type your PIN here')
<tweepy.oauth.OAuthToken object at 0x02C0CE90>
>>> print "ACCESS_KEY = '%s'" % auth.access_token.key
ACCESS_KEY = 'access key code'
>>> print "ACCESS_SECRET = '%s'" % auth.access_token.secret
ACCESS_SECRET = 'access secret code'
```

Copy the two Application codes and save them in the same text file you created for the Consumer codes. You'll need all four codes for authenticating and communicating with Twitter from here out. It's pretty simple to take these new codes and post an update to Twitter. In fact, you can do it with about six additional lines of code as follows:

```
>>> ACCESS_KEY = 'your just-obtained access key'
>>> ACCESS_SECRET = 'your just-obtained access secret'
>>> auth = tweepy.OAuthHandler(CONSUMER_KEY, CONSUMER_SECRET)
>>> auth.set_access_token(ACCESS_KEY, ACCESS_SECRET)
>>> api = tweepy.API(auth)
>>> api.update_status("Hello from the Apress Book Sample")
```

Figure 7-10 shows what this would look like if you went to **twitter.com** and looked at the timeline.

paulferrill Paul Ferrill
Hello from the Apress Book Sample
15 Feb

Figure 7-10. *Twitter timeline of Python message*

Now we have everything we need to write the **tweetmylocation** script. Putting together all of the pieces gives us this:

```
import android, datetime, time, tweepy

CONSUMER_KEY = 'my consumer key'
CONSUMER_SECRET = 'my consumer secret'

ACCESS_KEY = 'my access key'
ACCESS_SECRET = 'my access secret'

auth = tweepy.OAuthHandler(CONSUMER_KEY, CONSUMER_SECRET)
auth.set_access_token(ACCESS_KEY, ACCESS_SECRET)
api = tweepy.API(auth)

droid = android.Android()
droid.startLocating()
time.sleep(15)
loc = droid.readLocation()
droid.stopLocating()

if 'gps' in loc.result:
    lat = str(loc.result['gps']['latitude'])
    lon = str(loc.result['gps']['longitude'])
else:
    lat = str(loc.result['network']['latitude'])
    lon = str(loc.result['network']['longitude'])

now = str(datetime.datetime.now())
outString = 'I am here: ' + now + ' ' + lat + ' ' + lon

api.update_status(outString)
```

Figure 7-11 shows what the result of running the **tweetmylocation** script would look like if you went to **twitter.com** and looked at the timeline (with the exception of the fake GPS locations).

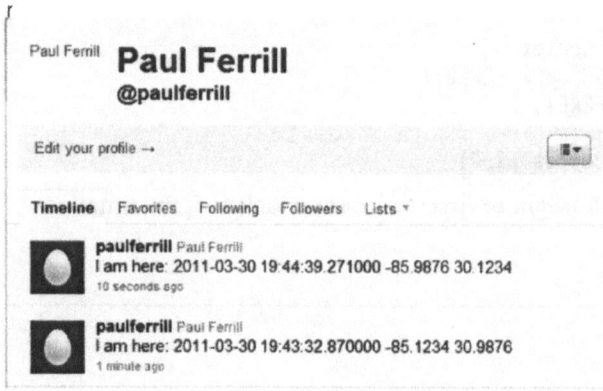

Paul Ferrill **Paul Ferrill**
@paulferrill

Edit your profile →

Timeline   Favorites   Following   Followers   Lists ▾

paulferrill Paul Ferrill
I am here: 2011-03-30 19:44:39.271000 -85.9876 30.1234
10 seconds ago

paulferrill Paul Ferrill
I am here: 2011-03-30 19:43:32.870000 -85.1234 30.9876
1 minute ago

Figure 7-11. Twitter timeline of location messages

Track My Travel

Now that we know how to use the location functions, it's a pretty simple task to query every so often and save that information to a file. This could be useful for such things as tracking how long and how far you travel in one day on your cross-country trip. To make this application work we're going to have to make a few basic assumptions. First, since this script will need the GPS and will be taking periodic location readings, it's probably going to need the device to be plugged into a charger, or else the battery will run dry in short order. Second, we're going to rely on a Python timer to schedule our measurements, which means that the script will be running continuously. While that's not a big deal, it's just another reason to have your device connected to a power source and not rely on the battery.

With those little details out of the way, let's talk about a few housekeeping items. It's a good programming practice to make as few assumptions about your environment as possible, so we'll try to follow that and configure everything we need in the script. First of all, we want to have GPS available for the most accurate location information. At present, you must manually turn GPS on, so we need to prompt the user to do that. Here's a little snippet that will issue a call to the **startLocating** API function and wait for the GPS to show up in the return from **readLocation**:

```
droid = android.Android()
droid.startLocating()

while not droid.readLocation()[1].has_key('gps') :
    print "Waiting on gps to turn on"
    time.sleep(1)
```

Next, we need the ability to write out a log containing time and location for later retrieval. The biggest thing here is picking a known directory on the device's sdcard or creating our own. Python's OS module makes these tasks easy. The simplest thing to do is to create our own directory for storing files. Choosing a name is probably the biggest decision at this point. To actually create the directory, we'll use **os.mkdir**. Here's what that might look like:

```
import os
os.mkdir('/sdcard/logs')
```

You could use the os.path.exists function to check for the directory before you make the call to os.mkdir. From a programming perspective, this makes more sense. Adding this in would give us the following:

```
if not os.path.exists('/sdcard/logs'):
    os.mkdir('/sdcard/logs')
```

Python does file I/O in much the same way as other programming languages. First, open a file for writing to obtain a file object. Make sure you pass the 'a' parameter to implicitly open the file for appending. If you don't, you'll just create a new file each time. Then write to the file using the write method on that file object. Here's a short snippet of what that might look like:

```
f = open('/sdcard/logs/logfile.txt','a')
f.write('First header line in file\n')
f.close()
```

Reading files with Python is even easier. If you want to open a file and read each line, you can use something like the following:

```
f = open('/sdcard/logs/logfile.txt')
for line in f:
    print line
f.close()
```

Python file objects are *iterable*, meaning you can read a file line by line with the for line if f: syntax. You could use this approach to read the log file and create an e-mail with all the entries. I'll leave that option up to the reader. That should be all we need to put this script together. Here's what the final version looks like:

```
import android, os, time, datetime

droid = android.Android()
droid.startLocating()

while not droid.readLocation()[1].has_key('gps') :
    print "Waiting on gps to turn on"
    time.sleep(1)

if not os.path.exists('/sdcard/logs'):
    os.mkdir('/sdcard/logs')

# Now we'll loop until the user closes the application

while True:
    loc = droid.readLocation()

    lat = str(loc.result['gps']['latitude'])
    lon = str(loc.result['gps']['longitude'])
    alt = str(loc.result['gps']['altitude'])
```

```
now = str(datetime.datetime.now())
f = open('/sdcard/logs/logfile.txt','a')
outString = now + ',' + lat + ',' + lon + ',' + alt + '\n'
f.write(outString)
print outString
f.close()

time.sleep(1)
```

Because we explicitly wait for the GPS in this script, there's no need to check for a gps entry to be in the results from **readLocation**. It's also not a bad practice to give the user some feedback when a program is running. In this case, we just print the same line out to the console that we write to the file. For testing purposes, we can use the **telnet** command as we did earlier to send simulated GPS information to the emulator. Figure 7-12 shows an example along with the help for the **geo fix** command.

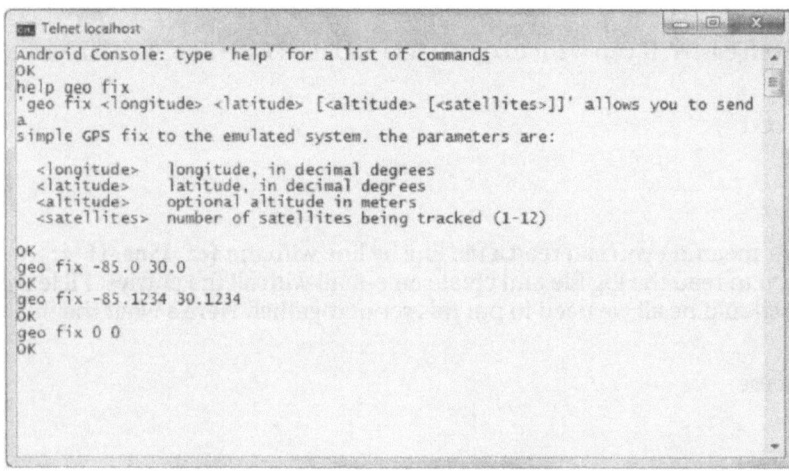

Figure 7-12. *Android console used to simulate GPS*

Here's a sample of a log file run using the emulator and the simulated GPS data using the Android console **geo fix** command:

```
2011-02-16 11:32:35.178488,30,-85,0
2011-02-16 11:32:36.287759,30,-85,0
2011-02-16 11:32:37.331069,30.1234,-85.1234,0
2011-02-16 11:32:38.449301,30.1234,-85.1234,0
2011-02-16 11:32:39.555303,30.1234,-85.1234,0
2011-02-16 11:32:40.639048,0,0,0
2011-02-16 11:32:41.749413,0,0,0
2011-02-16 11:32:42.849682,0,0,0
2011-02-16 11:32:43.936020,0,0,0
2011-02-16 11:32:45.041614,0,0,0
2011-02-16 11:32:46.106619,0,0,0
2011-02-16 11:32:47.181367,0,0,0
```

```
2011-02-16 11:32:48.297515,0,0,0
2011-02-16 11:32:49.374033,0,0,0
2011-02-16 11:32:50.509526,30.1,-85.0999983333,0
2011-02-16 11:32:51.612404,30.1,-85.0999983333,0
2011-02-16 11:32:52.727394,30.1,-85.0999983333,0
2011-02-16 11:32:53.838587,30.1,-85.0999983333,0
2011-02-16 11:32:54.977258,30.1,-85.0999983333,0
```

You can easily switch to the SL4A console screen from the notifications drop-down screen. You can also terminate the script from there by pressing the Menu button and choosing Stop All (see Figure 7-13).

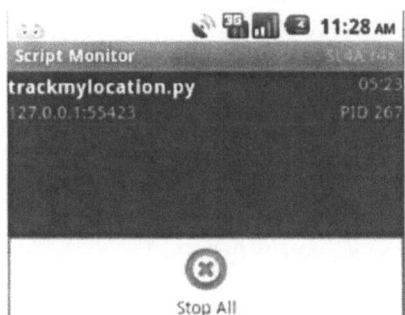

Figure 7-13. *Script Monitor showing the trackmylocation.py application running*

WiFi Scanner

Knowing what WiFi access points are available from your current location can be a good thing to know. It would take about three steps if you were to use your phone to search for available networks. An SL4A script could do it with one click. The steps are actually pretty simple. The first thing you have to do is turn the WiFi on with:

```
>>> droid.toggleWifiState(True)
```

The `toggleWifiState` function will actually turn the WiFi on if you pass it the `True` parameter. Once you have the WiFi turned on, you can start scanning with:

```
>>> droid.wifiStartScan()
Result(id=0, result=False, error=None)
```

You want to give it some time to do the scanning and then read the results with:

```
>>> scan = droid.wifiGetScanResults()[1]
```

Here's the output of a scan from a hotel room, which is actually just a Python dictionary:

```
>>> pprint.pprint(scan)
[{u'bssid': u'00:1d:7e:33:ba:a4',
  u'capabilities': u'[WEP]',
  u'frequency': 2462,
  u'level': -83,
```

```
   u'ssid': u'moes'},
  {u'bssid': u'00:23:33:a4:08:80',
   u'capabilities': u'',
   u'frequency': 2412,
   u'level': -70,
   u'ssid': u'hhonors'},
  {u'bssid': u'00:23:5e:d4:e8:90',
   u'capabilities': u'',
   u'frequency': 2462,
   u'level': -76,
   u'ssid': u'hhonors'},
  {u'bssid': u'00:23:5e:1e:e8:40',
   u'capabilities': u'',
   u'frequency': 2462,
   u'level': -85,
   u'ssid': u'hhonors'},
  {u'bssid': u'00:23:5e:d4:e3:f0',
   u'capabilities': u'',
   u'frequency': 2412,
   u'level': -89,
   u'ssid': u'hhonors'},
  {u'bssid': u'00:02:6f:77:e8:c4',
   u'capabilities': u'',
   u'frequency': 2447,
   u'level': -92,
   u'ssid': u'Comfort'},
  {u'bssid': u'00:02:6f:88:2b:52',
   u'capabilities': u'',
   u'frequency': 2412,
   u'level': -93,
   u'ssid': u'Comfort'},
  {u'bssid': u'00:02:6f:85:b3:cf',
   u'capabilities': u'',
   u'frequency': 2462,
   u'level': -94,
   u'ssid': u'Comfort'}]
```

It's easy to take the output from `wifiGetScanResults` and populate an alert dialog box. This would give you a quick and easy way to scan for a WiFi access point with a single click. Here's the code to do that:

```
import android
import time

def main():
    global droid
    droid = android.Android()
```

```
    # Wait until the scan finishes.
    while not droid.wifiStartScan().result: time.sleep(0.25)

    # Build a dictionary of available networks.
    networks = {}
    while not networks:
        for ap in droid.wifiGetScanResults().result:
            networks[ap['bssid']] = ap.copy()

    droid.dialogCreateAlert('Access Points')
    droid.dialogSetItems(['%(ssid)s, %(level)s, %(capabilities)s' % ap
                          for ap in networks.values()])
    droid.dialogSetPositiveButtonText('OK')
    droid.dialogShow()

if __name__ == '__main__':
    main()
```

Figure 7-14 shows what you'll get when you run this script on your device. You'll probably see only access points that broadcast their ssid or that you're attached to.

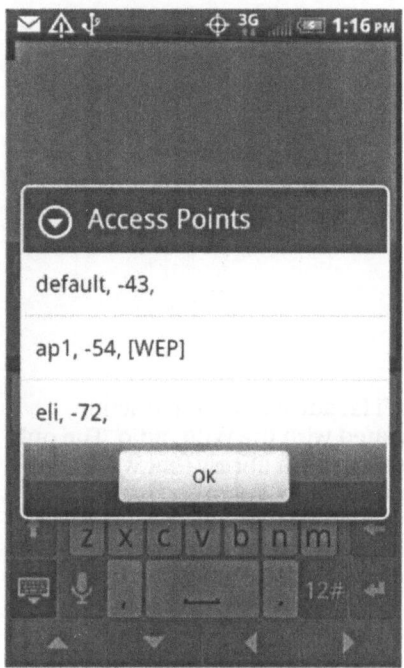

Figure 7-14. *Output of WifiScanner script*

HTTP Server

Python knows how to do HTTP and provides a number of library functions to make creating an HTTP server drop-dead simple. The library you'll want to use is `SimpleHTTPServer`. If you were to run the following code from your desktop, it would launch a web server from the current directory on port 8000:

```
import SimpleHTTPServer
SimpleHTTPServer.test()
```

We can expand on this theme a bit for an Android device by setting the working directory to where the camera app saves pictures and then launching the HTTP server. This will, in effect, make a way to retrieve your pictures from the camera over a local network. Here's the code:

```
import SimpleHTTPServer
from os import chdir
chdir('/sdcard/DCIM/100MEDIA')
SimpleHTTPServer.test()
```

Figure 7-15 is a screenshot of what you would see running this script in the emulator. It also shows the result of pressing the hardware Back button. SL4A will prompt you before it actually exits your application as shown.

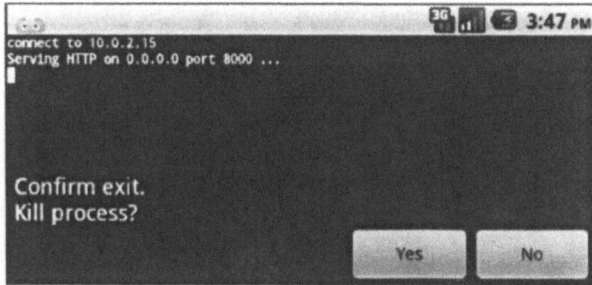

Figure 7-15. *SimpleHTTPserver Script running in the emulator*

Now all you need to know is the IP address of your device. The WiFi facade contains a function, `wifiGetConnectionInfo`, which will return the current IP address associated with the WiFi radio. The only problem is that it returns the value as a long integer. Not to fear, there's a Python library that will help with that. You'll actually have to import two libraries to get what we need. Here's a short script that will get the current IP address and display it using a `makeToast` popup.

```
import android, socket, struct

droid = android.Android()

ipdec = droid.wifiGetConnectionInfo().result['ip_address']

ipstr = socket.inet_ntoa(struct.pack('L',ipdec))

droid.makeToast(ipstr)
```

Now we're going to take this code and add it to our four-line web server to display the IP address of the device. Here's what the updated code looks like:

```
import android, socket, SimpleHTTPServer, struct
from os import chdir

droid = android.Android()

ipdec = droid.wifiGetConnectionInfo().result['ip_address']
ipstr = socket.inet_ntoa(struct.pack('L',ipdec))

chdir('/sdcard/DCIM/100MEDIA')

print "connect to %s" % ipstr
SimpleHTTPServer.test()
```

Figure 7-16 shows what the screen will look like with the server running. Notice that you'll also get a log of all activity in the main window.

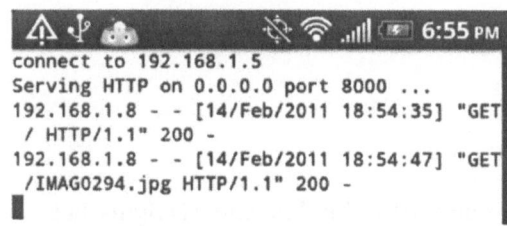

Figure 7-16. *Status screen from httpd2.py Script*

Figure 7-17 shows a screenshot of what I see in a browser when I run the SimpleHTTPServer2 code:

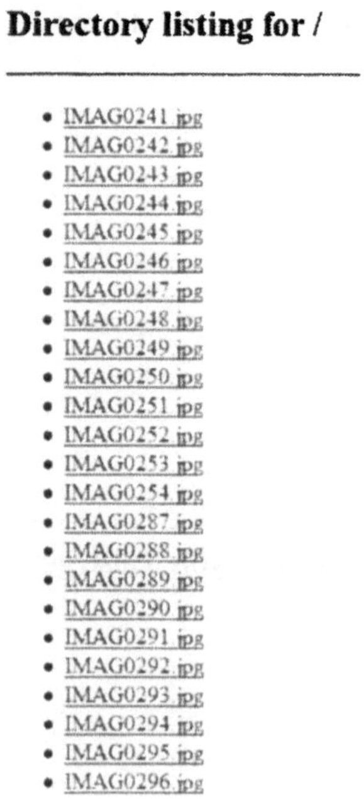

Directory listing for /

- IMAG0241 jpg
- IMAG0242 jpg
- IMAG0243 jpg
- IMAG0244 jpg
- IMAG0245 jpg
- IMAG0246 jpg
- IMAG0247 jpg
- IMAG0248 jpg
- IMAG0249 jpg
- IMAG0250 jpg
- IMAG0251 jpg
- IMAG0252 jpg
- IMAG0253 jpg
- IMAG0254 jpg
- IMAG0287 jpg
- IMAG0288 jpg
- IMAG0289 jpg
- IMAG0290 jpg
- IMAG0291 jpg
- IMAG0292 jpg
- IMAG0293 jpg
- IMAG0294 jpg
- IMAG0295 jpg
- IMAG0296 jpg

Figure 7-17. Example of the SimpleHTTPServer app

All you have to do to transfer one of the pictures from your device to a local machine is right-click with your mouse and choose Save As.

Killing a Running App

There are several ways to kill a running application. The brute force way is to use the Settings menu on your device and choose Applications and then Manage Applications. This will display a list of currently running applications and should contain entries for SL4A and Python For Android. If you choose Python For Android, you should then see a screen like Figure 7-18.

Figure 7-18. *Application info for Python for Android*

If you press the Force Stop button, it will cause the application to exit. A second option is to switch to the notifications page on the device and select the SL4A Service, as shown in Figure 7-19.

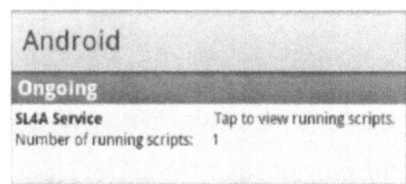

Figure 7-19. *Example of SimpleHTTPServer app*

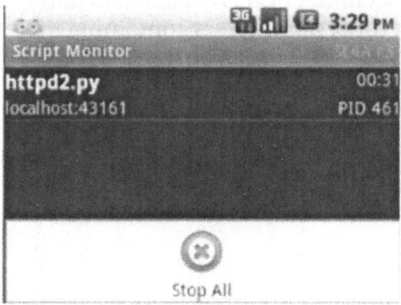

Figure 7-20. *SL4A Script Monitor screen*

This screen provides a control page allowing you to see all active SL4A scripts, including how long they have been running. Pressing the Stop All button will force the currently running script to exit. If you select the `httpd2.py` line, as shown in Figure 7-20, you'll be switched to the screen displayed by that script. Once there, you can press the hardware Back button and exit the script that way (refer to Figure 7-15).

URL File Retriever

There are times when downloading files from the Internet to a specific location on your Android device is not something you can easily accomplish. You may actually launch a program like your music player, depending on how your device handles embedded links on a web page, when what you really wanted was to download a copy. It can get very frustrating; that is, unless you write a script in Python to do it for you.

This simple script relies on one of Python's standard library modules, `urllib`, to do the bulk of the work. It also uses the Android clipboard to pull the link from which to download. By default, all files are downloaded into the download directory on the `sdcard`. You are given the opportunity to rename the file before the download is initiated. Figure 7-21 shows the Filename dialog box. If you choose the Cancel button instead of Ok, you will simply exit the script.

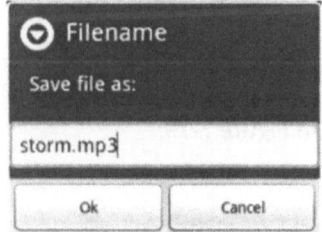

Figure 7-21. *Filename dialog box*

The other piece of code in this little script that really works well is the progress bar. The `urlretrieve` function accepts one mandatory and three optional parameters. You must pass in a URL to be retrieved, so that's the only required parameter. The second parameter is a filename that specifies where to store the downloaded file. The third parameter is actually a function reference, which the Python documentation calls a reporthook. This will be called once the network connection is established and after each block read completes. The reporthook will have passed to it three parameters containing the count of blocks transferred so far, individual block size, and the total size of the file to be transferred. This is perfect for the progress bar and will make it simple to implement:

```
import android
import urllib
import os

downloads = '/sdcard/download/'
```

```python
def _reporthook(numblocks, blocksize, filesize, url=None):
    base = os.path.basename(url)
    try:
        percent = min((numblocks*blocksize*100)/filesize, 100)
    except:
        percent = 100
    if numblocks != 0:
        droid.dialogSetMaxProgress(filesize)
        droid.dialogSetCurrentProgress(numblocks * blocksize)

def main():
    global droid
    droid = android.Android()

    url = droid.getClipboard().result
    if url is None: return

    dst = droid.dialogGetInput('Filename', 'Save file as:', os.path.basename(url)).result
    droid.dialogCreateHorizontalProgress('Downloading...', 'Saving %s from web.' % dst)
    droid.dialogShow()
    urllib.urlretrieve(url, downloads + dst,
        lambda nb, bs, fs, url=url: _reporthook(nb,bs,fs,url))
    droid.dialogDismiss()

    droid.dialogCreateAlert('Operation Finished',
                            '%s has been saved to %s.' % (url, downloads + dst))
    droid.dialogSetPositiveButtonText('OK')
    droid.dialogShow()

if __name__ == '__main__':
    main()
```

When the progress bar is first initialized, it has a max value of 100. If you look closely when the program is starting up, you might see that. Once it has started the actual download, it will have the information needed to populate the progress bar with the right numbers. Figure 7-22 shows what the progress bar will look like in the middle of downloading a file.

Figure 7-22. Progress dialog box for URL downloader script

Python FTP Server

The converse of downloading files to your Android device is obviously uploading to it. The same reasoning applies here as well as for the upload utility. There are times when you don't have a cable but you'd like to be able to upload a file from a laptop or other computer to your device. While there are a number of options for this problem, the most obvious solution is to implement an FTP server. This would give you the ability to both upload and download files should you so choose.

Implementing an FTP server is not quite as easy as HTTP, at least not using the Python Standard Library. A quick Google search for *Python FTP server* turns up pyftpdlib as the first result. This is a pure Python library that implements a full-fledged FTP server. If you browse the source code of the project, you'll see one large file named ftpserver.py. That's the only file you'll need from this project. Download it to your host machine and then push it to your device with the ADB command as follows:

```
adb push ftpserver.py /sdcard/sl4a/scripts/
```

That will place the server code in the same directory as the rest of the SL4A Python scripts. It will allow the Python import command to load the library without any path issues:

```
import android, socket, struct
import ftpserver

droid = android.Android()

authorizer = ftpserver.DummyAuthorizer()
authorizer.add_anonymous('/sdcard/downloads')
authorizer.add_user('user', 'password', '/sdcard/sl4a/scripts', perm='elradfmw')
handler = ftpserver.FTPHandler
handler.authorizer = authorizer
ipdec = droid.wifiGetConnectionInfo().result['ip_address']
ipstr = socket.inet_ntoa(struct.pack('L',ipdec))
droid.makeToast(ipstr)
server = ftpserver.FTPServer((ipstr, 8080), handler)
server.serve_forever()
```

Once the FTP server is running, you can connect to it with any FTP client. FireFTP is a really nice Firefox add-on that gives you a two-pane display (see Figure 7-23) for easy drag-and-drop file operations between host (on the left) and client (on the right).

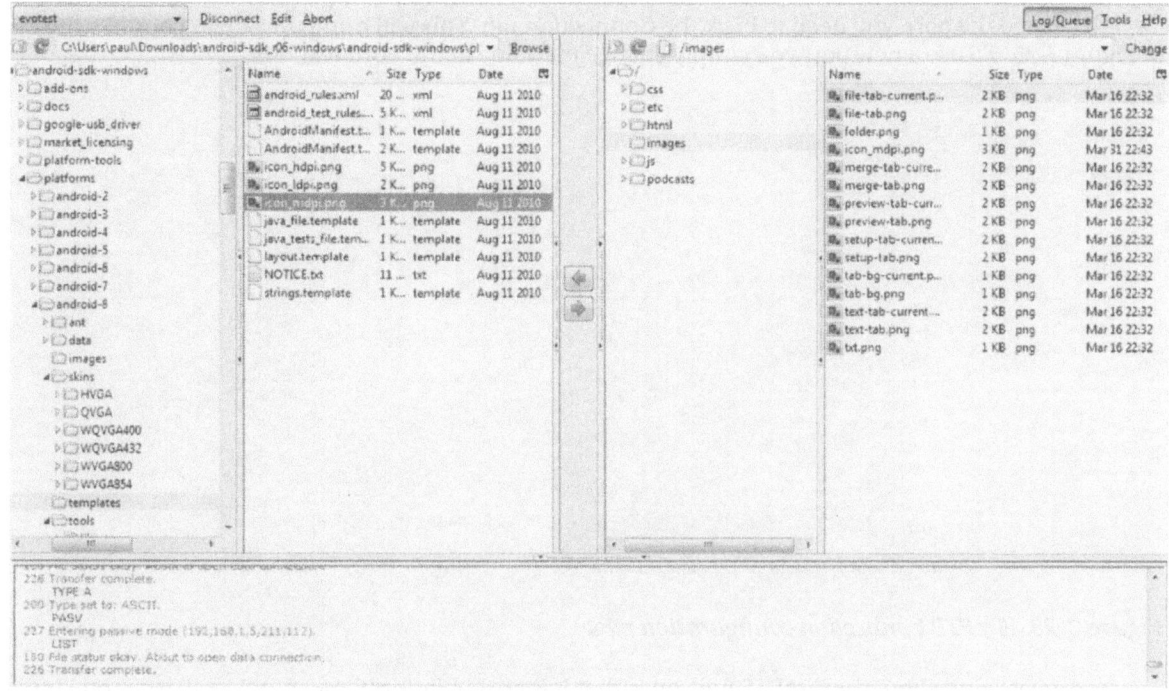

Figure 7-23. *FireFTP connected to Android phone*

FTP uses IP port 21 by default, but for this example I chose to use port 8080. You'll need to configure your FTP client to use an alternate port if you use this example as is. In the Firefox FireFTP add-on, this is done using the Edit Connection tool. Figure 7-24 shows the first tab of this dialog box.

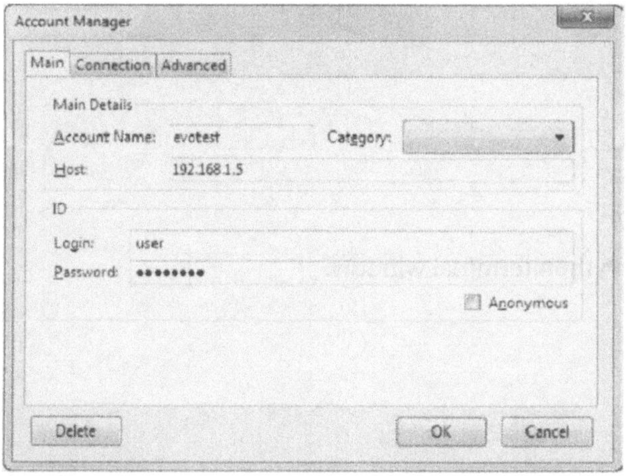

Figure 7-24. *FireFTP Account Manager main page*

To change the port, you need to click the Connection tab. This will bring up a dialog box like the one in Figure 7-25. To use a new port you simply change the value in the Port: text box.

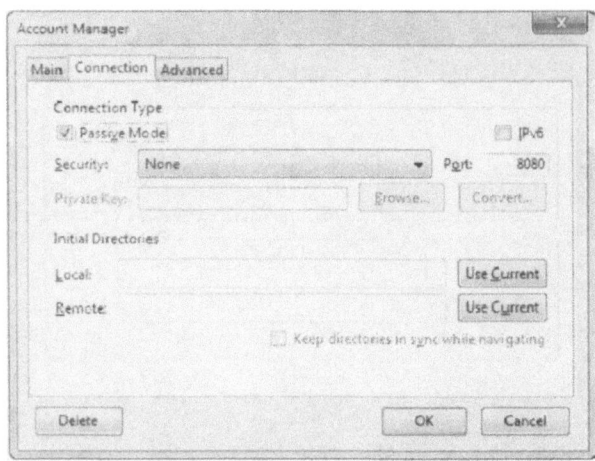

Figure 7-25. *FireFTP Connection configuration page*

The great thing about the FireFTP add-on is that it is cross-platform, meaning it will work on Linux, Mac OS X, and Windows. Couple this with our FTP server app, and you have a great way to move files to and from your Android device without a cable. The FTP server app outputs log messages to the Python standard output screen. If you want to see those you'll need to launch the app from SL4A using the Terminal icon (see Figure 7-26).

Figure 7-26. *Log screen for Python FTP server*

Figure 7-27 shows the FTP logs you'll see in the Python terminal window.

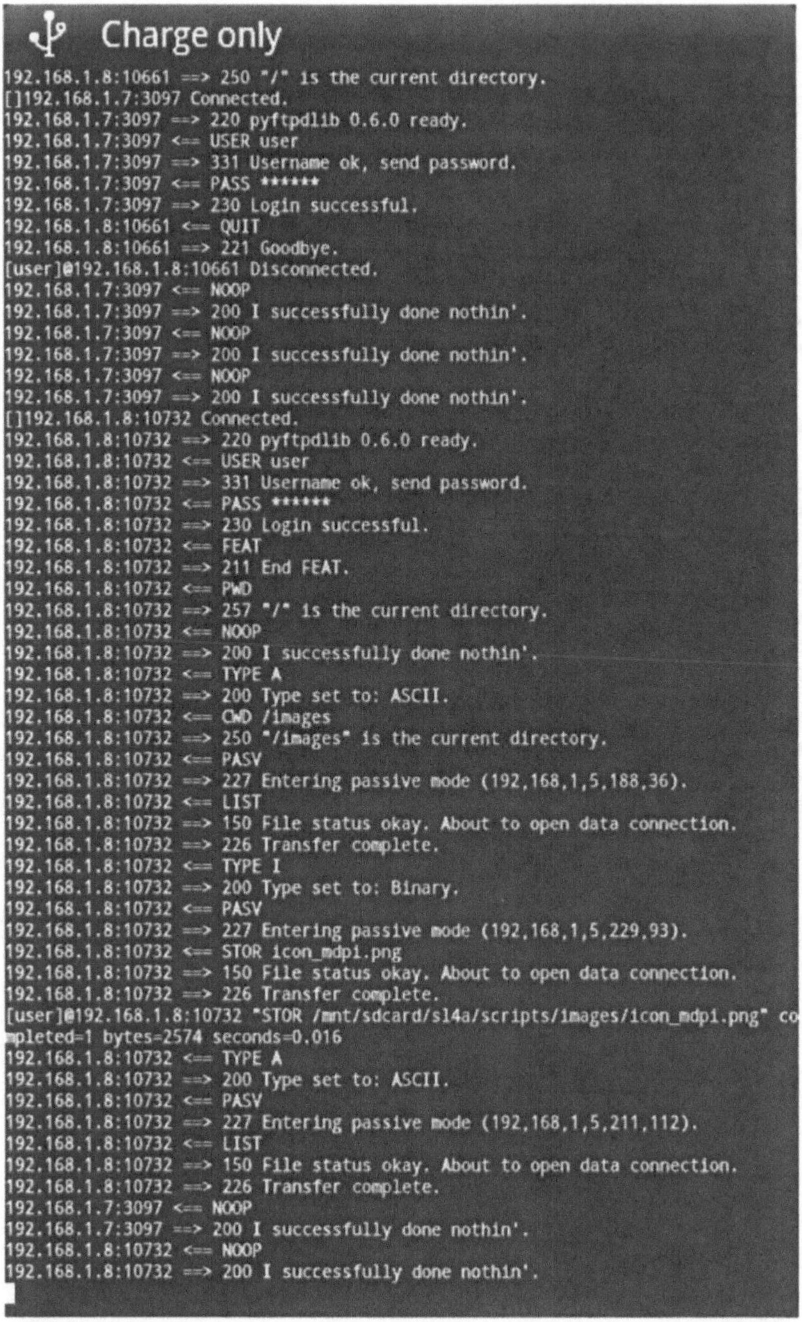

```
     Charge only
192.168.1.8:10661 ==> 250 "/" is the current directory.
[]192.168.1.7:3097 Connected.
192.168.1.7:3097 ==> 220 pyftpdlib 0.6.0 ready.
192.168.1.7:3097 <== USER user
192.168.1.7:3097 ==> 331 Username ok, send password.
192.168.1.7:3097 <== PASS ******
192.168.1.7:3097 ==> 230 Login successful.
192.168.1.8:10661 <== QUIT
192.168.1.8:10661 ==> 221 Goodbye.
[user]@192.168.1.8:10661 Disconnected.
192.168.1.7:3097 <== NOOP
192.168.1.7:3097 ==> 200 I successfully done nothin'.
192.168.1.7:3097 <== NOOP
192.168.1.7:3097 ==> 200 I successfully done nothin'.
192.168.1.7:3097 <== NOOP
192.168.1.7:3097 ==> 200 I successfully done nothin'.
[]192.168.1.8:10732 Connected.
192.168.1.8:10732 ==> 220 pyftpdlib 0.6.0 ready.
192.168.1.8:10732 <== USER user
192.168.1.8:10732 ==> 331 Username ok, send password.
192.168.1.8:10732 <== PASS ******
192.168.1.8:10732 ==> 230 Login successful.
192.168.1.8:10732 <== FEAT
192.168.1.8:10732 ==> 211 End FEAT.
192.168.1.8:10732 <== PWD
192.168.1.8:10732 ==> 257 "/" is the current directory.
192.168.1.8:10732 <== NOOP
192.168.1.8:10732 ==> 200 I successfully done nothin'.
192.168.1.8:10732 <== TYPE A
192.168.1.8:10732 ==> 200 Type set to: ASCII.
192.168.1.8:10732 <== CWD /images
192.168.1.8:10732 ==> 250 "/images" is the current directory.
192.168.1.8:10732 <== PASV
192.168.1.8:10732 ==> 227 Entering passive mode (192,168,1,5,188,36).
192.168.1.8:10732 <== LIST
192.168.1.8:10732 ==> 150 File status okay. About to open data connection.
192.168.1.8:10732 ==> 226 Transfer complete.
192.168.1.8:10732 <== TYPE I
192.168.1.8:10732 ==> 200 Type set to: Binary.
192.168.1.8:10732 <== PASV
192.168.1.8:10732 ==> 227 Entering passive mode (192,168,1,5,229,93).
192.168.1.8:10732 <== STOR icon_mdpi.png
192.168.1.8:10732 ==> 150 File status okay. About to open data connection.
192.168.1.8:10732 ==> 226 Transfer complete.
[user]@192.168.1.8:10732 "STOR /mnt/sdcard/sl4a/scripts/images/icon_mdpi.png" co
mpleted=1 bytes=2574 seconds=0.016
192.168.1.8:10732 <== TYPE A
192.168.1.8:10732 ==> 200 Type set to: ASCII.
192.168.1.8:10732 <== PASV
192.168.1.8:10732 ==> 227 Entering passive mode (192,168,1,5,211,112).
192.168.1.8:10732 <== LIST
192.168.1.8:10732 ==> 150 File status okay. About to open data connection.
192.168.1.8:10732 ==> 226 Transfer complete.
192.168.1.7:3097 <== NOOP
192.168.1.7:3097 ==> 200 I successfully done nothin'.
192.168.1.8:10732 <== NOOP
192.168.1.8:10732 ==> 200 I successfully done nothin'.
```

Figure 7-27. *Log screen for Python FTP server*

Summary

This chapter showed you the basics of writing short scripts using the Python language and some actual usable scripts you can take and modify to meet your needs. Python is a great language for this and provides a wealth of libraries to accomplish virtually any computing task you might have.

Here's a list of take-aways for this chapter:

- **Python libraries**: A quick Google search will turn up tons of them, but you need to know whether they are written in pure Python or not (*pure Python* means that all the code is written in the Python language). Some libraries are just wrappers around some C-based library and they deliver a compiled binary of the real library. They won't work unless they've been cross-compiled to run on the Arm architecture.

- **Use e-mail to send stuff**: Sending an e-mail message with SL4A is a piece of cake. This chapter showed you how to build a message and send it through Gmail. You're bound to think of any number of other uses for this kind of utility. Now you have the building blocks to put one together to meet a specific need.

- **Location, location, location**: That's what they say in real estate, anyway. Every Android device has the capability to provide location information from multiple sources. Some are more accurate than others, but you don't always need extreme accuracy. You also need to keep in mind trivial things (for example, GPS doesn't work when you're indoors).

- **The Web is a big deal**: Turning your little Android device into a web server takes a total of two lines of code in Python. This chapter only barely scratched the surface of what you could do here. Just make sure you don't totally ignore security when you launch your file browser out in public.

CHAPTER 8

Python Dialog Box–based GUIs

This chapter will take a look at the options available for building dialog box–based graphical user interfaces (GUIs) with SL4A.

■ **Note** This chapter will discuss the use of the Android dialog box API functions to build applications that present real-world user interfaces. Some background in these areas would be helpful but not absolutely required.

There are two basic approaches to user interaction with SL4A. First, there are the Android API calls for using the stock dialog boxes such as alerts. This is the easiest and most straightforward way to present information to the user and receive input back. We'll cover this method here. The second approach uses HTML and JavaScript to build the user interface (UI) and then Python behind the scenes to handle any additional processing. I'll show you how to do a UI with HTML in the next chapter.

UI Basics

SL4A includes a UI facade to access the basic dialog box elements available through the Android API. It's pretty simple to build a script using these elements. Essentially, all you have to do is set the text you want displayed for the buttons, items, and title and then make a call to showDialog. You can obtain the results of a user's action using the **dialogGetResponse** call.

When coding a user interface, it's important to expect the unexpected. Your script needs to be able to handle every action a user might perform including doing nothing. I'll start with a little refresher on setting up a few of the dialog boxes and then work into an example application. If all you need to do is show the user a brief message, you can use the **makeToast** API function. The SL4A help page gives a simple example that also showcases the **getInput** API function. Here's what the code looks like:

```
import android

droid = android.Android()
name = droid.getInput("Hello!", "What is your name?")
print name  # name is a named tuple
droid.makeToast("Hello, %s" % name.result)
```

This will first display an input dialog box like Figure 8-1. It has a title (Hello!) and a prompt (What is your name?). By default, the **getInput** function displays a single line text box for the user input and the Ok button. It should be noted that the most recent versions of SL4A have deprecated the **getInput** function and replaced it with **dialogGetInput**.

Figure 8-1. *Input dialog box with title, prompt, input box, and Ok button*

When the user presses the Ok button, the **getInput** will return a result object as a named tuple. If you use the Python IDLE tool to run your code remotely on either the emulator or a real device, you'll be able to see the result of the print name code. I'll be using IDLE a good bit in this chapter because it makes things easier when you need to step through code or just see the results of different API calls. In this case, the result will look something like this:

```
Result(id=0, result=u'Kentucky Rose', error=None)
```

Each result is assigned a unique **ID** for tracking purposes, and here we get **id=0**. The second element of the tuple is **result** and contains the text string the user typed into the text box. Every result also includes an **error** element to provide feedback to the caller on any error condition that might have been encountered. In this instance, we see that **error=None,** meaning there were no errors. When Ok is pressed, you should see a popup message like Figure 8-2 displayed for a short period of time.

Figure 8-2. *makeToast dialog box showing user input*

The main API call we'll be using to create our dialog boxes is **dialogCreateAlert**. It accepts two optional arguments to set the dialog box title and a message string to display inside the dialog box. The message string is a good place to describe to your user what you want them to do in the dialog box. Figure 8-3 shows the result of the following code:

```
droid.dialogCreateAlert('Settings Dialog','Chose any number of items and then press OK')
droid.dialogShow()
```

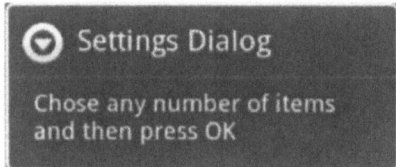

Figure 8-3. Basic alert dialog box with a title and message

The alert dialog box can be compared to a popup dialog box on a desktop machine. It allows you to create up to three buttons providing three different return values. To create a button, you must use any of **dialogSetNegativeButtonText**, **dialogSetNeutralButtonText**, and **dialogSetPositiveButtonText** API calls to enable the button and set the text to be displayed. Here's the code to add two buttons for a positive and negative result:

```
droid.dialogSetPositiveButtonText('Done')
droid.dialogSetNegativeButtonText('Cancel')
```

Figure 8-4 shows what our dialog box looks like now that we've added buttons to the text. The basic alert dialog box simply displays text and returns nothing. This can be useful to communicate information, but once you show an alert dialog box you must either dismiss it with a call to **dialogDismiss,** or the user must press the return hardware button.

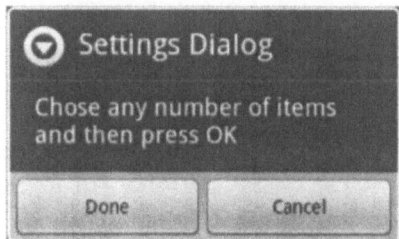

Figure 8-4. Alert dialog box with two buttons

To find out which button the user pushed, you must call **dialogGetResponse** like this:

```
>>> response = droid.dialogGetResponse()
>>> response
Result(id=10, result={u'canceled': True}, error=None)
```

If you need the user to give you some type of text input, you'll want to use the **dialogGetInput** function. Here's what the code would look like to prompt for a message and set the result equal to the variable ans:

```
ans = droid.dialogGetInput("Message Title","Message Text","Default").result
```

Figure 8-5. getInput dialog box

If the user presses the Cancel button, you'll see an empty return that looks like this:

```
Result(id=0, result=None, error=None)
```

When you make a call to `dialogGetResponse`, it will return the last action the user accomplished. So if you have a multichoice dialog box up for display and the user simply presses Cancel, your result will be the output of the button labeled *Cancel*. For example, here's the result of several passes at the Settings dialog box from the Python IDLE console:

```
>>> droid.dialogSetItems(['one','two','three','four','five','six','seven','eight','nine'])
Result(id=16, result=None, error=None)
>>> droid.dialogShow()
Result(id=17, result=None, error=None)
>>> droid.dialogGetResponse()
Result(id=18, result={u'canceled': True, u'which': u'positive'}, error=None)
>>> droid.dialogShow()
Result(id=19, result=None, error=None)
>>> droid.dialogGetResponse()
Result(id=20, result={u'item': 2}, error=None)
>>> droid.dialogShow()
Result(id=21, result=None, error=None)
```

The first line creates an alert dialog box with nine elements added to the two buttons defined from the previous example. Figure 8-6 shows the resulting dialog box.

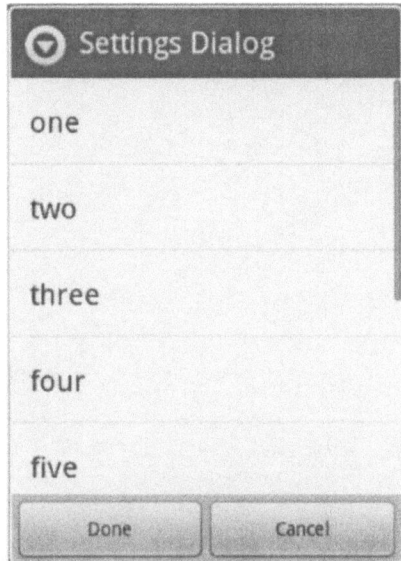

Figure 8-6. Alert dialog box with list of items and two buttons

Let's look at all of these by using the `Result id` to identify each one. The first response, `id=18`, returns a Python dictionary with two elements named `'canceled'` and 'which'. Their values are `'True'` and `'positive'`, respectively. This tells us that the user canceled the operation without selecting any of the items by pressing the positive button, which in our case is labeled `'Done'`.

The next result, `id=20`, is an example of the user selecting one of the items in the list. Notice that the result is simply `{u'item': 2}`. Once again, we have a dictionary returned as the result, but this time it has only one element: `'item'`. The value of `'item'` is 2, which translates to the text line `'three'`. That's because Python uses zero-based indexing. You don't see any values for the buttons because the dialog box will close when the user selects one of the items in the list. For this type of user interaction, you really only need one button for the user to cancel everything.

One last example of what you would see using the Python IDLE console to examine dialog box button responses is here:

```
>>> droid.dialogGetResponse()
Result(id=22, result={u'canceled': True, u'which': u'neutral'}, error=None)
```

`Result id=22` is what you would expect to see if a user pressed the Cancel button. In our example, we defined the positive and neutral buttons, hence the dictionary values. The last UI dialog box we need for our settings script is `dialogCreateInput`. In the next section, we'll use it to prompt the user when we need input.

Book Title Search

Now let's take the previous example showing how to display a list of items and use the `dialogCreateInput` function call to prompt for a book title and then do a Google Book Search before displaying the results. Figure 8-7 shows our dialog box prompting for a search term. Once we have our term, we fire it off to the Google search API and then fill the alert dialog box with a list of returned titles.

Figure 8-7. *Input dialog box for Google Book Search*

The code to do the search looks like this:

```
service = gdata.books.service.BookService()
service.ClientLogin(email, pw)

titles = []
for bookname in service.get_library():
    titles.append(bookname.dc_title[0].text)

droid.dialogCreateAlert()
droid.dialogSetItems(list)
droid.dialogShow()
```

This code will display a dialog box like the one shown in Figure 8-8.

George Washington,
Spymaster: How the Am...

George Washington
Carver: From Slave to Sc...

George Washington: The
Founding Father

George Washington and
slavery: a documentary ...

Figure 8-8. *Alert dialog box with list of results*

Now that we have that out of the way, we'll take a quick look at a few other UI elements that you might want to use at some point.

Convenience Dialog Boxes

The dialog box facade includes a number of convenience functions like the date picker. Figure 8-9 shows what you should see as a result of the following code:

```
droid.dialogCreateDatePicker(2011)
droid.dialogShow()
```

Arguments to this function are optional, but if used, should be integers representing year, month, and day, in that order. If no inputs are provided, the dialog box will default to an initial date of January 1, 1970.

Figure 8-9. *Date picker dialog box initialized with Jan 01, 2011*

To read the user's response, you'll need to call **dialogGetResponse** as follows:

```
>>> droid.dialogGetResponse()
Result(id=27, result={u'year': 2011, u'day': 6, u'which': u'positive', u'month': 3},↵
 error=None)
```

If you use Python's IDLE utility, you can easily examine the results returned from these functions. Assigning the result to the variable **date** lets you easily address the different named values:

```
>>> date = droid.dialogGetResponse().result
>>> date
{u'year': 2011, u'day': 7, u'which': u'positive', u'month': 3}
>>> date["year"]
2011
>>> date["month"]
3
>>> date["day"]
7
```

The other helper dialog box is the **createTimePicker** function. Just like **createDatePicker**, you can provide inputs to set the initial time to display. The following code will produce the dialog box shown in Figure 8-10.

```
>>> droid.dialogCreateTimePicker()
Result(id=9, result=None, error=None)
>>> droid.dialogShow()
Result(id=10, result=None, error=None)
```

Notice that you get a result object back from the dialogCreateTimePicker immediately because it's letting you know that you successfully set up a time picker. Now you can proceed to using the dialogShow call to actually display the dialog box. Here I chose to not use a preset time, so the dialog box displays 12:00 AM or midnight.

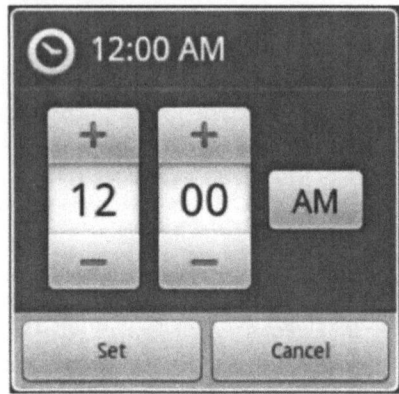

Figure 8-10. *Time picker dialog box with default time displayed*

Both the date and time picker dialog boxes accept a starting value if you know what you want to display. For the time picker, the first input should be an integer representing the hour, and the second input should be an integer representing the minute to display. A third optional input parameter is a Boolean to set 24-hour mode and is set to false by default. If this parameter is passed in as **true**, you will see values for hours up to 24.

Often you will want to echo an asterisk after each character of a password is typed. This dialog box will display immediately without the need to call **showDialog**. It will echo each character typed so that the user will have some feedback as to what characters have been pressed. Typing a new character will cover the previous one with an asterisk. Figure 8-11 shows what this dialog box looks like with the last character still showing.

Figure 8-11. *Get Password dialog box with last character typed displayed*

You will have to make a call to `dialogGetResponse` to return the password entered or to determine which button was pressed. Here's what that would look like using IDLE:

```
>>> droid.dialogGetPassword()
Result(id=5, result=u'Password', error=None)
>>> droid.dialogGetResponse()
Result(id=6, result={u'which': u'positive', u'value': u'Password'}, error=None)
>>> droid.dialogGetPassword()
Result(id=7, result=None, error=None)
>>> droid.dialogGetResponse()
Result(id=8, result={u'which': u'negative', u'value': u''}, error=None)
```

In the first line (`id=5`), a password was entered and the Ok button pressed. You can see it returns the result `'Password'`. Using a call to `dialogGetResponse` shows that the positive button was pressed and a value of `'Password'` was returned. For the next call to `dialogGetPassword`, the user simply pressed the Cancel button. The result here (`id=7`) shows `'None'`. Using another call to `dialogGetResponse` shows that the negative button was pressed, in this case Cancel, and that an empty value was returned.

Progress Dialog Boxes

Keeping the user informed of what your application is doing is always a good idea. If you need to do some type of processing that will take more than a few seconds, you should think about using a progress dialog box. SL4A provides an API facade for both a horizontal progress bar and a spinner dialog box. The biggest challenge in using a progress dialog box is determining how to measure progress and then display it.

In a previous chapter I used a horizontal progress bar to show file download progress. In this case, the size of the file is used to determine how much progress has been made. You don't have to specify anything when you call `dialogCreateHorizontalProgress.` This will just display a progress dialog box with a scale of 0 to 100. Figure 8-12 shows what you'll get with the code:

```
droid.dialogCreateHorizontalProgress()
droid.dialogShow()
```

Figure 8-12. Horizontal progress bar with default options

Once the dialog box is displayed you can use **dialogSetMaxProgress** to change the value displayed for the maximum value. You must use **dialogSetCurrentProgress** to update the progress of your application. The following code would update the progress bar to 50%, assuming the max progress has been set to **4096**:

```
droid.dialogSetCurrentProgress(2048)
```

Figure 8-13 shows what this code will produce.

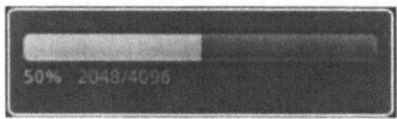

Figure 8-13. Horizontal progress bar at 50%

There are other times when you just need to let the user know that the application is doing some type of processing. This calls for the spinner progress dialog box. Here's all you need to do to start one up:

```
droid.dialogCreateSpinnerProgress("Spinner Test","Spinner Message")
```

Figure 8-14 shows what you'll get.

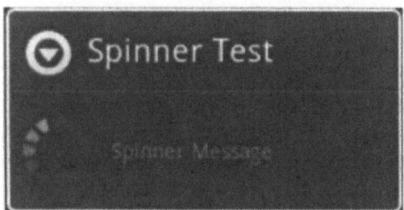

Figure 8-14. Spinner dialog box

Both progress dialog boxes require a call to **dialogDismiss** to close.

Modal versus Non–Modal Dialog Boxes

There are really only two options for dialog box behavior when you build a user interface. A modal dialog box or window is typically a child of another process or window, meaning it has a parent process or higher-level window to return to. Processing will wait or block until the user interacts with the new dialog box. In the case of an alert dialog box, it is essentially modal, meaning it will not close until you do something.

Here's some code to demonstrate what I'm talking about:

```python
# Demonstrate use of modal dialog. Process location events while
# waiting for user input.
import android
droid=android.Android()
droid.dialogCreateAlert("I like swords.","Do you like swords?")
droid.dialogSetPositiveButtonText("Yes")
droid.dialogSetNegativeButtonText("No")
droid.dialogShow()
droid.startLocating()
while True: # Wait for events for up to 10 seconds.
  response=droid.eventWait(10000).result
  if response==None: # No events to process. exit.
    break
  if response["name"]=="dialog": # When you get a dialog event, exit loop
    break
  print response # Probably a location event.

# Have fallen out of loop. Close the dialog
droid.dialogDismiss()
if response==None:
  print "Timed out."
else:
  rdialog=response["data"] # dialog response is stored in data.
  if  rdialog.has_key("which"):
    result=rdialog["which"]
    if result=="positive":
      print "Yay! I like swords too!"
    elif result=="negative":
      print "Oh. How sad."
  elif rdialog.has_key("canceled"): # Yes, I know it's mispelled.
    print "You can't even make up your mind?"
  else:
    print "Unknown response=",response
print droid.stopLocating()
print "Done"
```

This code will present a dialog box like the one shown in Figure 8-15.

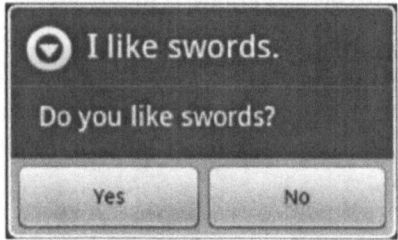

Figure 8-15. *An alert dialog box used to demonstrate a modal display*

If the user does nothing, the dialog box will time out and be dismissed. Using IDLE, you can see the results:

```
Timed out.
Result(id=7, result=None, error=None)
Done
```

If the user presses the Yes button, you should see this result:

```
Yay! I like swords too!
Result(id=7, result=None, error=None)
Done
```

Pressing the No button will show this:

```
Oh. How sad.
Result(id=7, result=None, error=None)
Done
```

If the user happens to press the hardware return button to cancel the app, you'll see the following in the IDLE main window:

```
You can't even make up your mind?
Result(id=7, result=None, error=None)
Done
```

The important thing is the use of events to implement a timeout feature. Normal modal dialog boxes don't time out unless the user cancels the entire application. Here the `eventWait` function call is used to wait either for one of the buttons to be pressed or 1000 ms, or 1 sec, and then resume processing. Events don't work unless an activity has been initiated such as `startLocating`. This will generate position events that must be filtered to look for just the events of interest. This is done using the line of code shown here:

```
if response["name"]=="dialog": # When you get a dialog event, exit loop
```

This line allows the script to key off the `'dialog'` event and continue processing while ignoring the location-based events.

Options Menu

Many Android applications make use of an options menu to allow the user to set preferences or any option for how the application behaves. SL4A provides a way to create options menu items using the `addOptionsMenuItem` call.

```python
import android
droid=android.Android()

droid.addOptionsMenuItem("Silly","silly",None,"star_on")
droid.addOptionsMenuItem("Sensible","sensible","I bet.","star_off")
droid.addOptionsMenuItem("Off","off",None,"ic_menu_revert")

print "Hit menu to see extra options."
print "Will timeout in 10 seconds if you hit nothing."

droid.webViewShow('file://sdcard/sl4a/scripts/blank.html')

while True: # Wait for events from the menu.
    response=droid.eventWait(10000).result
    if response==None:
        break
    print response
    if response["name"]=="off":
        break
print "And done."
```

The `webViewShow` call is necessary to present something other than a system screen to add in the options menu to. You are not allowed to alter the normal system options, so you need an application of some kind running that you can use to modify the options menu. Figure 8-16 shows what the results of running the previous script should look like if you press the hardware menu button.

Figure 8-16. *Example options menu*

Here's what you'll get if the user presses the Sensible button:

```
{u'data': u'I bet.', u'name': u'sensible', u'time': 1301074971174000L}
```

Notice that this result is actually the output of an event and includes the named items `data`, `name`, and `time`. You would then need to perform additional processing based on which menu option the user pressed.

File Listing with dialogCreateAlert

There are times when you need to get a list of files and display them in a dialog box like the one in Figure 8-17. Here's a short script that will do just that:

```python
import android, os

droid=android.Android()

list = []
for dirname, dirnames, filenames in os.walk('/sdcard/sl4a/scripts'):
    for filename in filenames:
        list.append(filename)

droid.dialogCreateAlert('/sdcard/sl4a/scripts')
droid.dialogSetItems(list)
droid.dialogShow()
file = droid.dialogGetResponse().result
print(list[file])
```

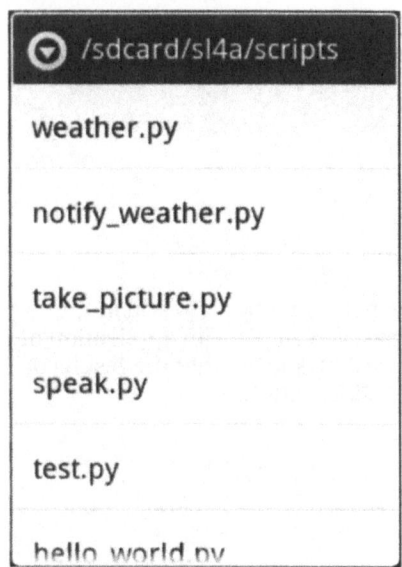

Figure 8-17. Simple file chooser dialog box

A slightly different take on this code would be to add the ability to drill down into subdirectories. This is pretty easy if you simply test to see whether the item selected by the user is actually a directory. If it is, you just clear the items and fill it up with the contents of the new subdirectory. The new dialog box would look something like Figure 8-18.

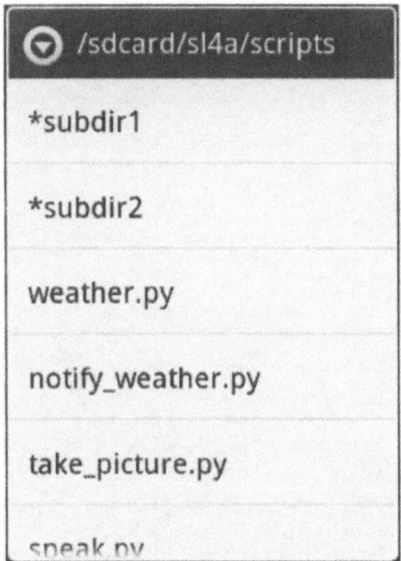

Figure 8-18. *Simple file chooser dialog box showing directories*

Notice that directories have an * in front and that the current path is displayed in the title string of the dialog box. Now we have a fully functional file chooser dialog box that we can use in some of the later examples. Here's the line of code I added to check to determine whether the selected item is a directory or not:

```
if os.path.isdir(start + '\\' + list[file['item']][1:]):
```

Here we use the `isdir` function to check against the full path name of the file, and we use Python's slicing notation to get everything after the asterisk.

Dialog Boxes as Python Objects

One way you can handle the processing or decision making from a user interface is to define a function in Python to help clean up the code and provide a more modular logic flow. Here's what the code for our UI list test code looks like:

```
# Test of Lists
import android,sys
droid=android.Android()

#Choose which list type you want.
def getlist():
  droid.dialogCreateAlert("List Types")
  droid.dialogSetItems(["Items","Single","Multi"])
  droid.dialogShow()
  result=droid.dialogGetResponse().result
```

```
    if result.has_key("item"):
      return result["item"]
    else:
      return -1

#Choose List
listtype=getlist()
if listtype<0:
  print "No item chosen"
  sys.exit()

options=["Red","White","Blue","Charcoal"]
droid.dialogCreateAlert("Colors")
if listtype==0:
  droid.dialogSetItems(options)
elif listtype==1:
  droid.dialogSetSingleChoiceItems(options)
elif listtype==2:
  droid.dialogSetMultiChoiceItems(options)
droid.dialogSetPositiveButtonText("OK")
droid.dialogSetNegativeButtonText("Cancel")
droid.dialogShow()
result=droid.dialogGetResponse().result
# droid.dialogDismiss() # In most modes this is not needed.
if result==None:
  print "Time out"
elif result.has_key("item"):
  item=result["item"];
  print "Chosen item=",item,"=",options[item]
else:
  print "Result=",result
  print "Selected=",droid.dialogGetSelectedItems().result
print "Done"
```

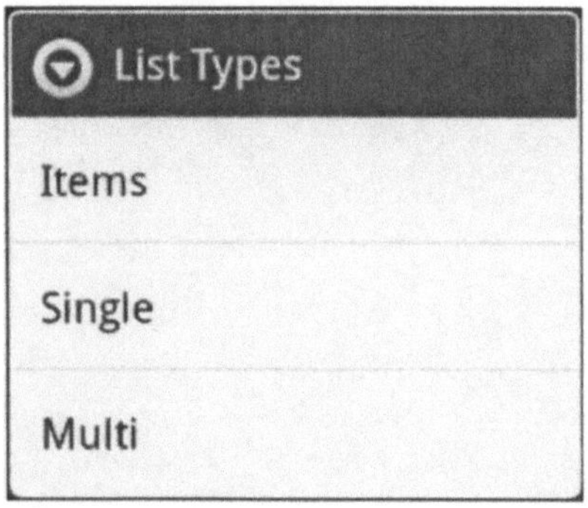

Figure 8-19. *Initial dialog box with list of choices*

The next dialog box presented depends on which choice the user makes. If the user chooses Items, they'll see a dialog box like Figure 8-20. This dialog box offers four items to choose from and two buttons. If the user chooses one of the items such as White, the code returns the following:

```
Chosen item= 1 = White
Done
```

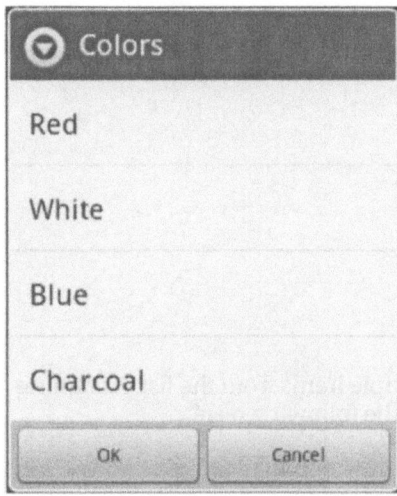

Figure 8-20. *Dialog box displayed from choosing Items*

Choosing Single from the initial dialog box will display a dialog box like the one shown in Figure 8-21. This dialog box demonstrates a slightly different way of prompting a user for a single input using radio buttons. In this dialog box, you need an Ok button to actually close the dialog box after picking a specific item. Selecting the Cancel button would give the user the option of exiting the dialog box without choosing anything. The result of choosing White from this dialog box would be the following:

```
Result= {u'which': u'positive'}
Selected= [1]
Done
```

■ **Tip**   If you run any application remotely that needs to reference the file system, you need to know that it will be looking on your local file system, not on the device or emulator. You can mirror the same structure you would find on either a device or emulator by creating a directory on your main drive named /sdcard and then adding a subdirectory named sl4a and then another named scripts below sl4a.

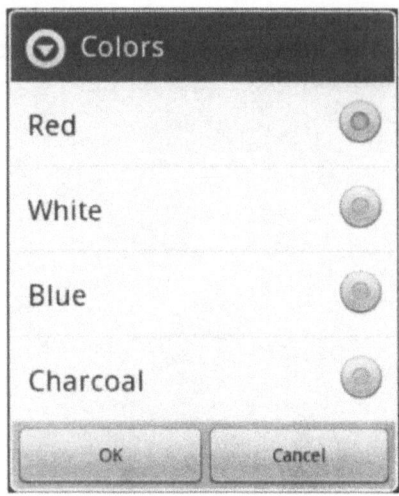

Figure 8-21. Dialog box displayed from choosing Single

The final option is the Multi option allowing a user to select multiple items from the list. Assuming the user chooses the options as shown in Figure 8-22, you would get the following result:

```
Result= {u'which': u'positive'}
Selected= [0, 1, 2]
Done
```

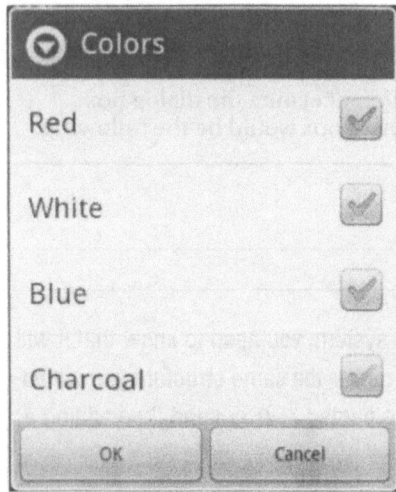

Figure 8-22. Dialog box displayed from choosing Multi

If the user were to select the Cancel button, you would see a result indicating that the negative response button was chosen, as in:

```
Result= {u'which': u'negative'}
Selected= []
Done
```

Podplayer App

One of the things I find annoying about my Android phone is the music player. If you have a large number of music files and you just want to listen to something like a podcast, it can be a problem. Part of the issue stems from the fact that the media player uses ID3 tags inside your MP3 files to sort your music by album, artist, or even individual songs. If the file you want to play happens to not have the ID3 tags set properly, you might not be able to find it using the media player interface unless it shows up under an Unknown tag.

SL4A has everything we need to build a simple little app to display the contents of a directory and then send a selected file to the media player. The first thing we'll use is the directory browser code we used earlier. Figure 8-23 shows what you'll see if you run the code starting in the /sdcard/sl4a directory.

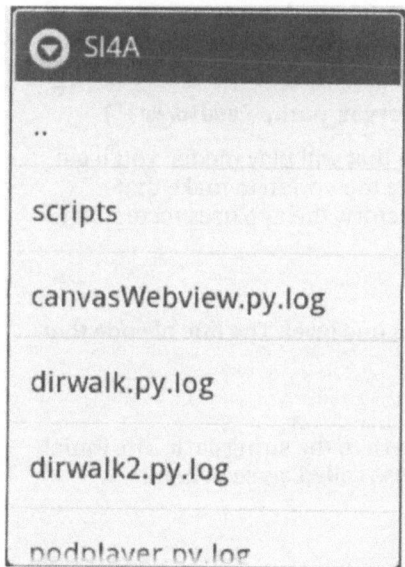

Figure 8-23. *File chooser dialog box*

All the work to populate the alert dialog box is done with a function named show_dir. The very first thing the code does is use the Python os.path.exists() function to determine whether the path specified in base_dir exists or not. If not, it will create the subdirectory using os.makedirs(base_dir). After this check, the code will use the Python os.listdir() function to retrieve a list of all directories and files in the base_dir directory. Here's what that code looks like:

```
nodes = os.listdir(path)

# Make a way to go up a level.
if path != base_dir: nodes.insert(0, '..')

droid.dialogCreateAlert(os.path.basename(path).title())
droid.dialogSetItems(nodes)
droid.dialogShow()

# Get the selected file or directory.
result = droid.dialogGetResponse().result
```

A couple of things need pointing out at this juncture. The 'if path != base_dir:' test is needed since we're going to use the programming construct of recursion to repeatedly display a new alert dialog box as the user moves around in the file system. This ensures that the user doesn't go anywhere outside the base_path directory and any subdirectories. It also makes a way to go up one directory using 'nodes.insert(0,'..')' if the user is not currently at the top level (see the first entry in Figure 8-23). The call to droid.dialogGetResponse() will block or wait until the user either selects a directory or file or exits the program using a hardware button.

When the user does something, there should be data in result to determine what the app does next. If the user selects a directory, the app will load the contents of that directory and create a new alert dialog box. If the user selects a file, it will check to make sure it's an mp3 file and then launch the media player using this line of code:

```
droid.startActivity('android.intent.action.VIEW', 'file://' + target_path, 'audio/mp3')
```

If you happen to have more than one app installed on your device that will play media, you'll get another dialog box prompt to choose which one to use. You'll also have the option to make that selection the default for the file type mp3. When the user chooses a directory, the app uses recursion to reload the next directory with the following line of code:

```
if os.path.isdir(target_path): show_dir(target_path)
```

The other option, if the user has opened a subdirectory, is to go up one level. The line of code that tests for this is as follows:

```
if target == '..': target_path = os.path.dirname(path)
```

So, if the user selects the line with '..', the code will set target_path to the string path. The initial value for path is set to the string base_dir when the show_dir function is called, as seen here:

```
def show_dir(path=base_dir):
```

■ **Note** Recursion is a great way to create a captive UI—meaning the same code will get executed multiple times until the user exits in a way that you desire.

Figure 8-24. *List of .mp3 files from podplayer.py*

The final UI for our Podplayer app is shown in Figure 8-24. Here's what the complete code looks like:

```python
import android, os, time

droid = android.Android()

# Specify our root podcasts directory and make sure it exists.
base_dir = '/sdcard/sl4a/scripts/podcasts'
if not os.path.exists(base_dir): os.makedirs(base_dir)

def show_dir(path=base_dir):
    """Shows the contents of a directory in a list view."""

    # The files & directories under "path".
    nodes = os.listdir(path)

    # Make a way to go up a level.
    if path != base_dir: nodes.insert(0, '..')

    droid.dialogCreateAlert(os.path.basename(path).title())
    droid.dialogSetItems(nodes)
    droid.dialogShow()
```

```
    # Get the selected file or directory.
    result = droid.dialogGetResponse().result
    droid.dialogDismiss()
    if 'item' not in result:
        return
    target = nodes[result['item']]
    target_path = os.path.join(path, target)

    if target == '..': target_path = os.path.dirname(path)

    # If a directory, show its contents.
    if os.path.isdir(target_path): show_dir(target_path)

    # If an MP3, play it.
    elif os.path.splitext(target)[1].lower() == '.mp3':
        droid.startActivity('android.intent.action.VIEW',
                            'file://' + target_path, 'audio/mp3')

    # If not, inform the user.
    else:
        droid.dialogCreateAlert('Invalid File',
                            'Only .mp3 files are currently supported!')
        droid.dialogSetPositiveButtonText('Ok')
        droid.dialogShow()
        droid.dialogGetResponse()
        show_dir(path)

if __name__ == '__main__':
    show_dir()
```

There are a few more things worth discussing in this example that Python makes really easy. Testing for a specific file extension takes just one line of code, like this:

```
os.path.splitext(target)[1].lower()
```

In addition, you should notice two other **os.path** methods used in this script, **os.path.join** and **os.path.isdir**. The **os.path library** module has quite a few methods available to make dealing with file systems and files a piece of cake.

Building the mysettings App

The basic idea behind the settings script is to build a little utility program that will create scripts tailored to a specific combination of phone settings. We'll present a dialog box with different settings to choose from and then let the user choose a filename in which to save them. All the user will need to do is create a link to the settings folder and will then have a way to configure the phone with two touches. We'll use multiple choice items so the user will be able to select the different features to enable.

We'll use standard Python code to write out our final script and save it to our directory. For this example we'll simply use a hard-coded directory, but you could give the user an option without too much extra coding. The biggest issue is making sure the directory chosen is on the sdcard and the user has permission to write to it. We'll use **/sdcard/sl4a/mysettings** as our target directory. The first thing the script will do when it runs is check to see whether that directory exists, and if not, it will create it. That requires a total of three lines of Python code:

```
import os
if not os.path.exists('/sdcard/sl4a/settings'):
        os.mkdir('/sdcard/sl4a/settings')
```

After executing this code, we know for sure we have a directory available in which to save our settings script. The user can create a shortcut to that directory for single-click access to the different settings scripts. Another thing our script doesn't do is check for any inconsistencies. It really doesn't make sense to turn Airplane mode on and set Wifi or Bluetooth to On. The intent behind the Airplane mode setting is to allow the script to turn Airplane mode off and set the others on. Most phones have a fairly easy way to turn Airplane mode on, so we'll not try to reproduce that. Figure 8-25 shows what our final settings dialog box will look like.

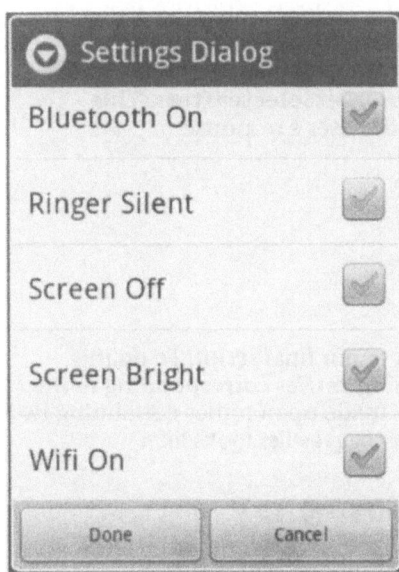

Figure 8-25. *Alert dialog box with list of items and two buttons*

When you click the Done button, you'll be presented with a new dialog box allowing you to name your script. To exit this dialog box, you must press either Done or Cancel. You could also use the hardware back button to exit the application if you so choose.

Figure 8-26 shows what the final dialog box prompting the user for a filename will look like.

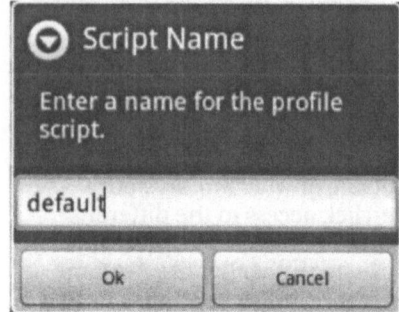

Figure 8-26. *Alert dialog box prompting for a name to save the settings script*

The last piece of code we need to look at handles the return from the multiple selection dialog box. First, you have to check to see which button the user pressed. If the Cancel button was pressed, we want to exit the script and not do anything. That requires the call to `dialogGetResponse` to determine which button was pressed. To actually read the response requires a call to `dialogGetSelectedItems`. This returns a list of the items selected. Here's the section of code that gets the user's response:

```
response = droid.dialogGetResponse().result

if 'canceled' in response:
    droid.exit()
else:
    response = droid.dialogGetSelectedItems().result
```

Once we have the selected values we can choose what to write out to our final script. To do this, we'll use some Python trickery to pull a specific line from a list containing entries corresponding to the positive and negative action we need to accomplish. The `toggles` list is made up of tuples containing two strings each so that the list has a total of five elements. Here's what our `toggles` list looks like:

```
toggles = [
    ('droid.toggleAirplaneMode(True)', 'droid.toggleAirplaneMode(False)'),
    ('droid.toggleBluetoothState(True)', 'droid.toggleBluetoothState(False)'),
    ('droid.toggleRingerSilentMode(True)', 'droid.toggleRingerSilentMode(False)'),
    ('droid.setScreenBrightness(0)', 'droid.setScreenBrightness(255)'),
    ('droid.toggleWifiState(True)', 'droid.toggleWifiState(False)'),
]
```

Now we can use the `enumerate` function, which takes an iterable; in this case, the list `toggles` and get a list of tuples containing the index of each item and the item itself as `i` and `toggle`, respectively.

```
for i, toggle in enumerate(toggles):
    if i in response:
        script += toggles[i][0]
    else:
        script += toggles[i][1]
    script += '\n'
```

Here's a sample of what the file looks like when the user selects Ok:

```python
import android

droid = android.Android()
droid.toggleAirplaneMode(False)
droid.toggleBluetoothState(True)
droid.toggleRingerSilentMode(False)
droid.setScreenBrightness(255)
droid.toggleWifiState(True)

droid.dialogCreateAlert('Profile Enabled', 'The "default" profile has been activated.')
droid.dialogSetPositiveButtonText('OK')
droid.dialogShow()
```

That's pretty much it. The first two lines in the script are required to import the android module and to instantiate our droid object.

```python
import android, os

script_dir = '/sdcard/sl4a/scripts/settings/'

if not os.path.exists(script_dir):
    os.makedir(script_dir)

droid = android.Android()

toggles = [
    ('droid.toggleAirplaneMode(True)', 'droid.toggleAirplaneMode(False)'),
    ('droid.toggleBluetoothState(True)', 'droid.toggleBluetoothState(False)'),
    ('droid.toggleRingerSilentMode(True)', 'droid.toggleRingerSilentMode(False)'),
    ('droid.setScreenBrightness(0)', 'droid.setScreenBrightness(255)'),
    ('droid.toggleWifiState(True)', 'droid.toggleWifiState(False)'),
]

droid.dialogCreateAlert('Settings Dialog', 'Chose any number of items and then press OK')
droid.dialogSetPositiveButtonText('Done')
droid.dialogSetNegativeButtonText('Cancel')

droid.dialogSetMultiChoiceItems(['Airplane Mode',
                                 'Bluetooth On',
                                 'Ringer Silent',
                                 'Screen Off',
                                 'Wifi On'])

droid.dialogShow()
response = droid.dialogGetResponse().result

if 'canceled' in response:
    droid.exit()
else:
    response = droid.dialogGetSelectedItems().result
```

```python
droid.dialogDismiss()
res = droid.dialogGetInput('Script Name',
                           'Enter a name for the profile script.',
                           'default').result

script = '''import android

droid = android.Android()
'''

for i, toggle in enumerate(toggles):
    if i in response:
        script += toggles[i][0]
    else:
        script += toggles[i][1]
    script += '\n'

script += '''
droid.dialogCreateAlert('Profile Enabled', 'The "%s" profile has been activated.')
droid.dialogSetPositiveButtonText('OK')
droid.dialogShow()''' % res

f = open(script_dir + res + '.py', 'w')
f.write(script)
f.close()
```

Summary

This chapter shows you the basics of interacting with a user via the available dialog boxes. Here's a list of takeaways for this chapter:

- **Dialog box basics**: The SL4A dialog box facade provides a number of standard ways to present information and get user input. Understanding how and when to use each one will help you build scripts that will be both useful and easy to use.

- **Understanding results**: It's important to understand what results to expect from the different input dialog boxes and how to handle each button a user could choose.

- **Modal and non-modal dialog boxes**: Use a modal dialog box when you need input from the user before you continue execution.

- **Using modules from the Python Standard Library**: These are great for handling routine file system chores.

- **Good programming practices**: There's no substitute for using good programming practices, including handling all possible actions a user can take.

- **Using multiple dialog boxes**: You can chain multiple dialog box types together to build a more complex UI with prompting through **createAlertDialog** and output with a list box recursively using the **dialogSetItems** function call.

CHAPTER 9

Python GUIs with HTML

This chapter will take a look at the options available for building graphical user interfaces (GUIs) with SL4A based on CSS, HTML, JavaScript, and Python.

Note This chapter will discuss the use of CSS, HTML, and JavaScript to build applications that present real-world user interfaces. Some background in these areas would be helpful if you have it, but it's not essential.

Here are the main topics for this chapter:

- HTML GUI basics

- Using cascading style sheets (CSS) to add some formatting to the HTML

- Creating commercial-quality user interfaces with CSS, HTML, JavaScript, and Python

The basic approach here uses HTML and JavaScript to build the user interface (UI) and then Python behind the scenes to handle any additional processing. CSS can be used to make the HTML fields and fonts cleaner in terms of appearance and consistency. Python can also be used to build an HTML file for displaying information without any user interface.

HTML and Basic Information Display

It's not uncommon when building applications to need a way to simply display a chunk of information to the user. This might be in the form of a list or even just a single continuous text box. Both are easily supported using HTML as the display mechanism. The HTML file could be generated programmatically or created using any text editor and then launched using the `webViewShow` API call.

We'll look at option number one first. In this sample code, we'll query the status of the battery and display everything you ever wanted to know in a simple HTML file. We'll then launch the file with a call to `webViewShow` and we're done. Here's the code to make it happen:

```python
import time

import android

# Simple HTML template using python's format string syntax.
template = '''<html><body>
<h1>Battery Status</h1>
<ul>
<li><strong>Status: %(status)s</li>
<li><strong>Temperature: %(temperature)s</li>
<li><strong>Level: %(level)s</li>
<li><strong>Plugged In: %(plugged)s</li>
</ul>
</body></html>'''

if __name__ == '__main__':
    droid = android.Android()

    # Wait until we have readings from the battery.
    droid.batteryStartMonitoring()
    result = None
    while result is None:
        result = droid.readBatteryData().result
        time.sleep(0.5)

    # Write out the HTML with the values from our battery reading.
    f = open('/sdcard/sl4a/scripts/battstats.html', 'w')
    f.write(template % result)
    f.close()

    # Show the resulting HTML page.
    droid.webViewShow('file:///sdcard/sl4a/scripts/battstats.html')
```

This creates a file in the scripts directory with the name battstats.html. If you wanted to keep a collection of these files, you could merely add the current time to the filename to generate a unique file each time. Figure 9-1 shows what you should see when the code displays the file:

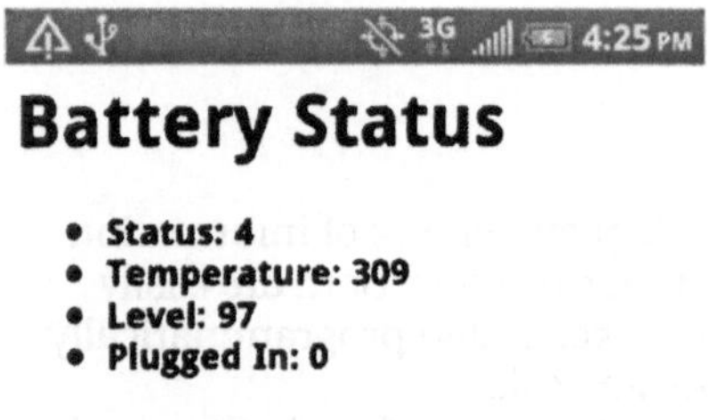

Battery Status

- **Status: 4**
- **Temperature: 309**
- **Level: 97**
- **Plugged In: 0**

Figure 9-1. Use of a simple HTML file to display battery status

A second example of this call is to take our WiFi scanner example from Chapter 7 and display the information using the HTML file method. In this case, you might want to add something such as a time and date stamp in the file and then append to the end each time. This way, you'll have a running log of the WiFi access points your device has seen. Here's the code to generate the file:

```python
import time
import android

if __name__ == '__main__':
    droid = android.Android()

    # Show the HTML page immediately.
    droid.webViewShow('file:///sdcard/sl4a/scripts/wifi.html')

    # Mainloop
    while True:

        # Wait until the scan finishes.
        while not droid.wifiStartScan().result: time.sleep(0.25)

        # Send results to HTML page.
        droid.postEvent('show_networks', droid.wifiGetScanResults().result)

        time.sleep(1)
```

While this code will simply show the current WiFi access points in range, you could create a log file and append your results to it. This file would grow over time until you delete it. The nice thing about saving it to a file and then displaying it as an HTML file is that you can scroll through it using the same finger motions as you would to view a web page. Figure 9-2 shows the results.

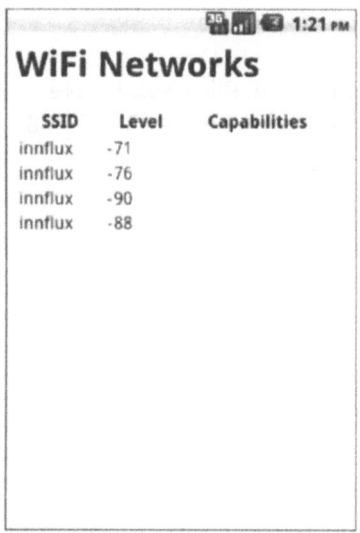

Figure 9-2. *Results of WiFi scan*

HTML and JavaScript

The next step beyond basic information display is to add some type of interactivity. This is where we have to bring JavaScript into the discussion. SL4A provides a mechanism for communication between a web page and Python. This is accomplished using events and some JavaScript code in the web page. The only real requirement for the JavaScript code is that you must instantiate the Android object with the code **var droid = new Android()** before you make any API calls. Once that's done you have access to the same set of API facades as you do from Python.

Here's an example that uses JavaScript to get a list of contacts and dynamically build a web page from the data. This technique can be used with any API call that returns data you'd like to display. Here's what the HTML file looks like:

```html
<html>
    <head>
    </head>
    <body>
        <h1>Contacts</h1>
        <ul id="contacts"></ul>
        <script type="text/javascript">
            var droid = new Android();
            var contacts = droid.contactsGet(['display_name']);
            var container = document.getElementById('contacts');
            for (var i=0;i<=contacts.result.length;i++){
                var data = contacts.result[i];
                contact = '<li>';
                contact = contact + data[0];
                contact = contact + '</li>';
                container.innerHTML = container.innerHTML + contact;
            }
        </script>
    </body>
</html>
```

Notice that all I'm doing here is calling the contactsGet routine and passing in the display_name qualifier. Here's what the Python code would look like to actually display the HTML file (the only thing this code does is load up the HTML file and then exit):

```python
import android

droid = android.Android()
droid.webViewShow('file:///sdcard/sl4a/scripts/contacts.html')
```

Figure 9-3 shows the result of our efforts.

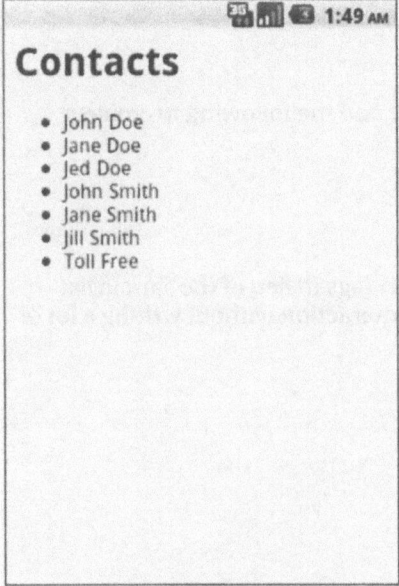

Figure 9-3. *Basic HTML display of contacts as a list*

This version is nice for simply displaying information but what if you wanted the user to be able to do something with what you present? We can make a slight modification to the HTML file and add a touch of interaction using a basic table and a hyperlink. Here's the HTML and JavaScript code:

```
<html>
    <head>
    </head>
    <body>
        <h1>Contacts</h1>
        <table id="contacts"></table>
        <script type="text/javascript">
            var droid = new Android();
            function call(number){
                droid.phoneDialNumber(number);
            }
            var contacts = droid.contactsGet(['display_name', 'primary_phone']);
            var container = document.getElementById('contacts');
            for (var i=0;i<=contacts.result.length;i++){
                var data = contacts.result[i];
                contact = '<tr>';
                contact += '<th>' + data[0] + '</th>';
                contact += '<td><a href="#" onclick="call(' + data[1] +
                        ');return false;">' + data[1] + '</a></td>';
```

```
            contact += '</tr>';
            container.innerHTML = container.innerHTML + contact;
        }
    </script>
    </body>
</html>
```

There are two slight modifications to the JavaScript code. First, we add the following to create a hyperlink to open the call dialog box:

```
function call(number){
            droid.phoneDialNumber(number);
        }
```

The other change is to create a table using the HTML <tr> and <td> tags in lieu of the simple list element tags. While the change is pretty simple, it creates a nice user interaction without writing a lot of code. Figure 9-4 shows the result.

Figure 9-4. *HTML display of contacts as a table*

HTML GUI Form Basics

Now we'll take a look at the basics of building GUIs with SL4A using CSS, HTML, and JavaScript. In general, the idea is to create an HTML form that uses Python to handle events generated by the form. So, for example, you could have a button on a form that causes something to happen when you press it. The SL4A wiki gives a simple example I've included here in Listing 9-1:

Listing 9-1. *text_to_speech.html*

```html
<html>
  <head>
    <title>Text to Speech</title>
    <script>
      var droid = new Android();
      var speak = function() {
        droid.postEvent("say", document.getElementById("say").value);
      }
    </script>
  </head>
  <body>
    <form onsubmit="speak(); return false;">
      <label for="say">What would you like to say?</label>
      <input type="text" id="say" />
      <input type="submit" value="Speak" />
    </form>
  </body>
</html>
```

Listing 9-2. *speakit.py*

```python
import android

droid = android.Android()
droid.webViewShow('file:///sdcard/sl4a/scripts/text_to_speech.html')
while True:
  result = droid.waitForEvent('say').result
  droid.ttsSpeak(result['data'])
```

Two files are needed to make up this program: the HTML file named **text_to_speech.html** and the Python launcher we'll call **speakit.py** (see Listing 9-2). Both must reside in the **/sdcard/sl4a/scripts** directory on the device. To launch the program, run the **speakit.py** file from the SL4A list of files. The Python code first launches the **text_to_speech.html** file using the **webViewShow** API call and then waits for an event to fire from the HTML page. The event is generated when the user touches the "speak" button.

Figure 9-5 shows what the screen will look like.

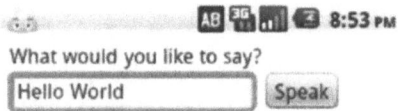

Figure 9-5. *Simple HTML page for text-to-speech demo*

The JavaScript code is enclosed by the **<script> </script>** tags and provides the connection to the calling Python script using the **postEvent** API call. To launch this HTML form requires a call to the **webViewShow** API as follows:

```
import android

droid = android.Android()
droid.webViewShow('file:///sdcard/sl4a/scripts/text_to_speech.html')
while True:
  result = droid.waitForEvent('say').result
  droid.ttsSpeak(result['data'])
```

Once the form is displayed, the Python code will block and wait for the **'say'** event to fire. This event will return the text to pass to the **ttsSpeak** API function in the data field of the result object. The web page will actually close when the user clicks the speak button, and the Python code will exit once control returns from the **ttsSpeak** function.

Simple HTML Forms

Now we're ready to tackle a little more complex problem with multiple input boxes and input types. This script will display a screen allowing the user to set a number of device preference settings including screen brightness and timeout, media volume, ringer volume, and the WiFi mode. The HTML for creating this type of form is pretty straightforward. Here's all you need:

```html
<body>
<div id="body">
<h1>My Settings</h1>
<form>
    <div class="container">
        <div>
            <label for="brightness">Brightness Level</label>
            <input size="5" id="brightness" type="text" />
        </div>
        <div>
            <label for="timeout">Timeout Secs</label>
            <select>
                <option value="0">0</option>
                <option value="1">1</option>
                <option value="2">2</option>
                <option value="3">3</option>
                <option value="4">4</option>
                <option value="5">5</option>
            </select>
        </div>
        <div>
            <label for="screen">Screen Off</label>
            <input id="screen" type="checkbox" />
        </div>
    </div>
    <hr />
```

```
    <div class="container">
        <div>
            <label for="media_vol">Media Volume</label>
            <input size="5" id="media_vol" type="text" />
        </div>
        <div>
            <label for="ringer_vol">Ringer Volume</label>
            <input size="5" id="ringer_vol" type="text" />
        </div>
    </div>
    <hr />
    <div class="container">
        <div>
            <label for="airplane_mode">Airplane Mode</label>
            <input id="airplane_mode" name="radio" type="radio" />
        </div>
        <div>
            <label for="wifi_on">Wifi On</label>
            <input id="wifi_on" name="radio" type="radio" />
        </div>
    </div>
    <div class="container buttons">
        <div>
            <input size="5" id="save" name="save" type="button" value="Save Settings" />
            <input size="5" id="cancel" name="cancel" type="button" value="Cancel" />
        </div>
    </div>
</form>
</div>
</body>

</html>
```

This will produce a page that looks like Figure 9-6. As you can see there are a few issues with how this renders on the small screen. The title is chopped off, the buttons don't completely fit on the page, and the horizontal rule lines seem to go off the page. While you could do some tweaking of the HTML to make it look pretty, the better way is to use CSS.

Figure 9-6. *Basic HTML form with no CSS*

Cascading Style Sheets

Formatting HTML with cascading style sheets (CSS) goes a long way toward creating and presenting a clean user interface. With CSS you can determine alignment, font, text flow, and size for all HTML elements on the page. This comes in really handy with small screens where you want to dictate exactly how each element on the page appears.

Here's a small snippet of CSS that I'll use to help spruce up our user settings page:

```
<html>
<head>
    <style>
        #body {width:100%;}
        .container {text-align:center;margin:auto;}
        .container div {text-align:left;width:75%;}
        h1 {text-align:center;margin:auto;}
        hr {width:75%;margin:0px auto;}
        label {display:block;float:left;width:60%;}
        .buttons div {text-align:center;margin:auto;}
    </style>
</head>
```

The body portion of the web form contains a number of standard elements like `<div>` tags, input boxes using the `<label>` and `<input>` tags, and a list of options to choose from in a drop-down box using the `<label>` and `<select>` tags. The preceding CSS code controls the width and appearance of the labels and alignment of the text. It also controls how the buttons, **h1** and **hr** HTML tags are formatted. You can do a lot more with CSS, but we'll stop here for this example. The remaining HTML looks the same as before.

Figure 9-7 shows what the HTML page will look like with the CSS added. While there's not a lot of difference, notice the width of the text boxes and the overall spacing of the elements. Feel free to go with the look you prefer.

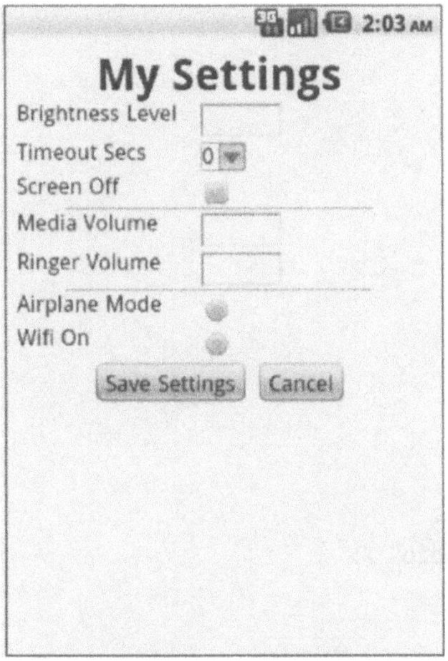

Figure 9-7. *HTML form with CSS added*

From the **speakit.py** example, we saw the use of the **droid.postEvent()** JavaScript code to send data back to the Python application using an event. This sent a single string value representing a phrase to be spoken. This form contains a number of elements with information that must be extracted and sent back to the Python code. There are a number of ways this can be accomplished, but we'll simply use a key/value string pair.

This can be done by adding a few more lines of code to our JavaScript to pass more information from the HTML form. Here's what it looks like:

```
<script type="text/javascript">
    var droid = new Android();

    function post_data(){
        var values = [
            ['airplane', document.getElementById('airplane_mode').value],
            ['wifi', document.getElementById('wifi_on').value],
            ['brightness', document.getElementById('brightness').value],
            ['volume', document.getElementById('volume').value],
        ];
```

```
            var q = '?';
            for (i=0;i<values.length;i++){
                var k = values[i][0];
                var v = values[i][1];
                if (q != '?'){
                    q = q + '&';
                }
                q = q + k + '=' + v;
            }

            droid.postEvent('save', q);
        }
    </script>
```

And here's the HTML that goes with this code:

```
<body>
<div id="body">
<h1>My Settings</h1>
<form onsubmit="post_data();return false;">
    <div class="container">
        <div>
            <label for="airplane_mode">Airplane Mode</label>
            <input id="airplane_mode" name="radio" type="radio" />
        </div>
        <div>
            <label for="wifi_on">WiFi On</label>
            <input id="wifi_on" name="radio" type="radio" />
        </div>
    </div>
    <div class="container">
        <div>
            <label for="brightness">Brightness Level</label>
            <input size="5" id="brightness" type="text" />
        </div>
        <div>
            <label for="volume">Media Volume</label>
            <input size="5" id="volume" type="text" />
        </div>
    </div>
    <div class="container buttons">
        <div>
            <input size="5" id="save" name="save" type="submit" value="Save Settings" />
            <input size="5" id="cancel" name="cancel" type="button" value="Cancel" />
        </div>
    </div>
</form>
</div>
</body>
```

The key to extracting the value from a specific HTML form element is the
`document.getElementById()` line. On the Python side, the values are then used to set specific settings on the phone. The Python code looks like this:

```
import android
import urlparse

droid = android.Android()
droid.webViewShow('file:///sdcard/sl4a/scripts/settings.html')
while True:
    result = droid.waitForEvent('save').result
    data = urlparse.parse_qs(result['data'][1:])

    droid.toggleAirplaneMode('airplane' in data)
    droid.toggleWifiState('wifi' in data)
    droid.setScreenBrightness('screen' in data and 255 or 0)
```

This example introduces another Python Standard Library tool named `urlparse`. This function will parse through the returned elements into a list of data items as key/value pairs. All that's left to do at that point is make the calls to the appropriate API functions to set the values.

SMS Merger

The SL4A home page includes links to a good number of example programs, including a few that demonstrate how to use the `webViewShow` API function. SMS Merger is definitely the most complete example of what can be done using a combination of Python, JavaScript, HTML, and CSS. This sample also gives us the opportunity to use Eclipse and its file management features to demonstrate how to build a complex application and eventually distribute it as an Android package (`.apk` file). That portion will actually be covered in Chapter 10.

To understand this sample program, it's important to break it down into the different components to see what each function does. Keep in mind that this program is a sample, not an actual fully tested and working application. It does have some quirks and even exposes a few bugs in the early versions of SL4A. The intent here is to examine the code to see what each function does and give you an idea of what you can build using the same techniques. I'll give you a summary of what to watch out for at the end of this section if you choose to run the code yourself. If you open up the `SMSMerge.zip` file, you should see something like Figure 9-8.

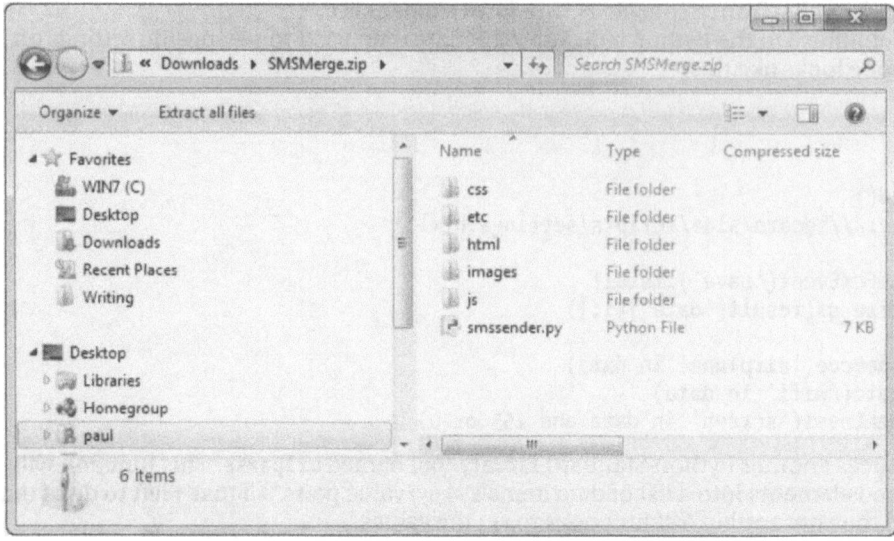

Figure 9-8. *Contents of SMSMerge.zip file*

Each of these directories contains information based on the name. The **/etc** directory contains a single file named **SMSSender.conf**, which stores all configuration information for the application. If you open the file with a text editor, you'll see something like this:

```
[locale]
prefix = +60

[merger]
informeveryratio = 10
informevery = 0

[application]
showonlycsvfiles = 0
showonlytextfiles = 1
showhiddendirectories = 0

[package]
version = 1.01
```

This is a great example of using standard Python coding practices that you would find in a typical open source application written for the desktop. It's based upon the Python Standard Library **ConfigParser** module. To use it, simply **import ConfigParser** and then instantiate it with **parser = ConfigParser()** to get access to the different methods. The section names are totally up to the programmer and should reflect a meaningful title. In this case, there are four named sections. When parsed, they turn into a Python dictionary of key/value pairs associated with the section name. Here's the code to load the **config** file section by section:

```
def load( self ):
    # Go through all the sections
    sections = {}
    # Some sections are meant to be ignored
    for section in self.sections():
        if section not in self.ignore:
            items = self.items(section)
            options = []
            for item in items:
                options.append( {"name":item[0],
                                 "value":item[1],
                                 "description": self.descriptions[section][item[0]]})
                sections[section] = options
        return sections
```

In Figure 9-9, you can see the available options on the setup page and get an idea of how they correlate to the values in the config file.

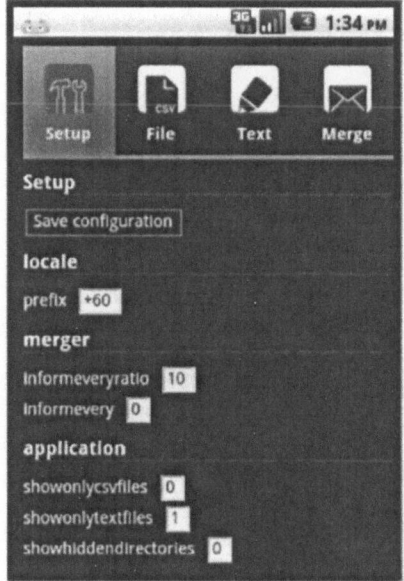

Figure 9-9. *Setup configuration page*

If you click on the label for any of the options, you'll get a pop up dialog box with a description of what the option does and what values are acceptable. Figure 9-10 shows what you would see if you click the showonlycsvfiles line. It uses a popup alert dialog box to give the user feedback about the consequences of setting this particular option.

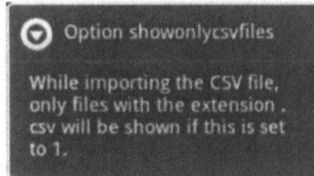

Figure 9-10. *Popup dialog box for showonlycsvfiles option*

Let's back up at this point and talk about the CSS file. In the earlier HTML example I used a pretty simplistic CSS file to define how the form would appear on the small screen. This application takes the CSS file to a whole new level. If you open the **zest.css** file in a text editor, you'll see the different sections and the techniques used to define the HTML element formatting. At the top of the file, you'll see two sections labeled **body** and **button**. Here's what the code looks like:

```
body {
        width:100%;
        padding: 0;
        font-size: 14px;
        background: black;
        color:white;
        font-family: Arial;
}
button{
        color:white;
        background: transparent;
        border: solid 1px #2986a5;
}
```

The body section defines the defaults for the entire body of the HTML page while the button section defines the defaults for buttons. For this application, there is a menu made up of four icons across the top of the page. These change depending on user interaction. Each button has a base color of white, a transparent background, and a one-pixel border around it with the hex color code of #2986a5.

Instead of plain buttons, the SMS Merger app uses a fairly common approach using image files. Each button uses two image versions for selected and not selected. When a user presses a button, the image is swapped, creating a highlighting effect. Figure 9-11 shows a view of the directory containing the different button images.

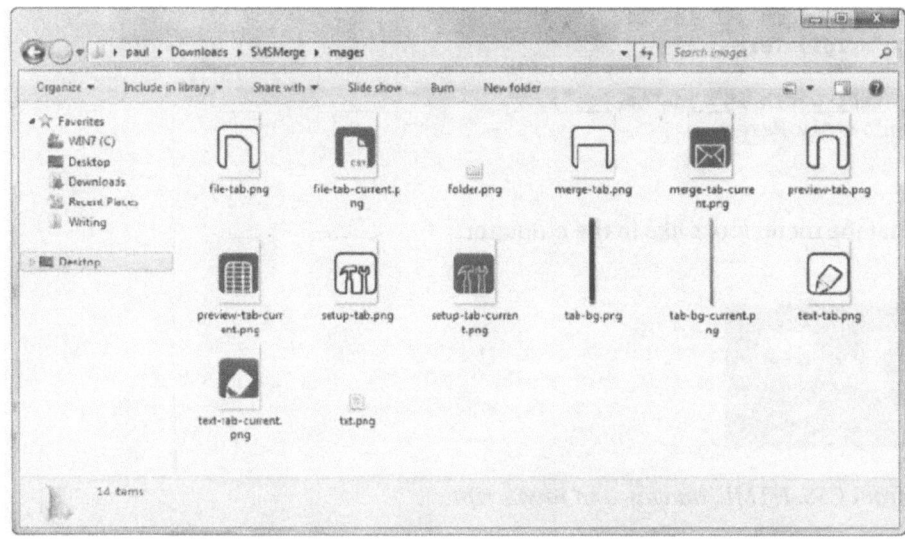

Figure 9-11. *Icons used for UI elements*

Here's a section of CSS code that defines what the menu will look like at the top of the page:

```
div#menu {
        background-image: url("../images/tab-bg.png");
        background-repeat: repeat-x;
        color: white;
        font-weight: bold;
        height: 96px;
}
div#menu div.current {
        background-image: url("../images/tab-bg-current.png");
        background-repeat: repeat-x;
}
div.icon {
        height: 67px;
        width: 100%;
        background-repeat: no-repeat;
        background-position: top center;
}
```

And here's the corresponding chunk of HTML:

```
<div class="col width-100" id="menu">
        <div class="col tabs width-25" id="bSetup">
                <div class="icon"></div>Setup
        </div>
        <div class="col tabs width-25" id="bFile">
                <div class="icon"></div>File
        </div>
```

```
            <div class="col tabs width-25" id="bText">
            <div class="icon"></div>Text
            </div>
            <div class="col tabs width-25" id="bMerge">
            <div class="icon"></div>Merge
            </div>
</div>
```

Figure 9-12 shows what the menu looks like in the emulator.

Figure 9-12. *Menu built from CSS, HTML, images, and JavaScript*

When you touch one of the buttons, such as the File button, you'll be presented with a new display as shown in Figure 9-13. The HTML code for this page looks like this:

```
<div id="dFile" class="nodisplay col width-100">
        <h1>File - <button id="bCSV">Load</button></h1>
        <p class="col width-100" id="csvfile"></p>
        <div class="col width-100 nodisplay" id="dFields">
                <h1>Fields (select phone number column):</h1>
                <div></div>
        </div>
        <div class="col width-100">
                <h1>File dialect:</h1>
                <p>End of line character: <span id="dialectLineterminator"></span></p>
                <p>Quote character: <span id="dialectQuotechar"></span></p>
                <p>Field delimiter: <span id="dialectDelimiter"></span></p>
        </div>
        <div class="col width-100">
                <h1>File preview:</h1>
                <div id="dPreview"></div>
        </div>
</div>
```

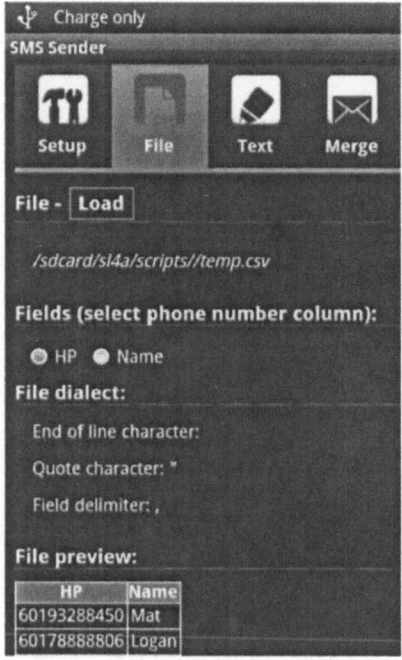

Figure 9-13. *File Load screen*

The File Preview section is built from the loaded CSV file and uses data provided by the Python code. Here's the code that actually reads the file and returns it to the JavaScript:

```python
def loadfile(self, data):
    self.log("Loading file")
    merger = self.merger
    filename = data["path"]
    if filename != "":
        self.log("Selected filename %s " % filename)
        try:
            reader = CSVReader( filename )
        except csv.Error, e:
            return { "error": "Unable to open CSV: %s" % e }
        fields = reader.getFields()
        self.log("Found fields: %s" % ''.join(fields))
        merger.setFields(fields)
        rows = reader.getRows()
        merger.setItems(rows)
        # Rows are now dicts, for preview, want them as list of values only
        values = []
        for row in rows:
            values.append( row.values() )
```

```
else:
    self.log("No file name")
    return {"filename":"","fields":[], "error": ""}
# Success and new file, return all info
return {"filename":filename, "fields":fields,
        "delimiter":reader.dialect.delimiter,
        "quotechar":reader.dialect.quotechar,
        "lineterminator": reader.dialect.lineterminator,
        "error": "", "rows":values }
```

The merge tab is where the real action takes place. It takes the CSV file with phone number and message text and merges it with either a message you type in manually or load from a file, and ultimately broadcasts the SMS messages. Figure 9-14 shows what this screen looks like.

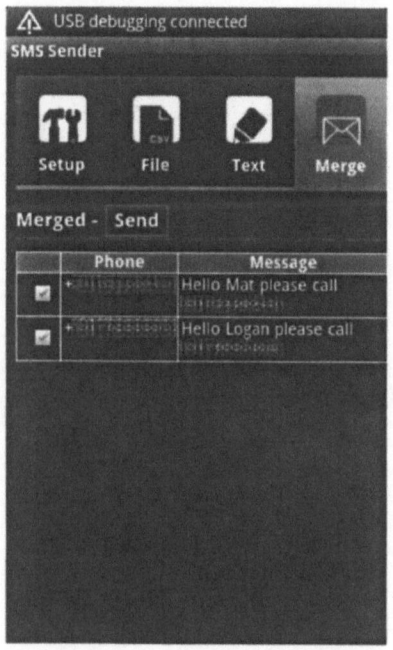

Figure 9-14. *Merge and Send SMS screen*

The Python code to perform the merge is not difficult to read at all. Here's what that looks like:

```
def merge(self, data):
    droid = self.droid
    merger = self.merger
    merger.prefix = parser.get( "locale", "prefix" )
    merger.setNumberColumn(int(data["phone"]))
    merger.setTemplate(data["text"])
    ret = {"success":False, "error":"", "messages":[]}
```

```
        # Valid template returns a list of merge fields that are not used by the given template
    missing = merger.validTemplate()
    if missing.__len__() == 0:
        ret["messages"] = merger.merge()
        ret["success"] = True
    else:
        droid.dialogCreateAlert("Incomplete text",
"The following merge fields are not being used by the template: %s.\r\n Would you like↵
 to edit the template text?" % ",".join(missing))
        droid.dialogSetPositiveButtonText("Yes")
        droid.dialogSetNegativeButtonText("No")
        droid.dialogShow()
        resp = droid.dialogGetResponse()
        # User wishes to load now
        if resp.result["which"] == "positive" :
            return {"task":"edittext"}
        else:
            ret["messages"] = merger.merge()
            ret["success"] = True
    return ret
```

There's also some JavaScript code behind this page as well:

```
/*
* Merge tab button event
* On Click, checks that CSV is loaded, checks that template text is loaded.
* Then fires an event to request Python to merge all SMS
* Receives sms as object {number,message} and displays them in a table
*/
buttons.merge.addEvent("click",function(){
    if(!csvLoaded()){
        if(loadCsv()){
            buttons.file.fireEvent("click");
            buttons.importCSV.fireEvent("click");
        }
    } else {
        var text=dta.getValue();
        if(text == ""){
            textNeeded();
            buttons.textTab.fireEvent("click");
        } else {
            handler.startLoad("Processing", "Merging")
            showOne(tabs,divs.mergeTab);
            phone = getMergeFields().phone;
            var resp = handler.postAndWait( {"task":"merge", "text":text.replace↵
("\n","\\u000A"), "phone":phone });
            if(resp.task=="edittext"){
                buttons.textTab.fireEvent("click");
                dta.fireEvent("click");
```

```
            }else{
                clearMergedSamples();
                var table = divs.mergeTab.getElement("table");
                resp.messages.each(function(m){
                    var clone = templateRow.clone();
                    clone.getElement("td.phone").setText(m.number);
                    clone.getElement("td.message").setText(m.message);
                    table.adopt(clone);
                });
            }
            handler.stopLoad();
        }
    }
});
```

Dependencies

Every software project has dependencies of some kind. When you choose a language in which to code, you have made a dependency choice. If your application will run on a specific operating system, you have made an OS dependency decision. External libraries often provide extra functionality that would be difficult to code otherwise. The price you pay is the pain involved in packaging the libraries and managing any updates that might break your code. All the sample scripts in this book depend on SL4A and Python.

The first version of SMS Merger used an external dependency for browsing and choosing files in the form of Open Intents (OI) File Manager. Here's a snippet of code from that version that launches the OI File Manager using the **startActivityForResult** API call and then extracts the filename from the returned map value:

```
def requestTemplateFromFile( self ):
    droid = self.droid
    map = droid.startActivityForResult( "org.openintents.action.PICK_FILE",
                        None, None,
                        {"org.openintents.extra.TITLE":"Choose file containing message",
                         "org.openintents.extra.BUTTON_TEXT":"Choose"})
    if map.result is None:
        self.requestMessage()
    else:
        filename = map.result["data"].replace( "file://", "" )
        text = open( filename, "r" )
        smscontent = text.readline().replace( "\n", "" )
        if self.validTemplate( smscontent ) is True:
            return smscontent
        else:
            self.warnInvalidTemplate( smscontent )
        # Loop
        return self.requestTemplateFromFile()
```

OI File Manager is a nice tool with a clean UI. It provides a simple way to choose a file and then return it to the caller. Figure 9-15 shows what it looks like.

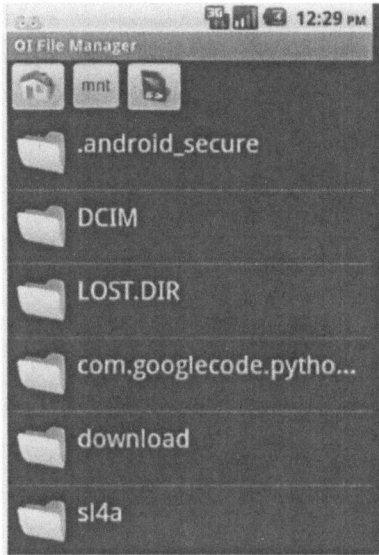

Figure 9-15. *Open Intents File Manager*

One downside of using an external application like OI File Manager is the need for an additional install that a user must accomplish. While this isn't a big deal for a programmer, it definitely isn't something you would want a typical user to do. A better solution would be to use HTML, JavaScript, and Python. Here's a Python function to create a list of files:

```python
def listdir(self, data):
    """ Creates two lists of files and folders in the path found in data

    data -- dict containing path and type (for filtering)

    """
    self.log("Loading directory content")
    base = data["path"]
    type = data["type"]
    # Check in the config whether we want to show only a certain type of content
    showHiddenDirectories = self.parser.getboolean( "application",
                                                "showhiddendirectories" )

    if type == "txt":
        if self.parser.getboolean( "application", "showonlytextfiles" ) is True:
            filter = ".{0}".format( type )
        else:
            filter = None
    elif type == "csv":
        if self.parser.getboolean( "application", "showonlycsvfiles" ) is True:
            filter = ".{0}".format( type )
        else:
            filter = None
```

```
        else:
            filter = None

        # List all directories and files, then filter
        all = os.listdir(base)
        files = []
        folders = []
        for file in all:
            # Separate files and folders
            abs = "{0}/{1}".format( base, file )
            if os.path.isdir( abs ):
                # Are we filtering hidden directories?
                if showHiddenDirectories is True or file[0] != ".":
                    folders.append( str( file ) )
            elif os.path.isfile( abs ):
                # Are we filtering by type?
                if filter is None or os.path.splitext( file )[1] == filter:
                    files.append( str( file ) )

        # Sort alphabetically
        files.sort( key=str.lower )
        folders.sort( key=str.lower )
        return {"files":files,"folders":folders}
```

Figure 9-16 shows an HTML and JavaScript version independent of any external application.

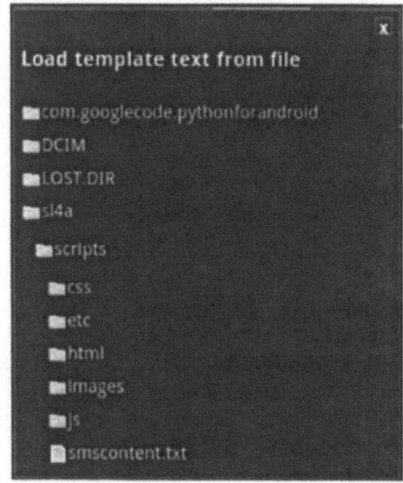

Figure 9-16. *HTML and JavaScript file browser*

The JavaScript code to create this window is lengthy but readable. It basically adds an event handler to the **importCSV** button to first call the Python code to do the actual loading of the CSV file and then build a table to display the results. It passes the path of the CSV file to the Python code as a return from the filebrowser function. The user chooses the CSV file to read by scrolling through the filebrowser window and touching the file, which closes the filebrowser window.

```
buttons.importCSV.addEvent("click",function(){
    // Override the onClose function to use the path of the CSV file
    filebrowser.onClose = function(a) {
        if(a){
            handler.startLoad("Loading","Loading CSV file");
            var resp = handler.postAndWait({"task":"loadfile","path":a});
            if(resp.error==""){
                // resp.filename will definitely be same as a?
                if(resp.filename!=""){
                    clearMergedSamples();
                    divs.csvFilename.setText( resp.filename );
                    divs.fields.removeClass("nodisplay").getElement("div").remove();
                    var newdiv = new Element("div").addClass("col").addClass("width-100");
                    resp.fields.each(function(r, k){
                        newdiv.adopt(new Element("div").addClass("col")
                                .adopt(new Element("input",{"type":"radio","name":"iField"})
                                .addEvent("click",function(){hideAll(valid);}))
                                .adopt(new Element("span").setText(r))
                        );
                    });
                    divs.fields.adopt(newdiv);
                    // Select the first item
                    divs.fields.getElement("input").setProperty("checked",true);
                    // More information about the loaded file
                    $("dialectQuotechar").setText(resp.quotechar);
                    $("dialectDelimiter").setText(resp.delimiter);
                    $("dialectLineterminator").setText(resp.lineterminator);
                    // Preview
                    var t=new Element("table",
                                    {"cellpadding":"0","border":"0"}),th=new Element("tr");
                    resp.fields.each(function(v){
                        th.adopt(new Element("th").setText(v));
                    });
                    t.adopt(th);
                    resp.rows.each(function(v){
                        var tr=new Element("tr");
                        v.each(function(w){
                            tr.adopt(new Element("td").setText(w));
                        });
                        t.adopt(tr);
                    });
                    divs.preview.empty().adopt(t);
                }
            }else{
                handler.alert("CSV import error",resp.error);
            }
            handler.stopLoad();
        }
```

```
        filebrowser.close();
    }
    filebrowser.setType("csv").setTitle("Load CSV file" ).show();
});
```

It's always a good idea to keep the user of your application informed of what's going on. When the SMS Merger app first starts, it needs to load the configuration file if one exists. The spinner dialog box is perfect to tell the user that the application is actually loading a configuration file instead of just leaving a blank screen visible. Figure 9-17 shows how the SMS Sender application uses the spinner to let the user know something is happening.

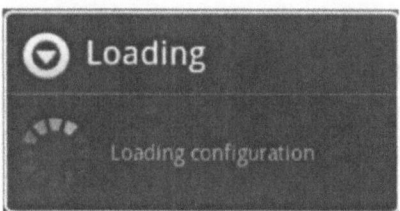

Figure 9-17. *Setup configuration page*

When you use the `webViewShow` API function to pass data between the HTML/JavaScript and the Python code, you must write an event handler on either side to receive the data. The SMS Sender example utilizes both JavaScript and Python event handlers to get the job done. Here's a chunk of code that sets up the different event handlers on the JavaScript side:

```
handler = new UIHandler();
window.addEvent("domready",function(){
    var buttons = {"saveconfig":$("bSaveConfig"),"file":$("bFile"),
                   "setup": $("bSetup"),"importText":$("bChooseText"),
                   "textTab":$("bText"),"merge":$("bMerge"),
                   "validate":$("bValidate"),"process":$("bProcess"),
                   "importCSV":$("bCSV"),"closebrowser":$("closeButton")},
        divs = {"preview":$("dPreview"),"filebrowser":$("filebrowser"),
                "browsercontent":$("browserContent"),"fileTab":$("dFile"),
                "fields":$("dFields"),"csvFilename":$("csvfile"),
                "setupTab":$("dSetup"),"textTab":$("dText"),"mergeTab":$("dCSVMerged")},
    dta=divs.textTab.getElement("textarea"),browserTitle=$("browserTitle"),
    tabs=[divs.setupTab,divs.mergeTab,divs.textTab,divs.fileTab],
    tabButtons=[buttons.setup,buttons.merge,buttons.textTab,buttons.file],
    validSpan=$("wValid"),invalidSpan=$("wInvalid"),valid=[validSpan,invalidSpan],
    templateRow=$("templateTable").getElement("tr");
    tabButtons.each(function(button,k){
        var current = "current";
        button.addEvent("click",function(){
```

```
        if(!button.hasClass(current)){
            removeClassFromAll(tabButtons,current);
            button.addClass(current);
            showOne(tabs,tabs[k]);
        }
    });
});
```

On the Python side, you must have corresponding event handlers. Here's how SMS Sender handles that:

```
class SMSSenderHandler(UIHandler):
    """ Handler class for this particular application. Extends UIHandler """
    def __init__(self):
        UIHandler.__init__(self)
        # Create the dispatch dictionnary which maps tasks to methods
        self.dispatch = {
            "loadfile": self.loadfile,
            "validate": self.validate,
            "loadfilecontent": self.loadfilecontent,
            "loadconfig": self.loadconfig,
            "send": self.send,
            "merge": self.merge,
            "listdir":self.listdir,
            "saveconfig":self.saveconfig
        }
```

Quirks and Gotchas with SMS Sender

Be aware that the SMS Sender example may not run depending on what version of SL4A you have installed. I ran into some issues with SLA4 r3 and the emulator not handling the passing of events correctly. This was a known bug at the time and was reported as such. There also is an issue with the HTML file chooser in that it doesn't seem to allow you to open up a subdirectory after you have opened either the text or CSV file. With that said, it does show off some of the ways you can communicate between Python and the HTML code in both directions.

Summary

This chapter has attempted to show you both the basics of writing scripts that use HTML to display information and interact with the user via the webViewShow API call.

Here's a list of take-aways for this chapter:

- **HTML basics**: Everything you ever learned about good HTML applies here. You can build simple output using an HTML file with just a few lines of code.

- **Learn some JavaScript**: The primary theme of this book is coding in Python, but to get the interaction in an HTML page you will have to write some JavaScript. It's not a difficult language to pick up, especially if you're at all familiar with C++ or Java. There are a multitude of resources on the Web to help get you started.

- **Don't forget design:** One of the biggest complaints about web pages created by programmers is that they don't look very appealing. The SMS Sender example uses a number of good design principles to separate actions and to keep similar functionality grouped together. Because the `webViewShow` API function uses HTML to create the user interface, it's a good idea to learn a little about good HTML page design.

- **CSS can help**: Using CSS is actually a good programming practice as well. It helps separate some of the design aspect from coding into one file. CSS helps to bring a consistent look and feel to HTML and works really well for the small screen.

CHAPTER 10

Packaging and Distributing

This chapter will take a look at ways to package and distribute scripts using Eclipse and QR codes. This chapter will cover these topics:

- Using QR codes to distribute scripts

- Building a distributable application

- Using Eclipse to create an .apk file

While much of this book has been about creating scripts for personal consumption, it is quite possible to build a commercial Android application using SL4A. Once that's done, you need a way to distribute your app so others can enjoy it. This chapter will look at several ways you can do just that.

QR Codes

The Quick Response (QR) code is a great way to publish your work if you have a relatively short script that you'd like to share. Most Android devices include a native barcode scanner app (ZXing), and SL4A even supports importing QR codes directly into the editor. It's also available from the Android Market. When you launch SL4A you should see a listing of files in the **scripts** directory on your device. If you press the hardware menu button, you'll see an Add button on the top left side (see Figure 10-1).

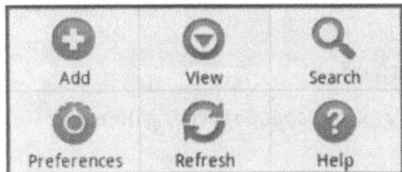

Figure 10-1. *Menu button popup dialog box*

If you press Add, you'll get a menu with options including files for any of the installed interpreters, Shell, and Scan Barcode (see Figure 10-2).

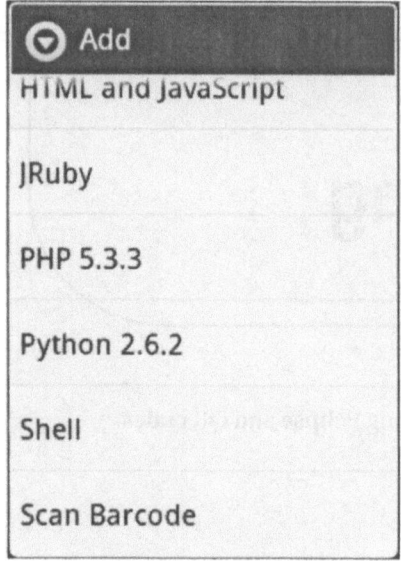

Figure 10-2. Add menu

If you do a quick Google search for SL4A QR codes, you'll find a number of entries in which people have shared their scripts on a blog or personal web site using a QR code. A QR code can only encode 4,296 characters of content, so your scripts will have to be short. There are several web sites where you can paste text and have a QR code created for you. The SL4A wiki references http://zxing.appspot.com/generator. Here are the instructions that go with it:

1. Open the Contents drop-down and choose Text.

2. On the first line of the Text Content, enter the name of the script (for example, hello_world.py).

3. Below that, paste the script content.

4. Open the Size drop-down and choose L.

5. Click Generate.

6. Embed the resulting barcode image or share it with your friends.

Figure 10-3 shows the result of generating a QR code from http://zxing.appspot.com/generator using the makeToast.py code shown here:

```
import android

droid = android.Android()
name = droid.getInput("Hello!", "What is your name?")
droid.makeToast("Hello, %s" % name.result)
```

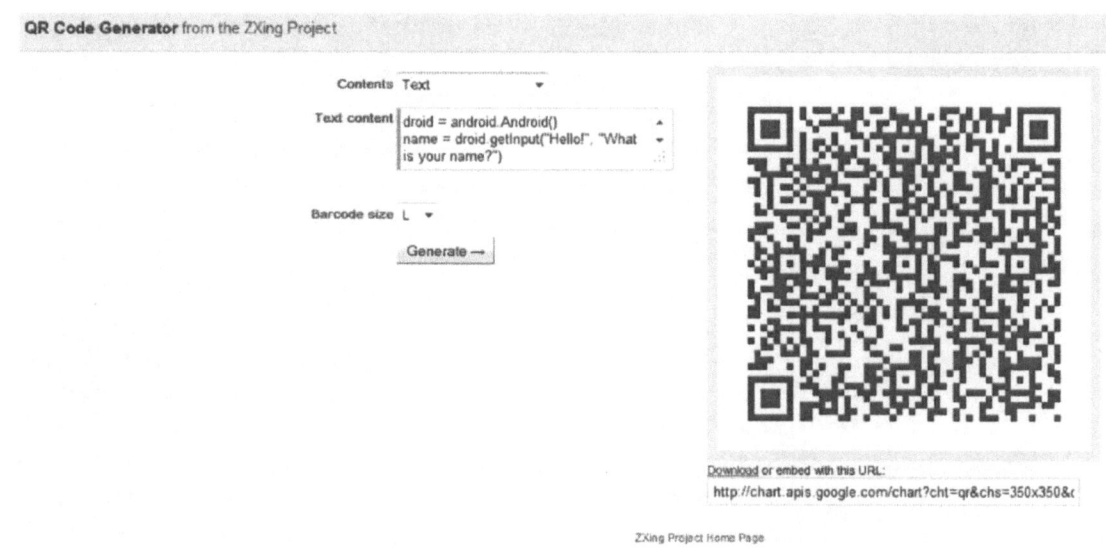

Figure 10-3. *QR code generation using http://zxing.appspot.com*

QR codes give you a nice option if you have a short script to share and a place to share it from, such as a blog or a web site.

Application Packages

Android applications are typically distributed in a single file or package with an `.apk` extension. An Android package is essentially an archive file similar to a `.jar` or `.zip` file. Each `.apk` contains a number of mandatory files that must be present, or the application will not install. The most important file is `AndroidManifest.xml`. This file describes the application in the context of resources and permissions that it needs. According to the Android docs, the manifest does a number of things in addition to declaring the application's components:

- Identifies any user permissions the application requires, such as Internet access or read-access to the user's contacts

- Declares the minimum API level required by the application, based on which APIs the application uses

- Declares hardware and software features used or required by the application, such as a camera, Bluetooth services, or a multitouch screen

- Specifies API libraries the application needs to be linked against (other than the Android framework APIs), such as the Google Maps library

You have a number of options for creating an Android project. One way is to manually create a new project from the command line. It involves using the `android` command along with a few parameters. Figure 10-4 shows the results of running this command from a Windows command prompt.

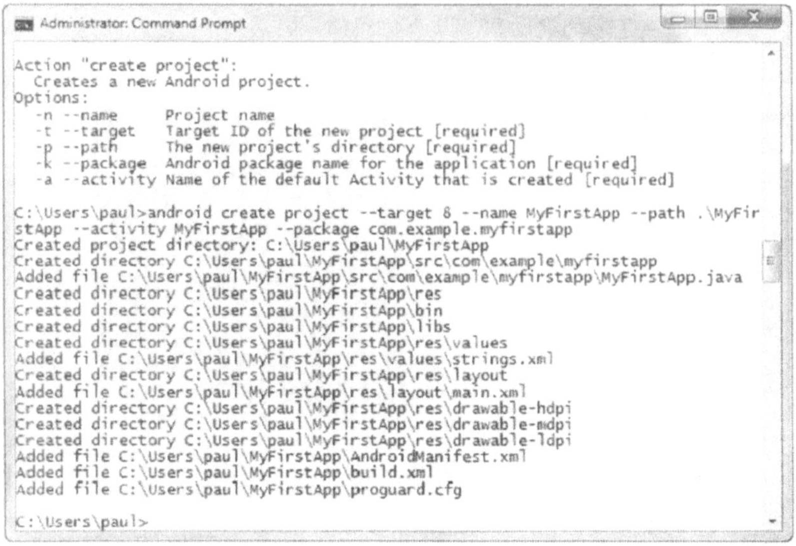

Figure 10-4. *Command-line project creation*

When you use the command-line **android** tool to build your project, it will set things properly in the **AndroidManifest.xml** file. Here's what that file looks like as a result of the command line from Figure 10-4:

```xml
<?xml version="1.0" encoding="utf-8"?>
<manifest xmlns:android="http://schemas.android.com/apk/res/android"
      package="com.example.myfirstapp"
      android:versionCode="1"
      android:versionName="1.0">
    <application android:label="@string/app_name" android:icon="@drawable/icon">
        <activity android:name="MyFirstApp"
                    android:label="@string/app_name">
            <intent-filter>
                <action android:name="android.intent.action.MAIN" />
                <category android:name="android.intent.category.LAUNCHER" />
            </intent-filter>
        </activity>
    </application>
</manifest>
```

The command-line method creates a bare-bones project skeleton that would take quite a bit of tweaking to make it work as an SL4A project. Fortunately for us, the SL4A folks have done most of the work already. The first thing you need to do is download the script template file from the SL4A project site (`http://android-scripting.googlecode.com/hg/android/script_for_android_template.zip`). Figure 10-5 shows what's inside the `script for android template.zip` file.

Name	Type	Compressed size	Password ...	Size	Ratio	Date modified
.settings	File folder					1/19/2011 4:18 PM
assets	File folder					1/31/2011 2:49 PM
libs	File folder					1/31/2011 2:09 PM
res	File folder					1/19/2011 4:18 PM
src	File folder					1/19/2011 4:18 PM
.checkstyle	CHECKSTYLE File	1 KB	No	1 KB	41%	1/19/2011 4:18 PM
.classpath	CLASSPATH File	1 KB	No	1 KB	59%	1/19/2011 4:18 PM
.project	PROJECT File	1 KB	No	1 KB	69%	1/19/2011 4:18 PM
.pydevproject	PYDEVPROJECT File	1 KB	No	1 KB	43%	1/19/2011 4:18 PM
AndroidManifest.xml	XML Document	2 KB	No	12 KB	87%	1/29/2011 10:04 AM
build.properties	PROPERTIES File	1 KB	No	1 KB	52%	1/19/2011 4:18 PM
build.xml	XML Document	2 KB	No	3 KB	65%	1/19/2011 4:18 PM
configure_package.sh	SH File	1 KB	No	1 KB	47%	1/19/2011 4:18 PM
default.properties	PROPERTIES File	1 KB	No	1 KB	33%	1/29/2011 10:04 AM
local.properties	PROPERTIES File	1 KB	No	1 KB	34%	1/19/2011 4:18 PM

Figure 10-5. *Contents of the script_for_android_template.zip file*

The `AndroidManifest.xml` file provided contains a list of items or properties to which you explicitly grant access. The template file available from the SL4A site has a complete list included, but with most of the entries commented out. It will look like the following:

```
<!-- <uses-permission
    android:name="android.permission.VIBRATE" /> -->
```

Each valid permission line should look like this:

```
<uses-permission android:name="android.permission.VIBRATE"></uses-permission>
<uses-permission android:name="android.permission.WRITE_EXTERNAL_STORAGE"></uses-permission>
```

Once you have the template downloaded, you're ready to get started building your distributable project, also known as an `.apk` file. The easiest way by far is to use Eclipse. I'll walk you through the steps using the dummy script template. Step number one is to import the template into Eclipse. Figures 10-6 and 10-7 show the two dialog boxes you'll need to navigate through.

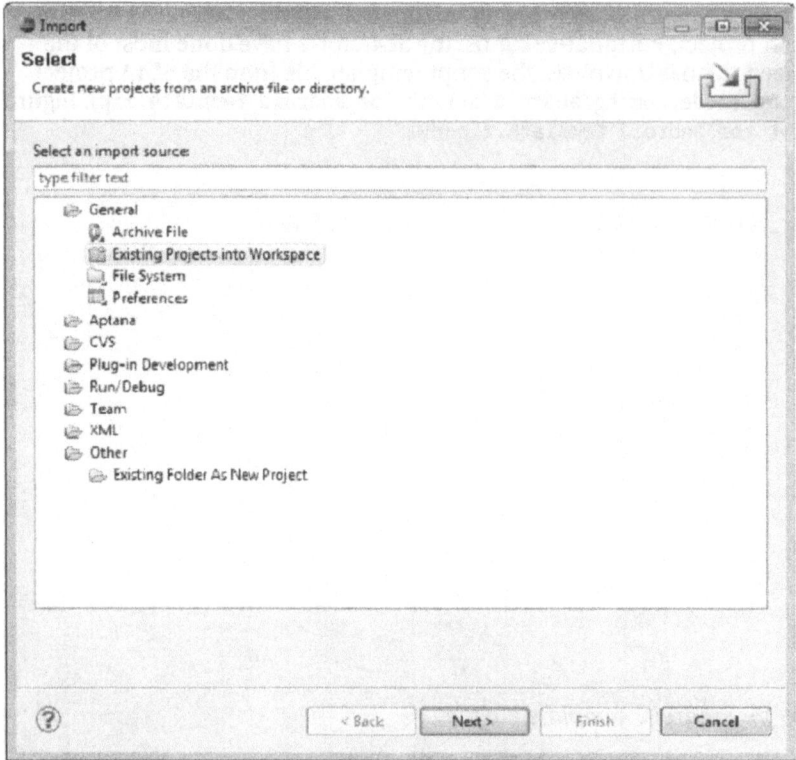

Figure 10-6. Eclipse project import dialog box

When you click the Next button, you should see a dialog box like the one in Figure 10-7. If you click the Browse button on the same line as the Select Archive File option, you'll be able to navigate to the directory and choose the `script_for_android_template.zip` file.

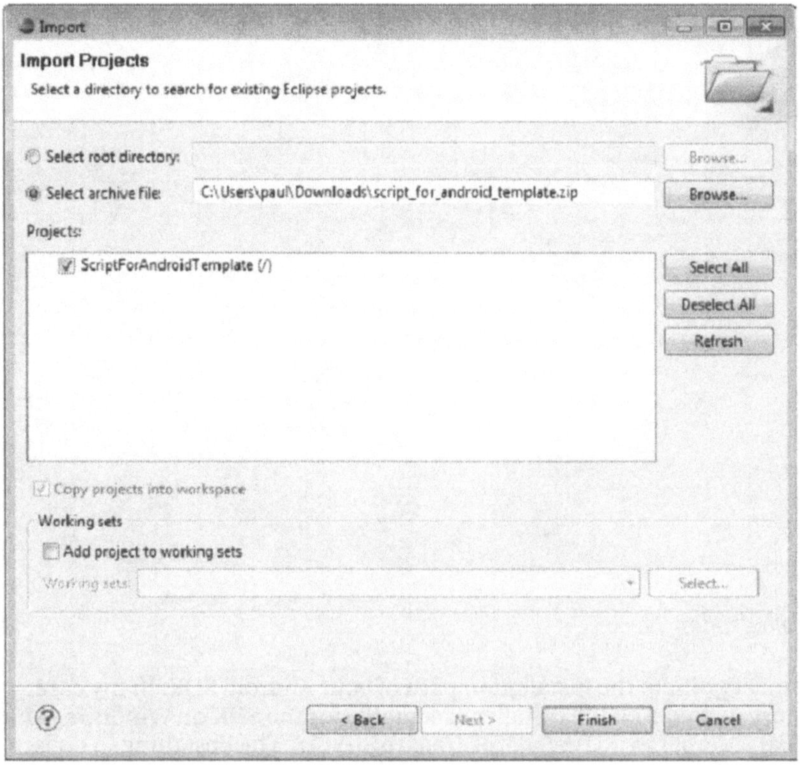

Figure 10-7. Eclipse project import dialog box: archive file selection

Before you build the project, you must make one change on the properties page. To do this, open the Preferences dialog box from the Window menu. Expand the Java menu item followed by Build Path. Your dialog box should look like the one in Figure 10-8 at this point. Select the Classpath Variables item and then click the New button. This will bring up another dialog box like the one in Figure 10-9.

▦ **Note** You may need to add a directory under `ScriptForAndroidTemplate` named gen. I got an error the first time I tried to build the project because this directory was missing. Later versions of the `script_for_android_template.zip` file may have this corrected.

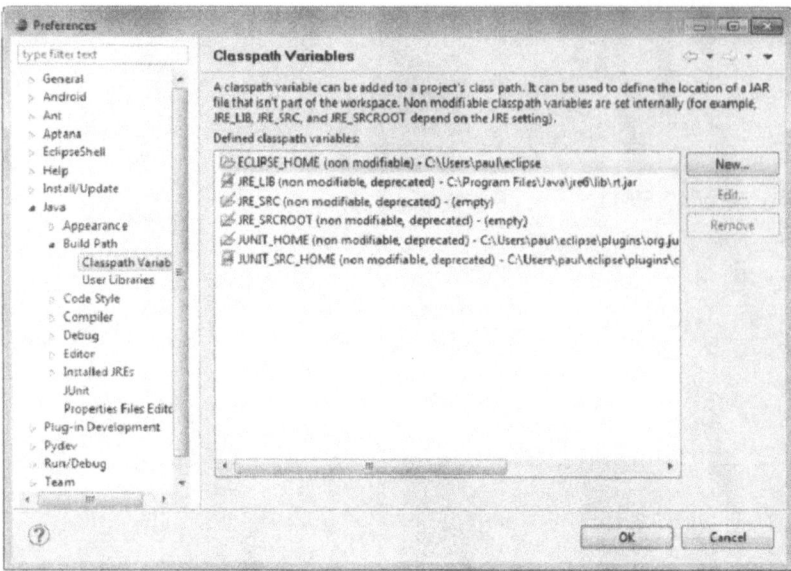

Figure 10-8. *Eclipse project preference dialog box*

The ANDROID_SDK variable must point to the installation path of your Android SDK. In my case, this is under my Downloads directory. If you used the installer executable for the SDK on Windows, your path will probably be something like `C:/Program Files/Android/android-sdk/`. The best thing to do is click the Folder button and navigate to the directory.

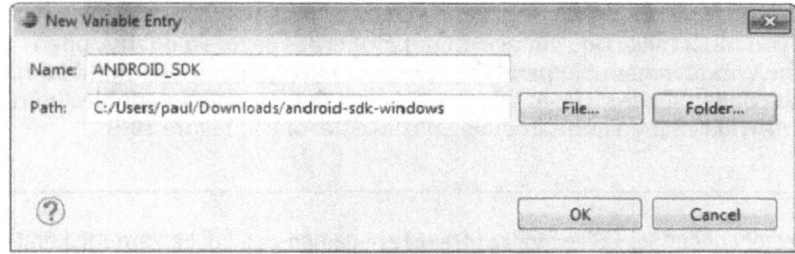

Figure 10-9. *New classpath variable entry dialog box*

If you expand the newly imported `ScriptForAndroidTemplate`, you should see something like Figure 10-10 in the Eclipse Pydev Package Explorer window.

Figure 10-10. *Explorer view of imported template project*

At this point, you should be ready to build the project. It's not a bad idea to run the Clean tool from the Project menu first to make sure you don't have any issues from old projects or previous builds. I make it a habit to do this every time, just for good measure. If the project builds successfully, you shouldn't see any entries on the Problems tab (see Figure 10-11).

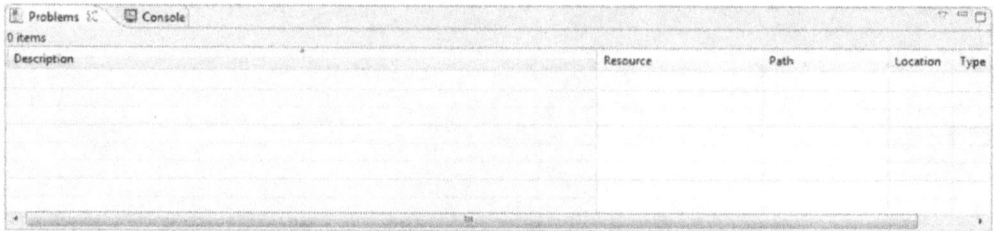

Figure 10-11. *Problems and console tabs should be empty*

At this point we have an Android application ready to be packaged. This is where Eclipse really shines. On the File menu, choose Export. You should see a dialog box like Figure 10-12.

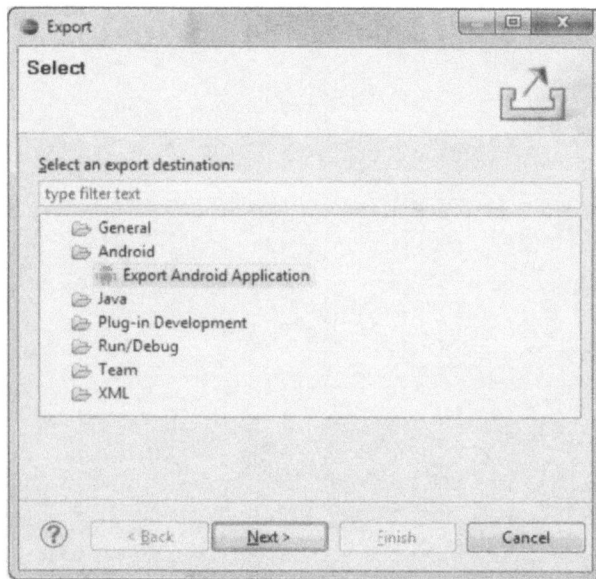

Figure 10-12. *Eclipse Android package export dialog box*

Clicking the Next button will bring up a dialog box like the one in Figure 10-13. This dialog box lets you know that you're about to export a project currently set as debuggable. That's not a problem while you're still developing, but you'll want to change it before you publish the application for anyone else to use.

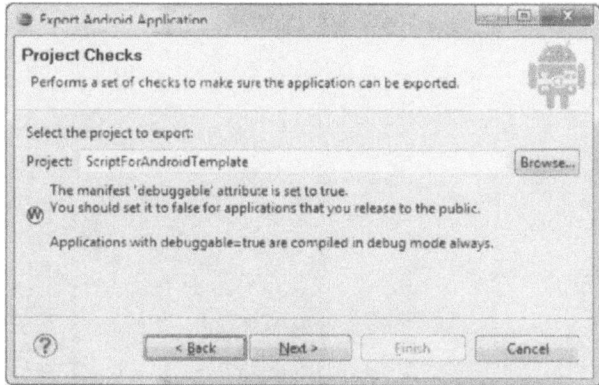

Figure 10-13. *Eclipse export project checks*

The next three dialog boxes deal with signing your application. Every Android application must be digitally signed before it can be installed. If this is the first time you've been through the process, you'll have to generate a new keystore and a key to use. Clicking the Next button of the dialog box in Figure 10-13 will present the dialog box shown in Figure 10-14.

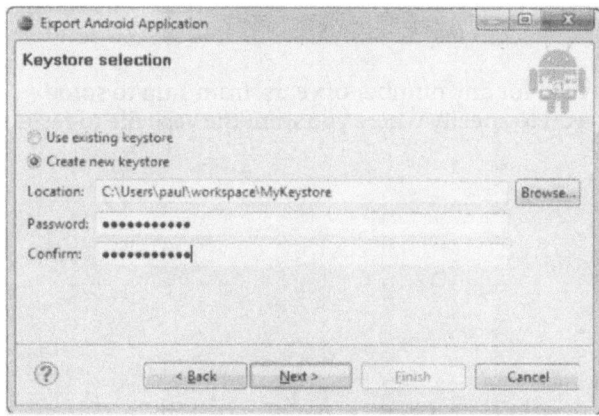

Figure 10-14. *Project keystore selection dialog box*

This is where you select a file to hold your keystore and a password to protect it. The password must be a minimum of six characters and should be something you will remember. Clicking the Next button will take you to another dialog box in which you will enter information to generate your new key. Figure 10-15 shows the Key Creation dialog box.

Figure 10-15. *Key creation dialog box*

Notice the Validity field. You could create a key valid for any number of years, from 1 up to some large number such as 99. The final dialog box allows you to specify where you want the .apk file to reside.

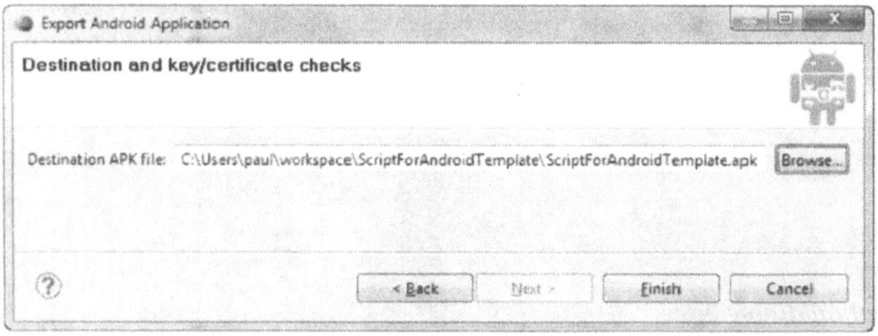

Figure 10-16. *Destination directory for .apk file*

Now that we have an .apk file generated, we can test it out in the emulator. There are two ways to do that: directly from Eclipse or using the ADB tool from the command line. I personally prefer the command line, but I'm pretty old school. To install using ADB, open a terminal window, change your current directory to the one you selected as the destination for the .apk file, and type the following:

```
adb install ScriptForAndroidTemplate.apk
```

If the installation completes successfully, you should see an entry in the emulator named Dummy Script, as in Figure 10-17.

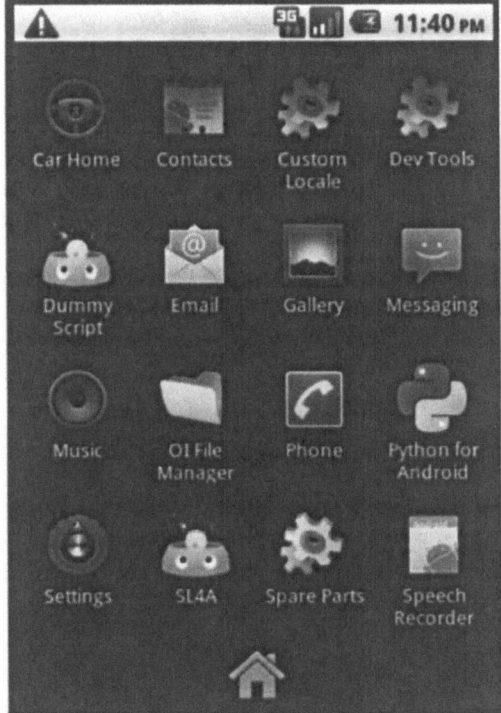

Figure 10-17. Emulator screen with dummy script installed

If you install the ScriptForAndroidTemplate.apk file to a device that does not have SL4A installed, you'll see a popup dialog box like the one in Figure 10-18.

Figure 10-18. Missing Python interpreter prompt

Clicking the Yes button will take you through the process of installing the Python interpreter for SL4A. Once that process has completed, you should be able to run the Dummy Script app by clicking it.

If, by chance, you happened to not get all the permissions set correctly in the `AndroidManifest.xml` file, you'll get a notification like the one in Figure 10-19.

Figure 10-19. Missing permission notification

To fix this issue, you must either edit the `AndroidManifest.xml` file by hand or open the file in Eclipse and make the change there. The Eclipse method is much safer and quicker, so we'll look at that here. To open the file simply double-click `AndroidManifest.xml` in the Package Explorer window. You should see a dialog box like the one in Figure 10-20.

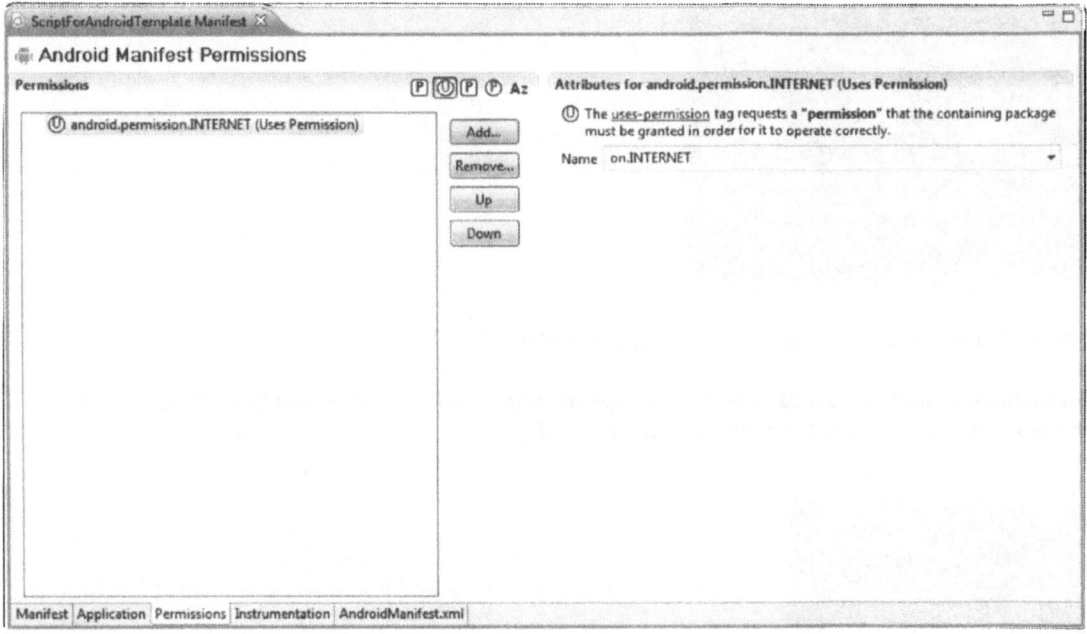

Figure 10-20. Eclipse Android Manifest permissions tab

You can see from Figure 10-20 that the only permission in this `AndroidManifest.xml` file is to allow access to the Internet. If you click the Add button, you'll be presented with a dialog box like Figure 10-21.

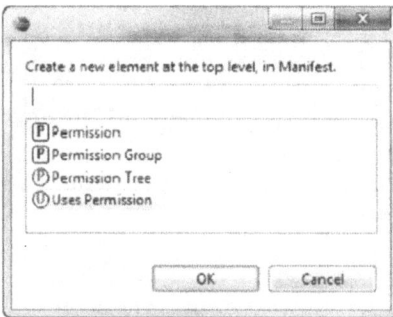

Figure 10-21. *Create a new Android Manifest permissions element*

We need to choose Uses Permission to add a new element. Select Uses Permission and then click the OK button. Next you need to choose a permission name using the drop-down box that contains all permissible values for you to choose from. We need the one labeled `android.permission.VIBRATE`. Figure 10-22 shows this value selected.

Figure 10-22. *Selection of android.permission.VIBRATE*

Once that's done, you can click the little disk icon under the Eclipse main menu to save your updates. Now you'll need to go back through the Project Clean and Export process to create a new `.apk` file.

Packaging Your Own Application

Now that you know how to package an application using a template, we'll use the same basic approach to package up our own application. The process is pretty simple for single Python script files. First, make a copy of the template in Eclipse by right-clicking the project and then choosing Copy from the menu. Next, right-click in an empty area of the Package Explorer window and choose Paste from the menu. This should present a popup like Figure 10-23. Give your new project a name and then click OK.

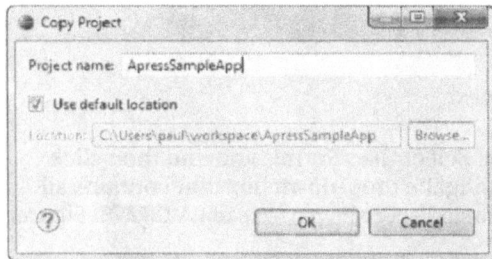

Figure 10-23. *Eclipse copy project dialog box*

Now comes the part where we insert our script. Make a copy of your script and paste it into the res/raw directory. The easiest thing to do here is delete the existing script.py file and rename your script to script.py. That way you won't have to change any of the other locations that reference script.py. You'll also need to rename the default package com.dummy.fooforandroid/*your_package_name*. You can use the Eclipse Refactor/Rename tool to do this for you. Then you need to update the package property in AndroidManifest.xml to reference *your_package_name*.

At this point ,you should be able to go through the build-and-export process to create an .apk file for your script.

Building with Ant

For the really hard-core command-line junkies, there's Ant. You'll need either a Mac OS X or Linux box if you want to take this route. The configuration scripts are .sh files, so they must be run from a terminal on either of those operating systems. To start, you need to download and extract the same template file used in the previous section. You'll also need to set the ANDROID_SDK variable to point to the root of your Android SDK. Here's what that would look like:

```
unzip -d <path/project_directory> script_for_android_template.zip
export ANDROID_SDK=<SDK_root>
```

Next, you need to execute the configure_package.sh script as follows:

```
sh configure_package.sh <your_fully_qualified_package_name>
```

If you were configuring for the actual dummy package in the template, the command would be this:

```
sh configure_package.sh com.dummy.fooforandroid
```

At this point, you need to copy your Python script into the **res/raw** directory and replace the existing **script.py** file. Again, it's easier if you just rename your script to **script.py**. You will need to hand edit **AndroidManifest.xml** to uncomment all permissions your script needs. The actual build-and-run process uses the **run-tests.sh** script. To build your package, you need to open a terminal window and navigate to the root of your project directory. The command **ant debug** will create an **.apk** file inside the project **/bin** directory named *<your_project_name>*-**debug.apk**. This file will be signed with a debug key and aligned using the **zipalign** tool.

Building a release version is a little more involved. For starters, you must sign your application with a suitable certificate. If you plan on publishing your application in the Android market, you must have a validity period ending after 22 October 2033. Debug certificates use the following defaults:

- Keystore name: **"debug.keystore"**

- Keystore password: **"android"**

- Key alias: **"androiddebugkey"**

- Key password: **"android"**

- CN: **"CN=Android Debug,O=Android,C=US"**

Your private release key must use different fields for all these values. You have two options when it comes to a private key: purchase one from one of the certificate-issuing vendors or create your own. The Java Development Kit (JDK) comes with a **keytool** utility that will generate a self-signed key for you. You'll also need the **jarsigner** tool from the JDK. Here's a sample command line to generate a private key:

```
keytool -genkey -v -keystore my-release-key.keystore -alias alias_name -keyalg RSA -keysize↵
2048 -validity 10000
```

With a valid key, you can build a release version of your application using the command **ant release**. By default, the Ant build script compiles the application **.apk** without signing it. You must use the **jarsigner** utility to actually sign the **.apk** file. You can accomplish it with this command:

```
jarsigner -verbose -keystore my-release-key.keystore my_application.apk alias_name
```

It's a good idea to verify that your **.apk** file is properly signed. You can also use **jarsigner** with this command:

```
jarsigner -verify my_signed.apk
```

You can add **-verbose** or **-certs** if you want more information. At this point, all that's left is to run the **zipalign** tool to ensure all uncompressed data is properly aligned. What actually happens with this tool is an adjustment of the final package so that all files are aligned on 4-byte boundaries. This greatly improves application-loading performance and reduces the amount of memory consumed by the running application. Here's the command line to run **zipalign**:

```
zipalign -v 4 your_project_name-unaligned.apk your_project_name.apk
```

That should be the last step needed to create a fully releasable Android application. As a final note, you might want to consider updating your template project to include the latest versions of the core SL4A executables as they are continually updated. To do this you'll need to download the most recent version of **script_for_android_teplate.zip** and extract the following files:

```
libs/script.jar
libs/armeabi/libcom_googlecode_android_scripting_Exec.so
```

Copy these files into the same location in your project and then do a Refresh ➤ Clean ➤ Build using Eclipse or rebuild using Ant.

Compiling SL4A

If you want to make sure you have the absolute latest and greatest version of SL4A, you must compile it from source. This might be a bit risky if you're looking for a stable release, but it also may fix an issue that your application needs. Either way, this is what you'll need to do if you want to compile SL4A. The first thing you'll need to do is get a copy of the SL4A source tree. You need to know that SL4A uses Mercurial as its source code management tool. You can get a copy of Mercurial clients for various Linux distributions, Mac OS X, and Windows on its download page (`http://mercurial.selenic.com/downloads`).

For the purposes of this chapter, I'll use TortoiseHg on a Windows 7 64-bit machine. The download page offers a number of options, including some that do not require administrator rights. I picked the TortoiseHg 2.0.4 with Mercurial 1.8.3 –x64 Windows option. This option provides integration with the Windows Explorer and makes it really simple to clone any repository to a specific location on a local drive. Once you have your client installed, you'll need to clone the source tree. In Windows, you can do that from the file explorer by right-clicking the directory where you want to create the clone and then choosing TortoiseHg and Clone as shown in Figure 10-24.

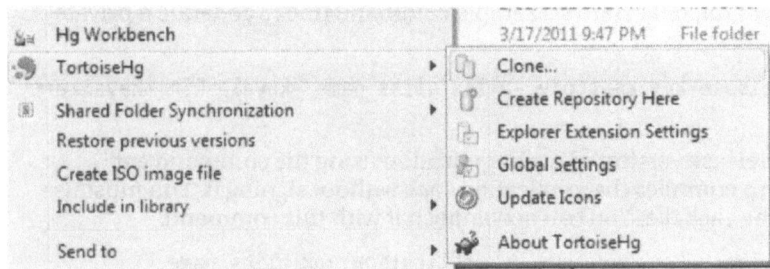

Figure 10-24. *Create clone of SL4A source tree*

Selecting the Clone option will launch another dialog box in which you must specify the source URL of the repository and the destination location on your local computer. The URL I used is as follows:

`https://rjmatthews62-android-scripting.googlecode.com/hg/`

The actual official URL is:

`https://android-scripting.googlecode.com/hg/`

As of this writing, this appears to be the most current location containing all patches and updates. Figure 10-25 shows the dialog box in which you must enter this URL.

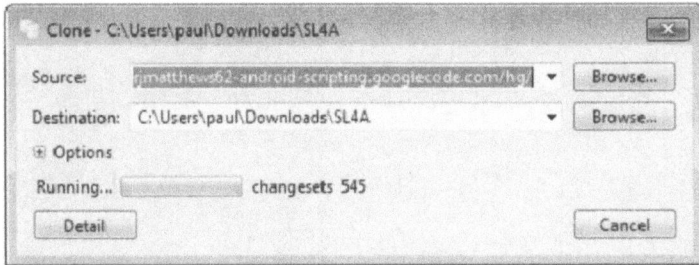

Figure 10-25. *Select SL4A source tree location*

Once you have the entire tree downloaded, you'll need to import it into Eclipse. To do this, open Eclipse and choose Import from the File menu. Because the files already exist on the local disk, you must use the Select Root Directory option. Click the Browse button to navigate to the location where you performed the clone operation. Figure 10-26 shows the dialog box as it should appear after choosing the cloned directory.

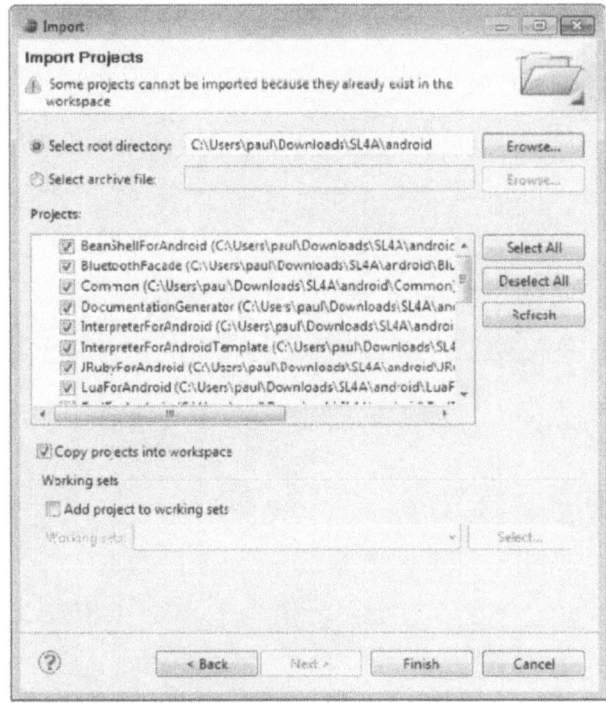

Figure 10-26. *Eclipse import from local directory*

At this point, you don't need all the projects from the cloned source tree. You can remove the following by right-clicking each and choosing Close Project:

- BeanShellForAndroid

- DocumentationGenerator

- InterpreterForAndroidTemplate

- JRubyForAndroid

- LuaForAndroid

- PerlForAndroid

- RhinoForAndroid

- TclForAndroid

You should now be ready to perform a Project ➤ Build followed by a Project ➤ Clean ➤ Clean all. I had to again add the gen directory to a number of the projects. Once that is done, you should do a Clean build, and all should be good. You should see an Eclipse window resembling Figure 10-27 at this point.

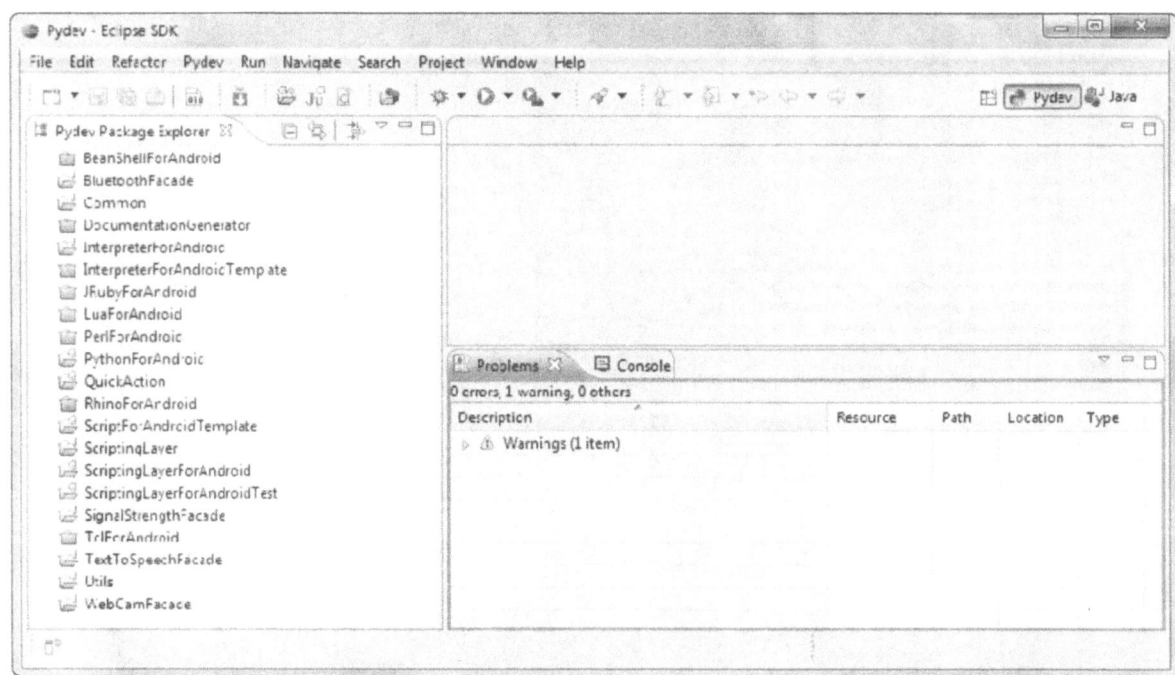

Figure 10-27. *Eclipse window after building SL4A*

Now we need to add our template project from which to create our final application. To do this, right-click the **ScriptForAndroidTemplate** folder and make a copy. Then paste the new copy by right-clicking in the Package Explorer area and choosing Paste. This will now be our target application. To connect this copy to the SL4A clone, you need to expand the project and right-click the **build.xml** file.

Select Run As and then Ant Build. You can rename your project at this point if you want. One more Clean build, and you should have a working **.apk** ready to test.

To test the app, either connect a real device to your workstation or simply use the emulator. From Eclipse you just have to right-click the copy of the template, choose Run As, and then choose Android Application (see Figure 10-28).

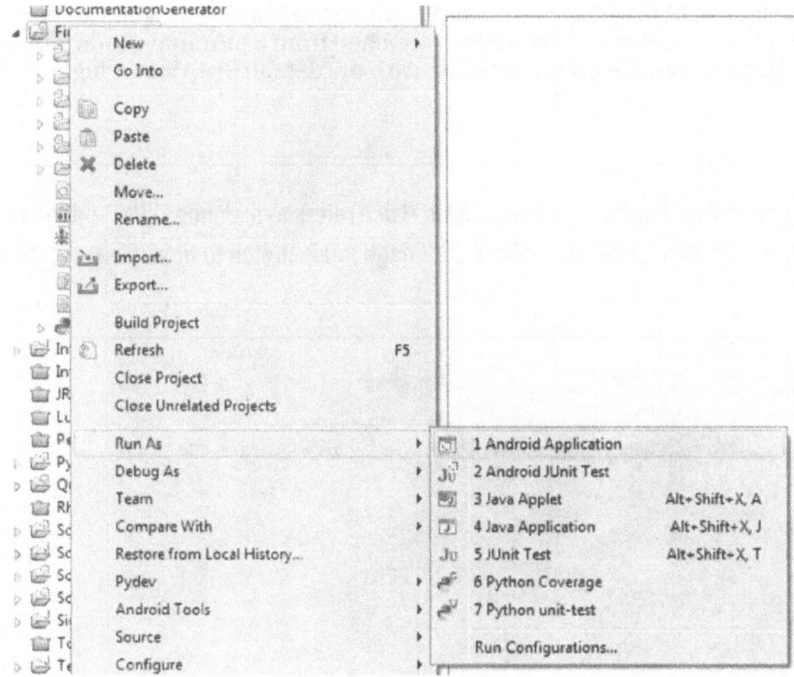

Figure 10-28. *Eclipse window after building SL4A*

At this point you have an **.apk** file for your application and an **.apk** for SL4A. If you distribute your application **.apk** file, it will prompt the user that Python 2.6.2 must be installed first (refer to Figure 10-18).

Finishing Touches

There are a few things you'll want to tweak if you intend to release your script to the public. The default template includes a resources directory named **res**. In this directory are a number of subdirectories that contain various files used by the application—including images representing the icon you will see when you browse for applications on the device and the name that will appear under that icon. To change the name you'll need to edit the **strings.xml** file in the **values** subdirectory. Here's what that file looks like in the default template:

```
<?xml version="1.0" encoding="utf-8"?>
<resources>
    <string name="hello">Hello World!</string>
    <string name="app_name">Dummy Script</string>
</resources>
```

To change the name, simply change the `"app_name">Dummy Script` line to reflect the name of your application. The other thing you might want to change is the application icon. To do this, you can use the **draw9patch** tool provided with the Android SDK. This can be launched from a terminal window by simply typing **draw9patch**. Figure 10-29 shows the **draw9patch** app with the default SL4A script logo loaded.

■ **Note** Android icons use the .png format as a default. The term *Nine Patch* refers to a standard PNG image that includes a 1-pixel wide border. It's typically used for buttons where the image must stretch to fit varying lengths of text labels.

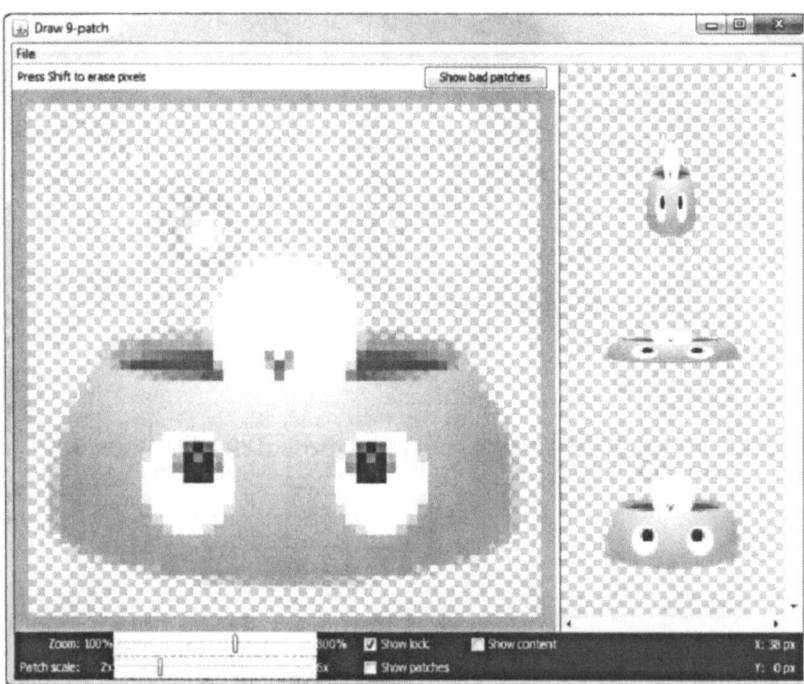

Figure 10-29. Draw9patch application with SL4A icon loaded

Once the program is running, you can either drag an image and drop it on the open window or use the File ➤ Open 9-patch option. When you're done, there's a Save 9-patch option on the File menu to save your work.

Winding Down

SL4A offers an ideal solution for both the aspiring programmer looking to develop a market-ready application and the savvy smartphone user wanting to automate some functions to make their mobile life easier. For the Python-literate, it represents the perfect opportunity to take advantage of their programming skills to use any Android device in much the same way as a desktop or laptop computer. For some, it might even be possible to replace a laptop with an Android-based tablet. This possibility will only become more likely as the processing and storage capabilities of mobile devices increase.

The really great thing about SL4A is its open source nature. As the project becomes better known, there will be more users translating into a wider audience and greater participation. New contributors to the development effort have added significant new features such as the ability to use any native Python library. Updates to other Android platforms such as Google TV should allow SL4A to run there as well. There's a fairly active forum on Google groups where you can ask questions and get help.

Trying SL4A out is not as hard as you might think. You really can't do anything directly harmful to your device, although it is possible to run up your data bill, depending on what your script does. The safest way to get started is to use the Android emulator. Working through the chapters in this book will give you a great foundation for using SL4A to make your Android device do things you never thought possible.

Summary

This chapter has described in great detail how to build distributable packages for your SL4A scripts. Here's a list of take-aways for this chapter:

- **Create QR codes**: QR codes give you a quick and easy way to distribute short scripts that anyone can directly load on an Android device.

- **Build .apk files**: If you want to distribute your application using the Android market, you'll have to learn how to build .apk files.

- **Use Eclipse**: It makes the process of building and testing distributable applications much, much easier.

- **Spruce up your app**: You really do need to spend some time creating an icon for your app if you want your users to actually use it.

Index

CPSIA information can be obtained at www.ICGtesting.com

234661LV00009B/2/P